THE HESYCHASTIC ILLUMINISM

AND

THE THEORY OF THE THIRD LIGHT

METAPHYSICS, METAPOLITICS AND ETHICS

DR NICOLAS LAOS

WHITE CRANE
PUBLISHING

THE HESYCHASTIC ILLUMINISM
AND THE THEORY OF THE THIRD LIGHT
METAPHYSICS, METAPOLITICS AND ETHICS

Dr Nicolas Laos

Produced, Designed, Illustrated and Edited by

White Crane Publishing Ltd
2nd Floor
2 Woodberry Grove
North Finchley
London
N12 0DR.
United Kingdom

www.whitecranepublishing.com

First Published 2014

British Library Catalogue-in-Publication Data:
A CIP record for this book is available from the
British Library.

ISBN: 978-1-907347-15-3 (Hardback)
First Edition.

The views of the author do
not necessarily reflect that
of the publisher.

White Crane Publishing

To the "Third Rome", namely the Patriarchate of Moscow,
and to the blessed memory of Saint Alexander Nevsky (1220–1263)

CONTENTS

INTRODUCTION

ILLUMINISM means belief in and proclamation and
advocation of a special personal enlightenment. The first
'illuminist' tradition in the Greek East was Plato's philosophy,
which expresses a quest for personal enlightenment through one's
participation in the transcendental truth of the world of ideas.
This tradition was eloquently delineated by Plato in his parable
of the Cave, which is presented in his book *The Republic*, Book VII,
514a–520a. The same tradition was further developed by Aristotle in
his *Metaphysics*. The previous tradition was perfected and arrived at
its zenith in the Greek East with the Hesychasts. The Hesychasts are
Christian Orthodox mystics who, in the Middle Ages, developed,
taught and vigorously defended the thesis that man can literally
be deified and experience God's uncreated Light. Maximus the
Confessor has explained that "spiritual knowledge", i.e. knowledge
obtained by the *nous* (mind), which, for the Hesychasts, is the
transcendental tank of God's uncreated Grace within the human
being, "unites knower and known", while "natural knowledge",
obtained by the ego, or the intellect, "is always a cause of change and
self–division".[1]

Hesychasm is a major spiritual phenomenon and a very influential
cultural movement in the history of the Eastern Roman Empire
(known also as the Byzantium or the Greek East) and of Russia
(which, from certain aspects, can be considered to be a kind of New
Byzantium). The purpose of this book is to articulate a systematic
interpretation of Hesychasm and to try to elucidate the position
of Hesychasm in the cultural history of humanity. Additionally,
the attentive reader will find in this book answers to several

---

1   G.E.H. Palmer, Philip Sherrard and Kallistos Ware, trans., The Philokalia, London: Faber and Faber,
1995, Vol. 2, p. 282.

ontological, psychological and political problems arising from present situations.

Before we study the essence of Hesychasm, we must clarify the meaning of the terms culture and spirituality. The means by which a historical actor (society/nation) attempts to improve the terms of its adaptation to reality and the outcome of the previous attempt constitute 'civilization'. Thus, civilization consists of institutions and technology. On the other hand, 'culture' is the result of a historical actor's reflection on its life. In other words, culture is a reflective attitude towards institutions and technology and expresses a historical actor's attempt to transcend institutions by means of myth. By the term 'myth', we mean neither an arbitrary imaginary creation nor a tale. A myth is a system through which experienced reality is translated into a symbolic language and thus it becomes a tradition, and, due to its symbols, it allows all members of the same culture to share common experiences exactly due to their participation in the same symbolic universe. In other words, myth is the core of culture.

The primary purpose of civilization is the achievement of rational control through technological construction, whereas the primary purpose of culture is the expression of the intentionality of consciousness through spiritual creation. However, civilization and culture are neither opposite nor incompatible to each other. Even though civilization primarily corresponds to technological construction and culture primarily corresponds to spiritual creation (art, philosophy, religion), culture is integrated into civilization and is the spiritual underpinning of civilization, and civilization safeguards the integration of culture in history.

In every historical segment, the structure of the established myth corresponds, or it should correspond, to the structure of the established system of institutions. Every major change in the fields of institutions and technology must be combined with and underpinned by a change in the field of myth. For, otherwise, there will be a serious conflict between civilization and culture, or between a historical actor's consciousness and its subconsciousness (values).

Following the terminology that is used by Harold G. Koenig, Michael E. McCullough and David B. Larson in their *Handbook of Religion and Health*[2], by the term 'spirituality', we mean one's personal quest for, or encounter with, the sacred and "ultimate questions about life, about meaning, and about relationship to the sacred or transcendent". More specifically, spirituality is the capacity to *see* what otherwise cannot be seen. Spirituality emphasizes the elements of personhood and mystical relationship, whereas 'religion' emphasizes the element of structural organization, since religion is an *organized* and hence formalized set of beliefs, rituals, behavioral rules and symbols.

The cultural identity of the historical West has three major pillars and has been historically expressed through three major philosophical zones, or traditions. The three major cultural pillars of the historical West are the following: (i) the Roman legal thought and system; (ii) the Greek scientific heritage and the Greek philosophical schools interpreted through the intellectual spectacles of the Roman legal thought and of the Franks' civilization; (iii) Christianity interpreted through the intellectual spectacles of the Roman legal thought and of the Franks' civilization.

The three major cultural zones, or traditions, through which 'Westernness' has been historically expressed are the following: (i) the Latino–Frankish rationalism, which, in the Middle Ages, was expressed in the form of scholasticism, and which, in the modern era, it was expressed in the form of Cartesianism; (ii) the Anglo–Saxon empiricism, which underpins analytical philosophy; (iii) the modern German voluntarism, which is associated with Friedrich Nietzsche's philosophy and with German romanticism. Rationalism is focused on the power of syllogistic reasoning ('I think therefore I am', or, according to the existentialist inversion, 'I am therefore I think'), empiricism is focused on the power of experience ('I experience therefore I am'), and voluntarism is focused on the power of will ('I will therefore I am'). The common feature of the previous three cultural zones is the ontological position that the reason/logos of reality is founded on the human subject's consciousness. By the term 'subject', we mean a historical being filled with reason and will, and more precisely a historical actor capable of acting on the basis of reason and will.

In contradistinction to the historical West, there is no such entity

---

2 H.G. Koenig, M.E. McCullough and D.B. Larson, Handbook of Religion and Health, New York: Oxford University Press, 2001.

as a 'pure subject' either in the classical Greek culture or in the Eastern Orthodox Christendom. As I shall explain in this book, both the classical Greek culture and the Eastern Orthodox Christendom emphasize the hypostatic mode of existence, or personhood, of the human being. By the term 'person', we mean a socialized individual and more specifically an–existential–otherness–in–communion. Therefore, Hesychasm, as a cultural phenomenon and as a spiritual tradition, is substantially different from the Latino–Frankish rationalism, the Anglo–Saxon empiricism and the modern German voluntarism.

THE THIRD LIGHT

The Western spirituality in general and the Western philosophy in particular know and identify two kinds of light: the one kind of light is the physical light, such as the light of the sun and the light of electricity, and the other kind of light is the intellectual light, which transcends the physical light, but, even when the intellectual light is considered to be 'supernatural' (whatever this ambiguous term may mean), it is deemed part of the created world, like the physical light. In other words, according to the Western theories of light, the only lights that are cognitively significant for man are created lights.

In contrast to the Western theories of light, Plato and the Hesychasts declare the existence of a third kind of light that is uncreated and yet can be experienced by the human being. In Plato's terminology, this third, uncreated, light is the light of the ideas, and, according to the Hesychasts' terminology, this third, uncreated, light is the uncreated light of God's glory and sovereign majesty, which, according to the New Testament, Christ revealed to three of his disciples (Peter, James, son of Zebedee, and John) during his Transfiguration (*Matthew*, 17:1–9; *Mark*, 9:2–8; *Luke*, 9:28–36; *2 Peter*, 1:16–18). The participation of man in the uncreated energies of God is what the Hesychasts mean by the term deification (divinization).

Plato's myth of the cave is a parable presented by Plato in his book *The Republic* (Book 7, section 7) in order to illustrate "our nature in its education and want of education" (514a). Imagine, says Plato, a cave in which prisoners are chained since their birth in such a way that all they can see are shadows thrown on a wall in front of them.

They would have the illusion that these shadows were reality. If, however, one of them were freed, and he managed to emerge into the sunlight, he would acquire a new kind of knowledge and he would realize how limited his vision was in the cave.

In his presentation of the myth of the cave, Plato identifies the following four different levels of knowledge and mental development:

i. Illusion, or conjecture (*eikasia*): it provides only the most primitive and unreliable opinions. Illusion is the level of knowledge at which one establishes arbitrary correspondences between reality and the things that are present in one's consciousness. At this level of cognitive development, a person cannot discriminate reality from that which he himself would wish to be real. Such a person cannot accurately discriminate things from their images.

ii. Belief (*pistis*): it is an experiential form of knowledge that allows one to distinguish between objects and their images ("shadows"), but it lacks epistemological and methodological rigor. As mentioned by Plato in the seventh book of the *Republic*, 515d, at the level of belief, man can discriminate the images of things from the prototypes, but he has not developed a scientific consciousness, yet.

iii. Rule–based reasoning, or logic (*dianoia*): it leads to systematic knowledge of the objects of consciousness through a disciplined application of the understanding. By the term science we mean an intentional and methodical enterprise whose purpose is to identify the reason of beings and things, and logic is an expression of a human subject's need to explain the course of the previous enterprise (science) to other human subjects by using formal language. However, Plato maintains, logic is not a cognitively self–sufficient system, and, therefore, it is not the *ne plus ultra* degree of mental development. Plato's argument about logic was mathematically confirmed in 1931 by the great mathematician and logician Kurt

Gödel, who published his seminal article "On Formally Undecidable Propositions of Principia Mathematica and Related Systems"[3]; in the previous article, Gödel proved that, for any computable axiomatic system that contains the finitary arithmetic[4], the following theorems hold: (i) if the system is consistent, it cannot be complete, and (ii) the consistency of the axioms cannot be proven within the system.

iv. Intelligence (*noeisis*): it is the supreme (*ne plus ultra*) level of knowledge, and it corresponds to the knowledge of the Good (Absolute). Plato calls the method that leads to the knowledge of the Good "dialectic". This is simultaneously a logical and supra–logical method of knowledge: it is logical in the sense that the knowledge of the Good presupposes that one's consciousness has progressed from the first level of knowledge to the third level of knowledge; it is supra–logical in the sense that a conscious being that has assimilated logic is aware of the limits of logic and has acquired an intuitive form of knowledge. Hence, as we read in Plato's *Republic*, 476b, as well as in the entire Platonic dialogue *Phaedo*, the relationship between the philosopher and the Good is not only a cognitive one but also an erotic one.

Plato's notion of 'intelligence' (*noesis*) is a kind of spiritual intuition about which we read in the Bible in *Luke*, 11:33–36, in *Mark*, 9:3ff, and in *Matthew*, 6:22 and 17:1ff. This kind of spiritual intuition is the core of Hesychasm.

Michael Psellos[5] (1018–ca.1081), a Hesychast and Neoplatonist

---

3   See: J.W. Dawson Jr., "Gödel and the Limits of Logic", Scientific American, Vol. 280, No. 6, 1999, pp. 76–81; J.W. Dawson Jr., Logical Dilemmas —The Life and Work of Kurt Gödel, Wellesley Mass.: A.K. Peters, 1997. The Italian mathematician Piergiorgio Odifreddi, commenting on Gödel's theorems, has pointed out that the axioms of proof cannot be demonstrated by appealing to themselves. Thus, Gödel has proved that the truth of mathematics transcends every possible formal system of mathematics.

4   For instance, the Peano Axioms, or the Zermelo–Fraenkel Axioms.

5   Psellos's essay on Christ's Transfiguration survives in two manuscripts (Parisinus Graecus 1182 and its apograph Athous Iviron 388), and it was edited for the first time in 1989 by P. Gautier. See: Paul Gautier (ed.), Michaelis Pselli Theologica, Vol. I, 11, Leipzig: Teubner, 1989; reviewed by J.A. Munitz in Classical Review, Vol. 41, 1991, pp. 229–230.

philosopher, has written extensively on the nature of light emanating from Christ during Christ's Transfiguration. He describes the relation between God's activity and man's as follows:

> We do not always participate in God, even though he is active, because of our lack of receptiveness towards participation. As the sun at midday is always shining, and not everyone is capable of gazing at it, except those who have healthy eyes, in the same way not everyone is capable of participating in God, even if he deploys the mental light more amply than sunlight, but only those who have a mental eye purified in their soul.[6]

Using the metaphor of the sun and its rays, Psellos proposes that man can see the rays, or activities of God, and not the essence of God. Additionally, Psellos is clear that this experiential knowledge of the uncreated energies of God varies according the spiritual elevation. Thus, in the context of Hesychasm, man is literally a partaker of the Divinity, and the relationship between God and man is based on personal freedom and not on any rational or natural necessity.

Many of the elements of holiness that the Hesychastic tradition envisions are strongly related to the mysticism of Biblical Israel's Patriarchs and Prophets. There are similarities between the Hesychasts' notion of *nous* (the tank of uncreated divine energies within the human being) and the Biblical term *Neshamah* (הְמָשְׁנ), which literally means breath, and it can be broadly understood as the 'soul proper' and the ability to become partakers of the Divinity. In the Old Testament, there are several references to the Neshamah, such as the following: *Isaiah*, 30:33: breath of God as hot wind kindling a flame; 2 *Samuel*, 22:16, and *Job*, 4:9: as destroying wind; *Job*, 32:8, and *Job*, 33:4: as cold wind producing ice; 1 *Kings*, 17:17, *Isaiah*, 42:5, *Job*, 27:3, and *Daniel*, 10:7: breath of man; *Genesis*, 2:7, and *Job*, 34:14 and 36:4: breath of life and God's breath in man; *Isaiah*, 2:22: man in whose nostrils is but a breath.

Furthermore, again avoiding speculation about parallel development, there are similarities between the Hesychasts' vision of God as uncreated Light and the Sufi's notion of prophetic inspiration, where "God guides to His Light whom He will", according to the *Quran*, Surah 24:35. In the *Quran*, Surah 24:35, spiritual realization is represented as a flash of illumination. The Sufi

---

6 Michael Psellos, De Omnifaria Doctrina, 95, ed. L. G. Westerink.

teacher Abu Hamid al–Ghazali (ca.1058–1111), utilizing the previous image and combining it with Neoplatonism, developed a mystical Islamic tradition that exerted significant influence on the Jewish mysticism throughout the Middle Ages.

In the present book, I attempt to show that Hesychasm fully confirms John Milbank's arguments[7] that Christian theology "offers a discourse able to position and overcome nihilism" and that it is very important to "reassert theology as a master discourse" and as "the discourse of non–mastery". According to the Hesychasts, the truth is universal (*katholiki*), but it exists *hypostatically*, and, therefore, in contrast to the rationalists' *universalia* (abstractions of genus), it is not coercive (i.e. it is not a logical necessity), and it transcends every formal system of knowledge. Thus, people are free to discard the Truth in the same way that they are free to discard Christ.

CHAPTER OUTLINES

Chapter 1 examines the transition from Paganism to Christianity. It explains why the Greek culture was Christianized, and it locates the origin of the Hesychastic anthropology and ontology in the classical Greek notion of hypostasis and in the Greek Church Fathers' distinction between the essence and the energies of God. Moreover, in this chapter, special emphasis is placed on the theology and the anthropology of Maximus the Confessor.

Chapter 2 examines the history of 'ratio' in the West, and it compares and contrasts the West's notion of ratio with the Greek notion of logos. Following a brief literary excursion to show why the West interpreted the Platonic term idea in a different way than the classical Greeks did, the discussion focuses on major ontological and epistemological questions.

Chapter 3 is devoted to the rise of bourgeois society and the Western modernity. In this chapter, I explain the cultural underpinnings of bourgeois society and modernity and their difference from the Greek East's culture.

Chapter 4 is devoted to a global study of Hesychasm. In this chapter, I am concerned with the following issues: the meaning of Hesychasm, the Hesychastic controversy, the vision and knowledge of God as Uncreated Light, the mind–body problem according to

---

7   John Milbank, Theology and Social Theory –Beyond Secular Reason, Oxford: Blackwell, 2006, p. 6.

Gregory Palamas, the passionate part of the soul according to Hesychasm, the principles of Hesychastic psychotherapy, the notion of Church freedom in the context of Hesychasm, and the Russian Hesychastic tradition.

Chapter 5 examines the political ramifications and the metapolitics of Hesychasm, and it explains the kind of civilization that can be created by Hesychasm. The political significance of religion and more generally of spirituality has been recognized and methodically studied by several distinguished scholars and research institutions, such as Douglas Johnston[8] (President of the International Centre for Religion and Diplomacy), Yale's Faith and Globalization Initiative, the Tony Blair Faith Foundation, the James A. Baker III Institute for Public Policy at Rice University, etc. However, Hesychasm, by falling outside all the major Western spirituality systems, and simultaneously by not being a 'school' of Oriental spirituality, has not received adequate scholarly attention.

Chapter 6 is concerned with the study of ethics and justice from a Hesychastic perspective. This chapter compares and contrasts Hesychasm with the major schools of moral philosophy and with the major theories of justice.

Finally, chapter 7, is concerned with the implications of Hesychasm for the management of international affairs.

Nicolas Laos
University of Indianapolis,
Athens Campus, Greece

July 2013

---

8 Douglas Johnston (ed.), Faith–Based Diplomacy —Trumping Realpolitik, Oxford: Oxford University Press, 2003.

ACKNOWLEDGEMENTS

I AM grateful to several scholars and policy–makers whose work has provided me with thought–provoking and intellectually challenging stimuli. Among them, I should first of all mention Professor Alexander Dugin (State University of Moscow), Dr John Nomikos (Research Institute for European and American Studies), Dr George Gavris and Dr Natella Speranskaja; with all of them I had useful personal contacts during the preparation of this book. Furthermore, I should acknowledge the significance of the intellectual stimuli that I have received from colleagues at North American and British Universities and think tanks in the context of research Programs and courses dealing with the ethos of the Founding Fathers of the United States of America and with contemporary humanistic movements and theories.

The Metropolitan Dr Daniel de Jesús Ruiz Flores of Mexico and All Latin America of the Ukrainian Orthodox Church and head of the Saint Andrew's Theological Academy of Mexico has been very supportive and encouraging. I am particularly grateful to Metropolitan Dr Daniel de Jesús Ruiz Flores for having signed my Doctoral Degree in Christian Philosophy and for having bestowed upon me important academic and ecclesiastical titles and distinctions, including the title of the Grand Commandeur de l' Ordre des Pauvres Chevaliers du Christ et des Saints Cyrille et Méthode. My gratitude extends to Metropolitan Archbishop Emeritus Dr Norman Sydney Dutton of the Anglican Episcopal Church International, who, in 2013, bestowed upon me the Ecclesiastical Noble Title of Duke of Bethphage and gave me opportunities to investigate the relation between Hesychasm and Anglican mysticism. In fact, I believe that there is a significant yet elusive and under–researched relationship between the spiritual quests of Anglican mystics and Hesychasm.

Even though I do not subscribe to any movement of religious syncretism, I have a fruitful and inspiring communication with the distinguished Islamic scholar Sheikh Imran N. Hosein about the interplay between spirituality and politics and about the relationship between the Orthodox Christian world and the Islamic world.

In 2013, the University of Indianapolis (Athens Campus, Greece) helped me to reconcile my interests in philosophy, spirituality and politics by appointing me as an Instructor of International Relations Theory. I should thank Mr Vasilis J. Botopoulos (University of Indianapolis Vice President), Professor Susie Michailidis (Vice Chancellor for Academic Affairs, University of Indianapolis Athens Campus), Professor Panayiotis Karafotias (International Relations Department Chair, University of Indianapolis Athens Campus) and my undergraduate and post–graduate students for offering me several fruitful academic experiences.

My publisher, David Campbell, and my editor (project manager), Alasdair Urquhart, have seen this text through several drafts with great efficiency and have been of great assistance throughout this project. I am always pleased and honored to co–operate with White Crane Publishing Ltd.

THE HESYCHASTIC ILLUMINISM

AND

THE THEORY OF THE THIRD LIGHT

1

FROM PAGANISM TO CHRISTIANITY

THE most important issue in the analysis of the Christianization of the Greco-Roman world is the study of the reasons for which the Greeks became Christians. If the Greeks had not become Christians, the Romans would not have become Christians either, since the latter were spiritually dominated by the first. And given the negative attitude of the Jews towards Christianity and the indifference of the other Eastern religious communities towards the Christian Gospel, Christianity could not have realized its triumphal march in the ecumene if it had not previously been accepted by the Greeks.

CHRISTIANITY AS THE COMPLETION AND PERFECTION OF THE GREEK PHILOSOPHY

In his *Physics*, V, 265a, Aristotle writes that God is the direct object of the universal love that characterizes the eternal natural beings (i.e. the celestial spheres), which imitate the perfectness of the divine mode of life through their harmonious motion. The classical Greek scholars see the 'cosmos' as a reality in which dwells the Word of God. Thus, according to classical Greek philosophy, it is only through his participation in the cosmos that man can actualize his divine potential.

In the context of classical Greek philosophy, participation in the cosmos leads to socialization and to individualization, too, because the human being lives as a member of a harmonious whole and simultaneously it turns inwards, into its own psyche,

1

in order to actualize its personal divine potential. As the previous awareness of individuality becomes deeper and more intense, the Greek individual gradually moves towards an existential crisis, because it encounters the tragedy of existence: the Greek individual does not exactly know how it can maintain *divine justice* (which is the necessary existential presupposition of every being and every reality) whilst simultaneously experiencing the divine element that dwells in its own self as *freedom of will*. In other words, the Greek individual seeks the perfect equilibrium between the maintenance of divine justice (which underpins socialization) and the actualization of free will (which underpins individualization).

According to classical Greek philosophy, 'theory' and 'theoretical life' are two terms that describe the best ideal in life. In the context of classical Greek philosophy, theoretical life means love for wisdom –i.e. the life of the philosopher– where wisdom is the object and the result of the operation of the philosophizing consciousness, which contemplates the cosmos and –together with the gods– experiences the pleasures of the mind. In *Nicomachean Ethics*, 1177a, Aristotle, who places God, as the ultimate source of significance in the world, at the top of his metaphysical system, argues that the communication between man and God takes place through the perfection of the human mind and the mental vigilance that is caused by mental pleasure. In addition, in *Metaphysics*, 1072b, Aristotle argues that "God is a living being, eternal, most good; and therefore life and a continuous eternal existence belong to God; for that is what God is".

On the other hand, the concept of theory (spiritual vision), which was coined by the classical Greek scholars, proved to be the limit of the development of the classical Greek thought. The classical Greek thought realized that the highest pleasure is 'theoretical life', i.e. the orientation of the mind towards the infinity of the Divinity, but it also realized that, without the finite and corruptible body, the human being cannot experience its mental life, and, therefore, the classical Greek thought realized that there was a tragic chasm between the 'absolute' and the 'partial'.

According to Aristotle's *Nicomachean Ethics*, 1177b11, man cannot continuously live in a state of pure theory, but only in rare, happy moments of his life, since the human being is a hylomorphic compound —compound of soul (or mind) and body— and, for this reason, man mainly lives in accordance with the terms of 'human life' and not in accordance with the terms of 'theoretical life'. In other words, due to his soul and with his soul, man turns towards and is attracted to mental pleasures, but, as a mortal being, i.e. because of the weak and corruptible character of his life, he lives in human societies and is engaged in practical pursuits. Thus, the more intense the experience of the pleasures of the mind is, the more intense the pain of death (i.e. the separation of soul and body) becomes.

Classical Greek philosophy discovered and analyzed the life of the spirit, but it proved to be unable to safeguard the unity of that life, which appeared to be fragmented between 'theoretical' and 'practical' life. In particular, in his *Nicomachean Ethics*, 1178b, Aristotle argues as follows: "Happiness...is co–extensive in its range with contemplation...But the philosopher being a man will also need external well–being, since man's nature is not self–sufficient for the activity of contemplation".

In order to find a creative solution to the aforementioned problem, the classical Greek thought needed a Logos[9] (Word) who could be spiritual —i.e. totally free from the logic of the material world— and simultaneously He could unite the material world with Himself. Thus, the classical Greek thought found the solution that it had been looking for in the Christian faith, since the latter is founded on the doctrine of the incarnation of the Divine Logos.

Justin Philosopher and Martyr[10] continued to hold Greek philosophy in high esteem after his conversion to Christianity. In particular, in his *Dialogue with Trypho*, II, 1, Justin writes the following: "philosophy is, in fact, the greatest possession, and most honorable before God, to whom it leads us and alone commends us; and these are truly holy men who have bestowed attention on philosophy". In addition, in *Dialogue with Trypho*, VIII, 1, Justin writes that he had found in Christianity "the only sure and profitable philosophy". Similarly, in his *Stromata*, IV, Clement of Alexandria argues that Greek philosophy proceeds from the same God who gave the Old and the New Testaments and that God's Providence raised up philosophers among the Greeks whilst raising up prophets among

---

9 In pre–Socratic philosophy, 'logos' means the principle governing the cosmos, the source of this principle, or human reasoning about the cosmos. In Stoicism, 'logos' means the active, material, rational principle of the cosmos; nous. Biblical Judaism understands 'logos' as the word of God, which itself has creative power and is God's medium of communication with man. In Christianity, 'logos' refers to the creative word of God, which is itself God and incarnate in Jesus (it is also called Word).

10 Justin (103–165 A.D.) was an early Greek apologist and martyr. He is considered a saint by many Christian denominations including the Orthodox Church and the Roman Catholic Church.

the Jews and the barbarians. In *Stromata*, I, 18:90, 16:80 and 5:28, Clement of Alexandria called the Gospel "the true philosophy", and he understood Greek philosophy, like the Mosaic Law, as instruction that prepared for Christian faith and paved the way for the Gospel.

Furthermore, in *Stromata*, VI, 7:55, Clement of Alexandria argues that "philosophy yearns for the wisdom which consists in rightness of soul and speech and in purity of life", and, in *Stromata*, I, 20:100, he argues that the primary task of the Greek philosophy is the defense of the Christian faith: "in rendering the attack of sophistry impotent and in disarming those who betray truth and wage war upon it, Greek philosophy is rightly called the hedge and the protective wall around the vineyard".

The New Testament offered the Greeks exactly what the classical Greek philosophers had been looking for: the self–revelation of the Absolute within the historical, material world. According to the New Testament, God, in Christ, became a human being. In *John* 12:45, Jesus Christ says that, if one wants to know what God is like, he should study the person and words of Jesus Christ. Similarly, in *Luke* 24:53, Jesus Christ is portrayed as the perfect example of a life lived according to God's will. Furthermore, in *Hebrews* 1:1–3, Paul writes that Jesus Christ is the complete expression of God in human body. In general, in the context of the New Testament, the following lessons follow from Christ's humanity: Christ is the perfect human leader, the perfect human model, the perfect human sacrifice, the perfect conqueror, and the perfect High Priest.

Christ —in the language of modern psychology— is the *Archetype*, the Divine Archetype, of the human being as the latter is restored to its proper and God–ordained path to perfection and divinization (deification). Speaking of Christ as the Archetype of restored man, Gregory the Theologian[11] has written in his *First Oration: On Easter and His Reluctance*[12]: "[Today] I am glorified with Him…, today I am quickened with Him,…let us honor our Archetype". Moreover, in his *Homily in Transfigurationem Domini* (*Patrologia Graeca*, Vol.

---

11 Gregory the Theologian (also known as Gregory of Nazianzus) was a 4th century A.D. Archbishop of Constantinople and philosopher, and also he is widely considered as one of the most accomplished rhetorical stylists of the early patristic era. He is a saint in both Eastern and Western Christianity.

12 See: Philip Schaff and Henry Wace (eds), A Select Library of Nicene and Post–Nicene Fathers of the Christian Church, Grand Rapids, MI: Wm. B. Eerdmans, 1991, Vol. 7, p. 30.

7, 552C), John of Damascus[13], speaking of the deification of man, refers to the divine image in man as it is "mingled" with Christ the "Archetype".

Finally, it should be mentioned that Greek philosophy exerted a significant influence on the Jewish civilization in general and on the Old Testament in particular. The part of the Jews that was Hellenised most rapidly was the one that was living in Egypt. Many Jews of Egypt used to take Greek names, such as: Apollonius, Artemidoros, Diodotus, Demetrius, Dionysus, Diophantus, Heracleia, Heracledes, Hermeias, Theodotus, Theodorus, Dositheus, Jason, etc. Even among the Maccabees —i.e. the Jewish nationalists (2 *Maccabees* 2:21)— one can find Greek names, e.g. two generals of the Maccabees' army had Greek names: Dositheus and Sosipatrus. Moreover, according to the fourth book of *Maccabees*, the Jews use the classical Greek term 'polity' in order to refer collectively to the faithful to the Torah.

During the Hellenistic era, many Jews of Egypt were taking Greek names, and also they were proud of their Greek education and were adopting Greek habits. The historiographer Demetrius, a Jewish courtier of Ptolemy IV, wrote an exposition of the Jewish religion following a philosophical style, which was indicating the Greek spiritual influence on the Jews of Egypt. Artapanus of Alexandria, another famous Hellenised Jew, wrote an allegorical novel in which Moses is presented as the founder of the Orphic Mysteries[14]. A Jew named Ezekiel composed a Greek tragedy on the theme of the Exodus. The Jewish epic poet Philo the Elder wrote an epic *On Jerusalem* in Homeric hexameters. Theodotus, another Hellenised Jewish epic poet, wrote an epic *On Shechem* (Shechem is mentioned in the Hebrew Bible as an Israelite city of the tribe of Manasseh) connecting the name of Shechem with Sikimios, the son of the Greek

---

13   John of Damascus was a Syrian Christian monk and priest, who died at his monastery, Mar Saba, near Jerusalem on 4/5 December 749 A.D. His fields of interest included theology, philosophy, music and law. He is a saint in both Eastern and Western Christianity, and the Roman Catholic Church recognizes him as a Doctor of the Church.

14   The Orphic cult was one of the most ancient Greek monotheistic systems. According to the initiates of the Orphic Mysteries, there is only one divine King–Lord, who is self–caused, and everything that has been created has been created by Him —the One— and all the different gods of the ancient Greek pantheon are different manifestations of the omnipotent One. See for instance: W.K.C. Guthrie, Orpheus and Greek Religion —A Study of the Orphic Movement, revised edition, Princeton, N.J.: Princeton University Press, 1993.

god Hermes. The Jewish philosopher Aristobulus of Paneas coined the theory that Pythagoras and Plato knew the Bible.

Additionally, during the Hellenistic era, the Jewish system of worship was also influenced by the Greek philosophical tradition, since it included not only chants and readings from the Bible but also interpretations of the Jewish religious texts, i.e. a philosophical task. The Greek philosophical influence on the Old Testament can be clearly identified in the Bible itself, since the expressions "God the Most High" and "I am that I am" are indications of Platonic influences on the Bible, and the epithets "Lord of the Powers" and "Almighty" (in Greek: "Pantocrator"), which were used by Hellenised Jews, were originally applied to Hermes.

In summary, Plato, with his theory of ideas, shows that teleology is the quintessence of spirituality and the core of philosophical life. From Plato's teleological perspective, everything has a *telos*, or purpose, and becomes meaningful through and due to its relation to ideas (macrocosmic reality), since, in the context of Plato's teleology, every microcosmic entity contains the vital or creative force of the cosmos, and truth corresponds to the common reality of the cosmos, i.e. to the common bond that unites all microcosmic beings into a cosmic harmony. The goal of Plato's philosophy is not the harmony of being itself, but man's harmonization with the transcendental truth of the ideas, which is simultaneously the truth of the world and the truth of consciousness. Furthermore, classical Greek philosophy and especially Aristotle realized and emphasized that mental, or philosophical, life cannot be experienced without the body. In the ancient Greek world, the awareness of the gap between the absolute (spirit/mind) and the relative (body) caused feelings of anxiety and tragedy. Thus, the ancient Greek spirituality solved the previous problem by endorsing the Christian Gospel, i.e. by endorsing the doctrine of the Incarnation of the Logos, which united the humanity and the Divinity into the hypostatic integrity of Jesus Christ. In this way, the essence of Greek philosophy was revived by and survived through Christianity.

GREEK PHILOSOPHY AND CHRISTIAN TRINITARIAN THEOLOGY

In the era of the early Church Councils, there was much confusion concerning the meaning of the Trinitarian formula. The Greek Fathers explained the doctrine of the Trinity by means of concepts that had been developed by Greek philosophers. Basil the Great[15]explains the important role of the Spirit in the Trinity in chapter nine of his work *On the Holy Spirit*, where he writes: "And He [the Paraclete = Holy Spirit], like a sun joining itself to the purified eye, will show you in himself the image of the invisible. And in the blessed vision of the image [i.e. the Son = Logos], you will see the intelligible beauty of the Archetype [Father = Nous]"[16]. Based on Basil's theological essays, Gregory of Nyssa[17]stresses that the Three Persons are 'hypostatic', i.e. essentially equal and the same; the only way to tell them apart is their mutual relations.

John of Damascus, in his essay entitled *An Exact Exposition of the Orthodox Faith*, defines 'nature' as the principle of motion and repose, and, on this ground, he identifies nature of subject with its substance. However, he adds that, according to some pre–Christian philosophers, such as Aristotle, in contrast to substance, which is simple being, nature is substance that had been made specific by essential differences so as to have, in addition to simple being, being in such a way. Thus, substance *qua* substance, to which belongs simple being, is amounted to unqualified subject. On the other hand, 'nature' as substance that had been made specific by essential differences relates to qualified substance, which is specified by the essential difference, i.e. it has not only being in the former sense, but also being in such a way according to its essential differences.

Furthermore, John of Damascus introduces the term 'hypostasis' in order to clarify the Trinitarian formula: in this case, 'hypostasis' means the existence of an individual substance in itself (i.e. an individual that is numerically different). Consequently, according to the consensus of the early Church Fathers, nature as a species is a common thing, which is predicated of hypostases and has its existence in them, while hypostasis is a particular thing in a numerical sense, as an individual of some kind. Therefore, according

---

15 Basil the Great (also known as Basil of Caesarea) was a 4th century Bishop of Caesarea in Cappadocia, Asia Minor. He is a saint in both Eastern and Western Christianity. Basil, Gregory of Nazianzus and Gregory of Nyssa are collectively referred to as the Cappadocian Fathers. The Cappadocian Fathers worked methodically in order to achieve a creative synthesis of Christianity with Greek philosophy.

16 Basil the Great, On the Human Condition, trans. and intro. by Verna Harrison, Crestwood, N.Y.: St. Vladimir's Seminary Press, 2005, p. 20.

17 St. John Damascene, An Exact Exposition of the Orthodox Faith, trans. E.W. Watson and L. Pullan, in Vol. 9 of Nicene and Post-Nicene Fathers, Second Series.

to John of Damascus, hypostasis not only possesses common as well as individual characteristics of the subject, but also exists in itself, whereas nature does not exist in itself, but is to be found in hypostasis. Thus, the God of Christianity, having a hypostatic form of existence, is not the same with the God of general, abstract 'monotheism' (e.g. Judaism and Islam). Christianity stresses the personhood of God, whereas general monotheism stresses merely the unity of God's nature.

Thus, through the distinction between hypostasis and nature, the Greek Church Fathers, and especially the Cappadocian Fathers, explained how it is possible for God to assume the human nature without losing or degrading His divinity. The hypostatic modes of existence of God imply that God's nature does not constrain Him, i.e. God's existence is characterized by absolute freedom. In particular, according to the New Testament, in the case of Jesus Christ, the same Hypostasis of the Word became the hypostasis of divine and human natures. Thus, according to *1 John* 23, "No one who denies the Son has the Father; whoever acknowledges the Son has the Father also".

In his *On the Holy Spirit, Against the Macedonians*, Gregory of Nyssa[18]stresses that the Trinity should not be understood as three separate Gods (e.g. Creator, Redeemer, Sanctifier). As Hans von Balthasar has written, after the Cappadocian Fathers, "it is no longer possible to infer Divine Persons on the basis of different regions of the world...[for] there is a 'common operation' which links their divine essence"[19]. Moreover, the energy or activity of grace that acts upon us is common to all three divine Persons (Hypostases), and it proceeds from the Father, acts through the Son, and is completed in the Holy Spirit.To explain the meaning of the Christian Trinitarian formula, one can use a metaphor about a poet, e.g. T.S. Eliot. The poetry of T.S. Eliot is his 'logos', or word; Eliot's word proceeds from Eliot's 'nous' (mind); and Eliot's word gives to its readers the 'spirit' of Eliot, i.e. a special feeling of participation in the personal world of Eliot. The spirit of Eliot remains with the readers of Eliot's word even when they do not have his poems in front of them. By

---

18   Gregory of Nyssa was a 4th century Christian bishop. He was a younger brother of Basil the Great and a good friend of Gregory the Theologian. He is a saint in both Eastern and Western Christianity.

19   Hans von Balthasar, Presence and Thought —An Essay on the Religious Philosophy of Gregory of Nyssa, trans. Mark Sebanc, San Francisco: Ignatius Press, 1995, p. 19.

analogy, God the Father is the Nous of God, God the Son is the Logos, or Word, of God, and the Holy Spirit is the Spirit of God. However, in the case of the Holy Trinity, the Nous of God (Father), the Logos of God (Son), and the Holy Spirit are not attributes or functions of a being, but they are three Hypostases of the same Divine Nature.

The above Trinitarian formula leads to the following ontological conclusions: God does not exist as a pure individual, i.e. without communion; but He exists as a communion of three Hypostases. Thus, 'communion' is an ontological category that describes God's mode of existence. In addition, communion comes from the three Hypostases of God, i.e. it is founded on concrete and free persons. By analogy, since, according to the Bible, man is the image of God, 'communion' is an ontological category that describes human personhood: no human being can exist without communion, i.e. no human being can exist as a pure individual, and communion comes from hypostases, i.e. from concrete and free persons. In general, a 'person' (or 'hypostasis') is an individual–in–communion, i.e. human personhood is impossible without communion, and any kind of communion that suppresses or eliminates individuality is inhuman and ungodly.

FROM GREEK PHILOSOPHY TO THE ANTHROPOLOGY OF THE GREEK CHURCH FATHERS

Within the Christian tradition, the writings of the Greek Fathers have always stressed the unity of body and soul. With respect to this issue, Jean–Claude Larchet has pointed out the following: "the Fathers strive constantly to defend a balance in understanding the constitution of the human being: the two substances which comprise him are distinct without being separated and united without being confused"[20]. Furthermore, paraphrasing Maximus the Confessor[21],

---

20   J.–C. Larchet, Thérapeutique des Maladies Mentales —L' Expérience de l' Orient Chrétien des Premiers Siècles, Paris: Les Éditions du Cerf, 1992, p.29.

21   Maximus the Confessor (ca. 580–662) was a Christian monk, theologian and scholar. He methodically and systematically supported the Council of Chalcedon's position that Jesus Christ had both a human and a divine will, fighting a heresy called Monotheletism (for Greek meaning 'one will'). Following the Asian legacy of transcendentalism, Monotheletism was an attempt to 'reduce' the human aspect of Christ by arguing that Christ had only one will —namely, the divine one. Maximus the Confessor is a saint in both Eastern and Western Christianity.

Larchet has written that "every action and every movement of the human being is at once an act of his soul and his body"[22] (i.e. a coincidence of action and movement, as Maximus the Confessor has stated elsewhere, which is ideally achieved by "one who brings the body into harmony with the soul [ho harmosamenos to soma pros ten psychen]"[23]).

In the context of the Greek Fathers' anthropology, the integral union of the body and the soul is characterized by a *hierarchy* of interaction, in the sense that the soul is *superior* to the body *in that interaction*. This is because the soul is immortal (by God's grace, and not due to its own nature) and immaterial, whereas, in man's fallen state, the body is material and mortal. This Patristic teaching is not easily understood, especially in the West, where the soul is often thought of as something that is naturally immortal and exists within the mortal human body, distinct and separate from it and unmarked by any essential interaction with the body. On the other hand, the Greek Fathers teach that the soul is created by God and thus it is God's grace that makes it immortal and that the soul not only "pervades (*chorousa*)" the "entire body (*holou...tou somatos*)", as Maximus the Confessor writes, but every member of the body responds to the presence of the soul, though the soul is incorporeal[24].

In the context of the Greek Fathers' anthropology, the concept of soul is understood as the personal way of carrying and manifesting the life–energy, i.e. as the essence of 'personhood', and not as a divine spirit in itself. In addition, following Paul's *1 Corinthians* 15:44, the Greek Fathers refer to the distinction between the spiritual body (*soma pneumatikon*) and the physical body (*soma psychikon*) —the latter term meaning literally the "psychic body", which is a special term used by Paul to refer to the physical body and to the concinnity of body and soul. The spiritual body is the body that the human being will have in the afterlife —after the death of the physical body— when the soul and the physical body are separated. It is a

---

22 J.–C. Larchet, La Divinization de l' Homme Selon Saint Maxime le Confesseur, Paris: Éditions du Cerf, 1996, p.30.

23 St. Maximus the Confessor, "Peri Theologias kai tes Ensarkou Oikonomias tou Hyiou tou Theou, Pros Thalassion" (Regarding theology and the incarnate economy of the Son of God, to Thalassios), in Philokalia ton Hieron Neptikon (Philokalia of the Sacred Neptic Fathers —hereafter, Philokalia), Athens: Ekdotikos Oikos "Aster", 1975, Vol. 2, p.90.

24 St. Maximus the Confessor, "Peri Diaphoron Aporion" (Regarding various difficult texts), in Patrologia Graeca, Vol. 91, 1100AB.

"resurrected" body that is both eternal and delicate and untouched by the materiality, disease, corruption, and mortality of the fleshly body in the present life.

The Greek Church Fathers teach that, even though, as a result of the Fall of Man, which is mentioned in the book of *Genesis*, humankind and the world were reduced in a condition of existence marked by illness and imperfection, human beings were still subject to God's grace and were not wholly separated from Him. In other words, man was never deprived of the potential for perfection. This understanding of man's Fall runs contrary to any idea of "original sin", the total deprivation of human nature after the Fall. Timothy Ware (Bishop Kallistos of Diokleia) has explained that, even before the Fall, "humans...were perfect, not so much in an actual as in a potential sense": the Forebears of humanity, "endowed with the image [of God] from the start" —namely, as "icons" of God and His "offspring"— "they were called to acquire the likeness [of God] by their own efforts (assisted of course by the grace of God)"[25]. This striving for perfection was not eliminated by sin, but, rather, it emerged as something even more significant in man's consciousness, as man had deviated from the path towards ensured perfection established by God.

In the context of the Greek Church Fathers' teachings about the Fall, salvation, and more precisely deification, are existential goals that constitute the purpose of man's historical life and should not be looked for in a primordial 'womb' to which people should ostensibly return. Therefore, reactionary forms of traditionalism, such as René Guénon's theory are totally incompatible with Orthodox Christianity. In contrast to the Greek Church Fathers, Guénon, a French intellectual and Sufi, sees human history as a narrative of decline, arguing that the relationship between God and man reached its climax at the moment of creation, which has been followed by an ever-widening gulf between the two. Thus, Guénon seeks to return to a primordial womb of humanity ("divine order"), and he ends up with an arbitrary syncretistic religious system that he has combined with Hindu hierarchical structures and with fascism's authoritarianism.

For the Greek Fathers, 'Paradise' is a symbolic image of that state of existence in which the human mind is united with the source of

---

25 Timothy Ware, The Orthodox Church, second edition, London and N.Y.: Penguin Books, 1993, p. 219.

the meaning of life, namely it is constantly oriented towards the Divine Archetype[26]. Thus, 'life in Paradise' does not signify a static condition of life, but it signifies a dynamic course towards man's existential perfection. In Paradise, the Forebears of humanity were not endowed from the start with all possible wisdom and knowledge, i.e. their perfection was not a realized one but a potential one. Thus, their Fall is not a penalty imposed on them by God according to some legalistic formula, but it is the result of their failure to realize their potential. As Protopresbyter John S. Romanides has pointed out, drawing on the theology of Theophilus of Antioch[27] and Irenaeus of Lyons[28], "the destiny of man was for him not to remain in the state in which God made him, since he was made to become perfect and, thus, to be divinized. He was made needing to acquire perfection, not because he was made flawed in nature and morally deficient, but because moral perfection is achieved only in total freedom"[29].

In contrast to various legalistic versions of Christianity that developed in the context of medieval Western theology, and also in contrast to the grotesque descriptions of afterlife by various Asian schools of mystical belief, the Greek Fathers teach that human nature was never totally deprived of God's grace after the Fall, and, moreover, that Christian soteriology has nothing to do with any legalistic notion of man's need to justify his sin before a wrathful, judgemental, Creator. Protopresbyter John S. Romanides has pointed out that, according to the first theologians of the Church, "the fall for them was not at all a judicial matter but rather the failure of man to attain the perfection and *theosis* (divinization) because he fell into the hands of him who has the power of death"[30].

---

26 The Bible contains many anthropomorphic expressions, and the Greek Church Fathers teach that these anthropomorphic expressions should not be taken literally, but symbolically.

27 Theophilus of Antioch was a 2nd century Bishop of Antioch and Christian apologist. In his Studia Biblica (p. 90), William Sanday, describes him as "one of the precursors of that group of writers who, from Irenaeus to Cyprian, not only break the obscurity which rests on the earliest history of the Church, but alike in the East and in the West carry it to the front in literary eminence, and distance all their heathen contemporaries". He is a saint in both Eastern and Western Christianity.

28 Irenaeus of Lyons (2nd century — 202) was Bishop of Lugdunum (now Lyons, France). He was a Greek from Smyrna in Asia Minor. He is a saint in both Eastern and Western Christianity.

29 J.S. Romanides, To Propatorikon Hamartema (Ancestral Sin), Athens, 1957, p. 126 (in Greek). For an English translation of this book, see: J.S. Romanides, The Ancestral Sin, trans. G.S. Gabriel, Ridgewood, New Jersey: Zephyr Publications, 2002.

30 Ibid, p. 112.

In the context of the Greek Fathers' spirituality, the narration of the *Genesis* is a story of human struggle for progress and existential perfection, and the Incarnation of the Divine Word is the historical manifestation of the Archetype of Perfect Man.

MAXIMUS THE CONFESSOR, THE GREEK HUMANISTIC LEGACY
AND THE SPIRIT OF ASIA

In general, all Christian heresies are based on the denial of the Incarnation of the Logos, i.e. on the denial of the dual nature of Christ. Apart from its particular characteristics and arguments, in essence, every Christian heresy rejects the doctrine that Christ maintains two natures —one divine and one human— and, therefore, from this viewpoint, every Christian heresy is a re–appearance of Arianism. The heresy of Arianism, which was founded by Arius (ca. 250 — 336 A.D.), a Christian presbyter from Alexandria, denies the dual nature of Christ and asserts that Christ was not God like the Father, but a creature made in time. The heresy of Monophysitism, which was primarily founded by Eutyches (ca. 380 — ca. 456 A.D.), an archimandrite at Constantinople, denies the dual nature of Christ and asserts that Christ has only one nature, his humanity being absorbed by his deity. In particular, the Archbishop of Constantinople Nestorius (ca. 386 — ca. 451 A.D.), having asserted that Mary ought not to be referred to as the "Mother of God" ('Theotokos' in Greek, literally 'God–bearer'), was denounced as a heretic, and, in combating Nestorianism, Eutyches fought Nestorius's heresy with a heresy —namely, Eutyches declared that Christ was a fusion of human and divine elements, causing his own denunciation as a heretic twenty years after the Ecumenical Council of Ephesus, at the Ecumenical Council of Chalcedon (451 A.D.).

In the 7th century, the Nestorians were concentrated in Persia, and the Monophysites were concentrated in Egypt, Palestine and Syria. Thus, when Emperor Heraclius defeated the Persians and recaptured great parts of the Middle East, a serious problem of religious fights between the Christian heresies emerged in the Byzantine Empire.

In order to prevent a new social upheaval and new schisms and also in order to enhance state unity, the Patriarch of Constantinople Sergius I (d. 9 December 638), adopted the compromising theological thesis of the Jacobite Syrians (this was the name of the Monophysites of Syria) with respect to the problem of Monophysitism. According to this compromising thesis, Jesus Christ had two natures (one divine and one human), but he operated with but one will and one energy, which were divine. Thus, the previous compromising thesis was called Monotheletism, which literally means only one will. Monotheletism was adopted by Byzantine Emperor Heraclius, for political reasons, as a politically convenient compromise between Monophysitism and Orthodoxy. Moreover, the Patriarch of Constantinople Sergius I adopted Monotheletism for two reasons: first, the Byzantine historiographer Theophanes, in his *Chronographia*, 506, writes that the parents of Sergius I were Jacobite Syrians, and, therefore, he was influenced by his parents' religious beliefs; second, the great patriotism of Sergius I urged him to adopt the heresy of Monotheletism.

In his *Epitome Historiarum*, XIV, 16, the Byzantine chronicler and theologian John Zonaras writes that Patriarch Sergius I and the Byzantine general Bonus, who held the rank of patrikios (in the sources he is often referred to as magister), undertook the responsibility of administration of the empire during Heraclius's absence on campaign against the Persians, and they played a leading role in the successful defense of the imperial capital Constantinople during the Avar–Persian siege of 626. Hence, Patriarch Sergius I was a politically significant and politically active religious leader who adopted a heresy because he put the interest of the state above the orthodox faith, i.e., eventually, he subordinated the truth of Christ to the raison d'état.

The politically convenient heresy of Monotheletism was also adopted by all the Patriarchates of the Eastern Roman Empire and by the Pope of Rome Honorius I (d. 638). However, two humble monks decided to go against this general consensus: the first was Sophronius, the Abbot of the Eucratas Monastery in Carthage, who later became Patriarch of Jerusalem and he played a leading role in the resistance of the Holy City against the Arabs; the second was Maximus the Confessor, a monk at the Eucratas Monastery in Carthage, who was later recognized by both Eastern and Western Christianity as one of the chief doctors of the theology of the Incarnation and of Christian asceticism.

Contrary to Patriarch Sergius's ethos, Maximus the Confessor neither succumbed to the lure of political power nor accepted to subordinate theological truth to the raison d'état. Maximus was born into Byzantine nobility, he was highly educated, and around the age of 30 he became the personal secretary to Emperor Heraclius. However, a few years later, he abandoned his privileged position at the court of Emperor Heraclius to become a monk. Moreover, when, in the middle of the Monothelite controversy, he was offered a patriarchal throne under the condition that he would give priority to the raison d' état over theological matters, Maximus the Confessor declined the offer. In fact, until the end of his life, he remained a simple monk, refusing to assume any position of authority in the Church.

Maximus the Confessor started his struggle against Monophysitism and Monotheletism from his monastic cell at the Eucratas Monastery, whose Abbot was Sophronius. His resistance against the imperial authority reached its climax when Emperor Constans II, the successor of Emperor Heraclius, issued the *Typos* in 648, which prohibited any discussion of the issue of "one will and one energy, or two energies and two wills" in Christ[31]. Maximus the Confessor despised this imperial edict, and additionally he denounced the intervention of the State in the affairs of the Church, promoting Leontius Byzantius's concept of separation of Church and State.

The resistance of Maximus the Confessor was not limited to words. He convinced the Pope of Rome Theodore I to challenge the authority of the Byzantine (i.e. Roman) Emperor and convene a Church Council. Never before had a Pope alone convened an ecumenical council. Moreover, the Papacy had long regarded ecumenical councils as the prerogative of the emperor. However, under the influence of Maximus the Confessor, Pope Theodore I convened the Lateran Council of 649, which was a synod held in the Basilica of St. John Lateran to condemn Monophysitism. According to A.J. Ekonomou, Maximus the Confessor and other monks from his order did all of "planning, preparation, and scripting" of the Council[32]. Pope Theodore I died on 14 May 649, while preparing for the Council. Maximus the Confessor convinced the local Church to elect the successor to Pope Theodor I without imperial approval. Due to the influence of Maximus the Confessor, in July 649, a deacon

---

31 See: A.J. Ekonomou, Byzantine Rome and the Greek Popes —Eastern Influences on Rome and the Papacy from Gregory the Great to Zacharias, A.D. 590–752, Lanham, MD: Lexington Books, 2007, p. 116.

32 Ibid, p. 116.

from Todi was consecrated as Pope Martin I, the first Pope of Rome consecrated without imperial approval. The Lateran Council of 649 was attended by 105 bishops, all but one from the Western Roman Empire, since the Churches of the Eastern Roman Empire remained obedient to Emperor Constans II. The Lateran Council of 649 denounced Monotheletism and the *Typos*, which had been issued by Emperor Constans II, and claimed for Rome the apostolic authority to weed out heresy.

In Rome, in 653, Pope Martin I was arrested under orders from Emperor Constans II, who supported Monotheletism. Pope Martin I was condemned without a trial, and he died of ill treatment before he could be sent to Constantinople. Maximus the Confessor was sent to Constantinople at the end of 655, and he was tried as a heretic. He was exiled to Thrace. In 662, Maximus the Confessor was placed on trial once more, and he was once more convicted of heresy. After this trial, Maximus the Confessor was tortured, having his tongue cut out, so he could no longer speak his rebellion, and his right hand cut off, so that he could no longer write letters. He died soon after, in August 662. The events of the trials of Maximus the Confessor were recorded by Anastasius Bibliothecarius, a 9th century Head of the Archives and Antipope of the Church of Rome.

Finally, Maximus the Confessor was vindicated by the Sixth Ecumenical Council, which was summoned by Emperor Constantine Pogonatus, it took place in Constantinople in 680–681, and it declared that Christ possessed both a human and a divine will. Thus, the Sixth Ecumenical Council condemned Monotheletism as heretical, and Maximus the Confessor was posthumously declared innocent of all charges against him. In fact, when the Sixth Ecumenical Council was finally convened, among those condemned for heresy were four Patriarchs of Constantinople, one Pope of Rome, one Patriarch of Alexandria, two Patriarchs of Antioch and a multitude of other Metropolitans, Archbishops and Bishops, and it was officially acknowledged that, all those years, Maximus the Confessor, a simple monk, was right and expressing Orthodoxy, whereas all those notable bishops were wrong.

Maximus the Confessor exerted a significant influence on the spiritual itinerary of the ecumene. His struggle against heresies inhibited the Orientalisation of the Greek spirit, prevented the subjugation of Christianity to the spirit of Asia and secured that the Greek philosophy would continue being the foundation of the orthodox exposition and interpretation of the Christian dogma. In particular, Maximus the Confessor's explanations regarding the 'logoi' of creation prevented the mingling of the Christian Logos doctrine with the abstract notion of monotheism[33] (e.g. the Muslims' notion of Allah) and with the abstract principle of cause and effect (known in the Oriental traditions as 'karma'). In order to achieve these results, Maximus the Confessor interpreted the mystical theology of Dionysius the Areopagite[34] in a manner that was fully compatible with the Orthodox Christian dogmas, thus making a substantial contribution to the development of the Orthodox Christian mysticism and depriving the Monophysites of the monopoly over the utilization of the Areopagite mysticism.

Maximus the Confessor starts from the principle that God is absolutely free, and, therefore, God creates without using any other resources apart from His own will. Hence, Maximus the Confessor stresses that the world and everything in it were brought into existence out of nothing ('ex nihilo'). The Creation is the realization of the Creator's will, and the Creator's will is not restricted by any necessity, such as the laws of logic, the principle of karma (or cause and effect), etc. In fact, this is the essence of God's hypostatic mode of existence, which I explained earlier in this Chapter. With respect to nature, the distance between God and His creation is expressed by Maximus the Confessor through the following terms: 'difference', 'distinction', 'distance', 'separation'[35]. Underlying the absolute difference between the nature (essence) of God and the nature (essence) of the creatures, Maximus the Confessor

---

33 Contra abstract monotheism, the God of Christianity is a communion of Three Hypostases (God the Father, God the Son and God the Holy Spirit). Thus, we read in 1 John, 2:23: "No–one who denies the Son has the Father; whoever acknowledges the Son has the Father also".

34 Dionysius the Areopagite was a judge of Areopagus who, as related in Acts 17:34, was converted to Christianity by the preaching of Paul during the Areopagus Sermon. According to Dionysius of Corinth (a 2nd century bishop of Corinth), Dionysius the Areopagite became bishop of Athens. A series of famous writings of a mystical nature, employing the language of Neoplatonic philosophy in order to elucidate Christian theological ideas, has been ascribed to Dionysius the Areopagite. In the Eastern Orthodox Church, Dionysius the Areopagite is venerated as a saint. In fact, in Greece, the Christian Orthodox Cathedral of Athens is dedicated to Dionysius the Areopagite.

35 See: Lars Thunberg, Microcosmos and Mediator —The Theological Anthropology of Maximus the Confessor, 2nd edition, Chicago: Open Court Publishing Company, 1995, pp. 51–60.

rejects the negative and pessimistic Origenist[36] and Gnostic views according to which, before coming into existence, beings pre–existed substantially united with the Divine Logos. Through sin, these fallen spirits would have attracted the divine–'karmic' punishment, which consisted essentially of taking an inferior, material form of existence. However, through a creative re–interpretation of the mystical theology of Dionysius the Areopagite, Maximus the Confessor refuted the previous view and articulated the concept of the divine logoi, stressing the personhood, and hence the freedom, of God and of man. In the context of a personal relationship, as opposed to relationships determined by logical necessities (e.g. karma), God and man are related to each other in a manner that reflects their freedom of will, and, therefore, their relationship is founded on love and not on any kind of necessity or mechanistic rules.

In his *Ambigua, 7* (*Patrologia Graeca*, Vol. 91, 1080A), Maximus the Confessor writes the following: "For we believe that a logos of angels preceded their creation, a logos preceded the creation of each of the beings and powers that fill the upper world, a logos preceded the creation of human beings, a logos preceded everything that receives its becoming from God, and so on". However, these logoi, which precede the beings and things in the world, do not exist *actually* before the creation of the corresponding beings and things in the world, since they are only wills of God. In other words, according to Maximus the Confessor, the logos of a being is not a substance, but the reason of that being's substance, and, therefore, it does not subsist in itself, but it only exists *potentially* in God, as a yet unmanifested possibility.

Following Dionysius the Areopagite, Maximus the Confessor names the logoi divine "wills"[37] (*thelemata*). Explaining the thought of Maximus the Confessor, J.–C. Larchet defined the logos of a being as "its essential reason, the one that fundamentally defines and

---

36 Origenism is the theological and philosophical system developed by Origen, an early Christian Alexandrian scholar and theologian (born ca. 185 A.D.). He was strongly influenced by the solipsistic philosophical traditions of Asia and Egypt, and, thus, his theological work was based on his belief that spirit is the only true substance. His solipsistic views were condemned at the Fifth Ecumenical Council, which took place in Constantinople in 553 A.D.; however, other parts of Origen's teachings are in agreement with the Orthodox Christian Dogmatics. For more details, see: John Karmiris, A Synopsis of the Dogmatic Theology of the Orthodox Catholic Church, trans. Rev. G. Dimopoulos, Scranton: Christian Orthodox Edition, 1973.

37 Maximus the Confessor, Ambigua, 7 (Patrologia Graeca, Vol. 91, 1085A).

characterizes it, but also its finality, the *scope* for which a being exists, briefly its reason of being in a double meaning of principle and end of its existence"[38]. Hence, in the context of Maximus the Confessor's theology, God is not related to the nature (essence) of the beings and things in the world, since the nature of the beings and things in the world is created whereas God's nature is uncreated, but God knows–recognizes the beings and things in the world as realizations of His will, and for this reason, His knowledge is equivalent to love.

Furthermore, according to Maximus the Confessor, the Logos (Word) of God is the One that gathers in Himself the multitude of logoi, since, as we read in *John* 1:3 and in *Colossians* 1:16, the world itself is made by Him. In Maximus the Confessor's own words: "we affirm that the one Logos is many logoi and the many logoi are One. Because the One goes forth out of goodness into individual beings creating and preserving them, the One is many. Moreover the many are directed towards the One and are providentially guided in that direction"[39].

Using Aristotle's concepts of being potentially and being actually, Maximus the Confessor explains that, within the Logos of God, all the logoi of the beings and things in the world exist potentially, and, through their actuality, they reveal the same work and presence of the Logos. In other words, in each creature, through its logoi, the Logos of God is made present and manifested. Thus, Maximus the Confessor compares our contemplation of the sensuous world with the meeting between Elizabeth and Mary the Mother of God, which is mentioned in *Luke* 1:39–56. In particular, according to Maximus the Confessor[40], in its material and bodily form, each and every human being represents John the Baptist in the womb of his mother Elizabeth, while the Logos of God is hidden in creatures as if in another womb (the womb of Mary the Mother of God).

Contra Origen and the Gnostics, who saw a decline in corporality and materiality, Maximus the Confessor writes that the creation of the world itself is a revelation of God's will, and the essence of this revelation is the presence of the Logos of God in the logoi of the creatures. This is considered by Maximus the Confessor to be an

---

38 J.–C. Larchet, Introduction à Saint Maxime le Confesseur, Ambigua, Paris: Suresnes, 1994, p. 20.

39 Maximus the Confessor, Ambigua, 7 (Patrologia Graeca, Vol. 91, 1081BC).

40 Maximus the Confessor, Ambigua, 6 (Patrologia Graeca, Vol. 91, 1068AB).

Embodiment of the Logos of God. In fact, Maximus the Confessor speaks about a triple Embodiment of the Logos[41]: in nature, in the Bible, and in the historic person of Christ.

In addition, contra Origen and Gnosticism, Maximus the Confessor's cosmology is highly dynamic. In fact, in order to refute theories that had been articulated by Origen and Gnostics and reflected the Oriental spirit of passivity, Maximus the Confessor stressed the movement of the beings of the natural world. According to Origen and many Oriental philosophies and religious systems, between the creatures and God, there is some connaturality (e.g. some Gnostics argued that the human soul is a spark of the divine nature), as they are both in a state of repose or rest in the original Unity (the Gnostics' One). But, for some reason (e.g. satiety), the spirits (or Aeons) went through a movement of decline, which implied their coming into a material life, which will (or must) be followed by their return to the original Unity. In other words, according to Origen and Gnosticism, movement is the cause of sin. On the other hand, according to Maximus the Confessor, movement is a natural characteristic of all beings, because the Divinity is unmoved, since it fills all beings, and everything that was brought from non–being to being is moved because "it tends towards some end"[42]. In Maximus the Confessor's own words: "The movement that it is tending towards its proper end is called a natural power, or passion, or movement passing from one thing to another and having impassibility as its end. It is also called an irrepressible activity that has as its end perfect fulfillment"[43].

Hence, in the context of the dynamic cosmology of Maximus the Confessor, the ontological perfection of man is understood as an end ('telos') to be progressively achieved in the future and not as a return to a lost paradise, nor as the negation of the material world. For this reason, according to Maximus the Confessor, movement is related to the concept of 'telos', or purpose: "nothing that came into being is perfect in itself, nor has a purpose in itself"[44]. Moreover, Maximus the Confessor goes on as follows: "If then rational beings come into

---

41 Maximus the Confessor, Questions to Thalassius, 15 (Patrologia Graeca, Vol. 90, 297B–300A). See also: H.U. von Balthasar, Cosmic Liturgy —The Universe According to Maximus the Confessor, San Francisco: St Ignatius Press, 2003, p. 292.

42 Maximus the Confessor, Ambigua, 7, Patrologia Graeca, Vol. 91, 1069B.

43 Ibid, 1072B.

44 Ibid, 1072C.

being, surely they are also moved, since they move from a natural beginning in being towards a voluntary end in well–being"[45]. Hence, the creation of the material world is not a negative event, but instead it is the necessary context in which rational beings can exercise their freedom of will and pursue their ontological perfection.

Maximus the Confessor stresses that Jesus Christ is the Archetype of Divinized Man, and not simply a great initiate who talks about the spiritual world and the moral improvement of man. The purpose of Jesus Christ is to operate as a practical, historic example of the manner in which the human being can be divinized. Therefore, Maximus the Confessor stresses that Jesus Christ has a divine nature and a human nature, and also that Jesus Christ has a divine will and a human will, i.e. that Jesus Christ is an integral man and an integral God. Otherwise, Jesus Christ's Work, which was to bridge the gap between God and man, remains incomplete. The two natures and the two wills of Jesus Christ imply that Jesus Christ is the perfect mediator between God and the material world, and, therefore, he is the perfect example for humans to follow in order to attain perfection. The Christology of Maximus the Confessor shows that the human being can be divinized (deified) without seizing to be a human being and without negating its material substance, but exactly because it is a human being[46]. In his book *Mystagogy* (*Patrologia Graeca*, Vol. 91), Maximus the Confessor stresses that man is a "mediator by nature" (between the Creator and the Creation) and a "microcosm" (a cosmos in small), recapitulating in himself the elements of the entire cosmos, in his body and in his soul. From this viewpoint, the Incarnation of the Logos of God is the necessary presupposition and the eternal symbol of the divinization of man.

ORTHODOXY VERSUS GNOSTICISM

Gnosticism (from Greek 'gnosis', which means knowledge) refers to a set of religious beliefs and spiritual practices based on the doctrine of salvation by a peculiar esoteric knowledge that promises to 'free' the soul from the material world. The roots of Gnosticism can be traced to non–Christian and pre–Christian Asian religious communities.

---

45   Ibid, 1073BC.
46   See: Thunberg, Microcosmos and Mediator.

In particular, Walter Bauer[47] and Christian Lassen[48] argue that Gnosticism is strongly related to the religions of India. According to Lassen, the Indian elements in the Gnostic 'schools' were derived from Buddhism, which exercised a considerable influence on the intellectual life of Alexandria. R.A. Lipsius[49] argues that the origins of Gnosticism are in Syria and Phoenicia. Adolf Hilgenfeld[50] argues that Gnosticism is strongly connected with later Mazdaism, i.e. the worship of Ahura Mazda, who, in Zoroastrianism, is the source of all light and good.

From the very beginning of Christianity, various Gnostics attempted to interpret Christianity in a way that made sense to them and particularly in a way that was leading to the subjugation of Christianity to the Asian traditions. In his Epistle to the Colossians, the Apostle Paul combated Gnostic teachings that had infiltrated the Colossian Church and were undermining Christianity in the following ways:

i.   The Gnostics taught that spirit is good, whereas matter is evil (*Colossians*, 1:15–20). Paul's answer was that both heaven and earth are realizations of God's Will and, hence, as we read in *Genesis*, 1:31, they have been created "very good". Moreover, in chapter 4, I shall explain the Hesychasts' thesis about the psychosomatic nexus and unity of the human being.

ii. The Gnostics insisted that one must follow certain esoteric ceremonies, rituals and restrictions in order to be saved or perfected (*Colossians*, 2:11, 16–23, 3:11). Simon Magus, the magician baptized by the Apostle Philip and rebuked by the Apostle Peter in *Acts*, 8:924, is a characteristic example of such a Gnostic teacher. Paul's answer was that the esoteric practices emphasized by the Gnostics were only shadows that ended when Christ came and that Christ –being the revealed Archetype

---

47   Walter Bauer, Orthodoxy and Heresy in Earliest Christianity, trans. and ed. R. Kraft and G. Kroedel, Philadelphia: Fortress Press, 1971.

48   Christian Lassen, Indische Alterthumskunde, Bonn: H.B. König, 1847.

49   R.A. Lipsius, Der Gnosticismus, Leipzig, 1860.

50   Adolf Hilgenfeld, Die Ketzergeschichte des Urchristentums, Leipzig, 1884.

of Divinized Man– is all one needs to be perfected. Furthermore, in chapter 4, I shall study the difference between the Hesychastic mystical practices and Oriental meditation.

iii. The Gnostics argued that Christ could not be both human and divine (*Colossians*, 1:15–20, 2:2–3). For instance, Cerinthus (ca. 100 A.D.), the founder of a Gnostic school in the Roman Province of Asia, depicted Christ as a heavenly spirit separate from the man Jesus. Paul's answer was that Christ was the Divine Logos in the flesh. In general, in presenting Christ as the Archetype of the new human being, and of Adam and Eve restored to the divine course appointed by God, there is present everywhere in the writings of the early Greek Fathers a clear soteriological leitmotif: that the Divine Logos –Christ– became man, so that man could achieve deification by grace. In his Logos *Peri tes Enanthropeseos tou Logou* (Discourse on the incarnation of the Word, *Patrologia Graeca*, Vol. 25, 192B), Athanasius the Great[51] has written that Christ "was made man, that we might be made God". This statement contains within it two essential elements in the deification of man: first, an affirmation of the restoration of man by his Creator; and, second, the indispensable affirmation of the humanity of Christ, who was simultaneously divine and human. The Orthodox Christology is founded on the notion of hypostasis, on the ontology of Maximus the Confessor and on the essence–energies distinction, which I shall study further in chapter 4.

iv. The Gnostics argued that one must obtain 'secret' knowledge[52] in order to be saved or perfected and that this knowledge was not available to everyone (*Colossians*, 2:2,

---

51 Athanasius the Great (d. 373), also known as Athanasius of Alexandria, was a 4th century Bishop of Alexandria. He is a saint in both Eastern and Western Christianity.

52 For instance, the Sethian Gnostics, one of the most influential Gnostic schools, believed that Seth, the third son of Adam and Eve, was the safeguard and keeper of a secret knowledge and believed Jesus to be a manifestation of Seth.

18). Paul's answer was that God's secret was His Logos (Word), and God's secret has been revealed to humanity through Christ. For He, Christ, is "our peace, the maker of the two [i.e. humanity and Divinity] into one" (*Ephesians*, 2:14), which were before separated and divided, now are one body and one unity "having, in him, destroyed their enmity" (*Ephesians*, 2:16–17). Moreover, as I shall explain in chapter 4, the Hesychasts elucidated the difference between the terms 'mind' (*nous*) and 'intellect'.

v.   The Gnostics were claiming to eschew the physical realm (material world) while simultaneously freely indulging their physical appetites and teaching that there is nothing wrong with bodily immorality (*Colossians*, 2:20–23, 3:1–11). Moreover, in his *Panarion*, 40:1:4, Epiphanius of Salamis[53] provides an example when he writes of the Archontics (a Gnostic school that existed in Palestine and Armenia) that "some of them ruin their bodies by dissipation, but others feign ostensible fasts and deceive simple people while they pride themselves with a sort of abstinence, under the disguise of monks". With respect to the Gnostics' asceticism, Paul's answer was that asceticism cannot conquer evil thoughts and desires, and, instead, it may lead to pride. With respect to the Gnostics' teachings about bodily morality, Paul's answer was that Christians follow a new life as representatives of Jesus Christ, and, therefore, they should live in harmony with their Archetype's ethos.

vi. The Gnostics were teaching that angels must be worshiped (*Colossians*, 2:18). In fact, some Gnostic schools used the term Archon to refer to several servants of the Demiurge, who was an emanation of the superior God and had created the mankind and the material world. Thus, Archons had the roles of the angels and demons of the Old Testament. For instance, according to Origen's *Contra Celsum*, a Gnostic school called the Ophites was

---

53   Epiphanius of Salamis was Bishop of Salamis and Metropolitan of Cyprus in the end of the 4th century. He is a saint in both Eastern and Western Christianity.

teaching the existence of seven Archons, beginning with Iadabaoth, who, similarly to the Mithraic Kronos and the Vedic Narasimha (a form of Vishnu), had a head of a lion. Paul's answer was that angels are not to be worshiped, whereas Christ is worthy of worship.

vii. Gnosticism promotes religious syncretism, i.e. the fusion of diverse religious beliefs and practices. Moreover, in the modern era, religious syncretism is promoted by several political and religious authorities that want to subordinate spirituality to historical needs and expediencies. Every kind of religious syncretism is opposite to Christianity.

Plutarch equates religion with worship. Even though Orthodox Christianity involves worship, it is not a mere community of worship, and, therefore, it is not merely a religion. Nowhere in the New Testament is the Church characterized as a religion, but rather as a "way" (*Acts*, 9:2), i.e. as a path and a way of life that leads to deification. According to *John*, 14:62, the ultimate "way" is Christ himself.

Orthodox Christianity can be characterized as a religion, but not in the way that the world's various faiths (irrespective of whether they are monotheistic or not) understand religion. Orthodox Christianity is founded on Christ's declaration: "I am the way and the truth and the life" (*John*, 14:6). Furthermore, Christianity is not merely an "Abrahamic faith", but Christ is the 'telos' and the fulfillment of the covenant between God and Abraham: "The promises were spoken to Abraham and to his seed. The Scripture does not say 'and to seeds', meaning many people, but 'and to your seed', meaning one person, who is Christ...You are all sons of God through faith in Christ Jesus" (*Galatians*, 3:16, 26). Thus, the God of Christianity is not the God of abstract monotheism. The God of Christianity is the Trinity of God the Father (Divine Nous), God the Son (Divine Logos), who is begotten from the Father, and God the Holy Spirit, who proceeds from the Father: three distinct hypostases (persons), yet they are one essence or nature.

2

THE ADVENTURE OF RATIO IN THE WEST

THE history of ratio in the West starts with the work of Augustine of Hippo (354–430 A.D.). In his early years, he was heavily influenced by Manichaeism and afterwards by the philosophy of Plotinus. After his conversion to Christianity and baptism (387 A.D.), Augustine wrote many works on Christianity and, in 395, he became bishop of Hippo. In the Roman Catholic and Anglican Churches, he is saint and pre–eminent Doctor of the Church, and many Protestants, especially Calvinists, consider him to be one of the theological fathers of Reformation. In the Eastern Orthodox Church, he is 'blessed' (instead of 'saint'), because the Eastern Orthodox Church does not accept some of Augustine's teachings because, at least to the eyes of the Eastern Orthodox Church, they reflect his Manichaean background[54].

The term 'ratio' is much broader than the term 'logic'. In modern philosophical language, rationalism is a method or a theory "in which the criterion of the truth is not sensory but intellectual and deductive"[55]. According to Augustine of Hippo's *De libero arbitrio*, II, 9, the term ratio means the logical capacity of the intellect to analyze and synthesize the objects of knowledge. Furthermore, Augustine of Hippo maintains that spiritual vision is the result of rational functions unique to human beings. In his *De trinitate*, 12, Augustine

---

54 The Greek Church Fathers do not interpret 'evil' and 'sin' in legalistic terms, and, therefore, they understand the notions of evil and sin in a substantially different way from Augustine.

55 V.J. Bourke, "Rationalism", in D.D. Runes (ed.), Dictionary of Philosophy, Totowa, NJ: Littlefield, Adams and Company, 1962, p. 263.

of Hippo divided ratio into "ratio inferior" and "ratio superior": ratio inferior is the capacity to judge physical reality in terms of super-sensible reality, and this level of perception yields the knowledge that Augustine calls 'scientia', i.e. the kind of knowledge that enables man to develop technology and institutions; ratio superior consists in a turning of the human mind towards the super–sensible reality, and, therefore, it discerns the ideal world in and through the human soul and it yields the knowledge that Augustine calls 'sapientia' (wisdom), i.e. the knowledge of super–sensible reality.

According to the Greek philosophy, when a scholar seeks the 'logos' of the world, he seeks two things: first, to collect, define and organize various elements into a coherent whole, the 'cosmos' (world); and, second, to find the existential telos (purpose), the ultimate meaning of the cosmos. In modern philosophical terms, the first endeavor is based on philosophical structuralism, whereas the latter is based on hermeneutics. According to Claude Lévi-Strauss, the purpose of structuralism is "to reduce apparently arbitrary data to some kind of order, and to attain a level at which a kind of necessity becomes apparent"[56]. According to Hans–Georg Gadamer, hermeneutics is an attempt "to clarify the conditions in which understanding takes place"[57], and "understanding is not to be thought of so much as an action of one's subjectivity, but as the placing of oneself within a process of tradition, in which past and present are constantly fused"[58].

In the context of the Greek philosophy, the quest for 'logos' consists in a synthesis between structuralism and hermeneutics. Hence, as we read in Plato's *Republic*, 476b, as well as in the entire Platonic dialogue *Phaedo*, the relationship between the philosopher and the Good is not only a cognitive one but also an erotic one. This is the erotic (intuitive) component of Plato's theory of intelligence. In Plato's dialogues *Theaetetus*, 154d–e, *Charmides*, 166c–e, *Philebus*, 38c–e, *Sophist*, 263e, and *Laws*, 893a, we realize that Plato understands dialectic as a form of inner dialogue that is motivated by the fact that the philosopher's soul seeks truth in order to achieve existential perfection. On the other hand, when a Latin scholar,

---

56   Claude Lévi–Strauss, The Raw and the Cooked, trans. John and Doreen Weightman, Chicago: The University of Chicago Press, 1969, p. 10.

57   H.–G. Gadamer, Truth and Method, London: Sheed and Ward, 1975, p. 263.

58   Ibid, p. 258.

such as Augustine, seeks the 'ratio' of the world, he mainly seeks to collect, define and organize various elements into a coherent whole, the 'cosmos' (world).

Augustine's distinction between ratio inferior and ratio superior led the medieval Western thought to the conclusion that ratio inferior cannot tell the 'real' truth, since the statements that are based on ratio inferior follow from the conscious processing of the sensuous world and not from the conscious processing of the universal reality. In the context of Augustine's thought, the 'real' truth is only the truth that follows from the conscious processing of the universal reality. Thus, Augustine's distinction between ratio inferior and ratio superior underpins the distinction between 'veritas' (truth) and 'ratio'. By contrast, in the context of the Greek philosophical tradition, 'reality', 'truth' and 'ratio' are united into one concept —namely, that of logos. Furthermore, in later years, Augustine's concept of ratio superior was identified with the concept of intellect (which was errantly considered to be a correct Latin translation of the Greek word nous, or mind), and Bernard of Clervaux (1090–1153) developed the concepts of 'intellectus fidei' (spiritual understanding through faith) and 'judicium rationis' (judgment based on discursive thinking). Thus, given the Latin West's way of understanding 'ratio', rationalism naturally gave rise to the quest for the control of ratio by an 'auctoritas' (authority), whose duty would be to make sure that man never misses the truth that meets the demands of disciplined thought and is governed by the intellect.

In his book *Scripta super libros Sententiarum* (Writings on the Books of the Sentences), Thomas Aquinas[59] (1224–1274) studies several epistemological questions —such as the source and the forms of knowledge, perception, intentionality, ratio, sensuous knowledge, imagination, memory, truth, objectivity, etc. In this book, he articulates a very important criticism of Augustine's epistemology.

According to Thomas Aquinas, ratio superior, which is identified with intellectual truth, is the knowledge of God. Thomas Aquinas argues that God knows all things in One, i.e. in Himself, and,

---

59   Thomas Aquinas (1225–1274) was an Italian Dominican priest and one of the most influential medieval philosophers and theologians. In the Roman Catholic Church, Thomas Aquinas is considered a saint (pronounced in 1323 by Pope John XXII).

therefore, He does not need any methodologies, syllogisms, analyses or syntheses, whereas man knows only under particular conditions and through particular mental processes. In *Scripta super libros Sententiarum*, III, 31, Thomas Aquinas writes that, "in the present life, it is true what the Philosopher [Aristotle] says, namely that, without images ['phantasmata'], the soul could neither develop science nor revise the things that it already knows; since images are for the intellect what sensibilia [i.e. sense–data] are for the senses". Thus, Thomas Aquinas discarded Augustine's qualitative distinction between ratio inferior and ratio superior, and, in his book *Summa Theologica*, Thomas Aquinas substituted his distinction between the supernatural end and the natural end of human life for Augustine's distinction between ratio inferior and ratio superior. The supernatural end of human life is, according to Thomas Aquinas, the object of theology and is based on faith, whereas the natural end of human life is the object of philosophy and, due to ratio, the knowledge of the natural end of human life can be attained by man himself.

The continuity of faith and reason, of grace and nature, is central to Thomas Aquinas's philosophical and theological system. For Thomas Aquinas, there is only one truth —namely, the divine truth— and the soul unites the sensible with the intelligible. Thomas Aquinas maintains that the soul is essentially different from the body, and, even though it is not self–existent, it is hierarchically the supreme intellectual creature of God, immortal, immaterial and capable of knowing the intelligible realm. However, according to Thomas Aquinas, because the soul is united with the body, the soul cannot know non–corporeal beings directly, but it can only know them through ratio, in the context of which general concepts are distanced from objects, i.e. through abstraction, which is a process by which higher concepts are derived from the usage and classification of concrete, individual forms.

According to Thomas Aquinas, in the sensuous world, the universal (general concept) cannot exist as such, apart from the individual; it is immanent in the individual as the essence specifically common to all members of the same species. This essence constitutes the thing specifically what it is. Therefore, Thomas Aquinas argues that knowledge starts from the sensuous world (i.e. he disagrees with Augustine's thesis that what Augustine calls ratio inferior leads to false knowledge) and is completed in what Augustine calls ratio superior, i.e. in the intellectual–speculative processing of sense–data, and that, in this way, man attains the knowledge of the universal, i.e. he can logically determine the kind (species) of a being. Furthermore, Thomas Aquinas argues that there is a group of truths, such as the mysteries of the Trinity and the Incarnation, quite incapable of justification by ratio. In this case, Thomas Aquinas argues that faith, which is a gift from the Creator, perfects the finite nature of man, but this does not reduce the significance or power of human reason (ratio). On the contrary, Thomas Aquinas maintains that, although the grace that confers faith comes from outside, yet, because it comes from the Creator who is responsible for the existence of the creature in question, it embraces the human being from inside, and, therefore, faith appears as intrinsic to the nature it perfects. Hence, Thomas Aquinas insists that we are obliged to comprehend the mysteries of faith through ratio. In other words, the 'Apollonian' element completely dominates the 'Dionysian' element in Thomas Aquinas's thought, and Thomas Aquinas completely ignores the Platonic notion of eros as a Dionysian epistemology.

For Thomas Aquinas, ratio governs the soul, and ratio's capability of knowing God is the noblest characteristic of the human being. In the context of Thomas Aquinas's thought, love, as a characteristic of the human being, is inferior to ratio, because will is determined by the knowledge of the good and, therefore, by ratio. In other words, because the intellect conceives the idea of the good and also knows what is good in each case, ratio determines will. Furthermore, in the context of Thomas Aquinas's thought, freedom, as a characteristic of the human being, is inferior to ratio, because freedom necessarily depends on knowledge, and, therefore, it is determined by ratio. In other words, according to Thomas Aquinas, the moral ideal of freedom is the necessity that is derived from knowledge.

Rationalism is the theory according to which knowledge is innate, independent of experience and self–confirmed. Hence, the opponent of rationalism is not faith in God —at least when the latter is based on ratio, as is the case in Thomas Aquinas's theology— but empiricism, i.e. the theory according to which knowledge is derived from experience. In fact, as I shall explain in chapter 4, in the Greek East, the Hesychasts fought Thomas Aquinas's theology and generally every kind of theological rationalism by giving priority to mystical experience and personhood over ratio and speculation about essences. The Hesychasts stress that to *talk about* God is not the same as *being* god (deification), and they choose the latter in accordance with Jesus Christ's statement: "You are gods" (*John* 10:34).

THE ROMAN CHURCH AS THE SOURCE OF MEDIEVAL RATIONALISM

There is an important cultural difference between Western Christian theology and Eastern Christian theology: the first is based on the Roman legal tradition, whereas the latter is based on the Greek philosophical tradition. The priority of the rationalist ethos of the Latin Christianity was to endow human life with a rational system of organization, whereas the priority of the Greek Christianity was to endow human life with an ultimate meaning, with a transcendental significance, or telos.

The Byzantine civilization is founded on the belief that the ultimate purpose of human life in this world is not to enjoy living benefits, and, therefore, according to the Byzantine civilization, the ultimate purpose of life is not the enjoyment of material goods. The Byzantine civilization believes that we must live in accordance with the commands of a transcendental, supra–rational, significance of life, on the basis of which and due to which 'praxis' (i.e. historical action) is a *means* towards the attainment of our ultimate purpose in this life —namely, our unification with the transcendental, supra–rational, significance of life, which, for the Byzantines, was the incarnate Logos of God. Thus, in the context of the Byzantine civilization and, more specifically, in the context of the Greek Christianity, even the most brutal material necessities are confronted in accordance with a certain symbolic constitution of external reality.

In contrast to Thomas Aquinas's thought, which ultimately succumbs to a form of objectivism, the Byzantine civilization and, more specifically, the Greek Christianity are based on the awareness that the reality of the world (external reality) does not exist in itself, i.e. it does not exist independently of the significance that is assigned to it by human consciousness, and, therefore, the Greek Christianity stresses that, through a mystical relation with the ultimate significance of the world, i.e. with the incarnate Divine Logos, man can attain his spiritual freedom from the world without refusing to

31

undertake his historical responsibilities in this world. In other words, instead of following Thomas Aquinas's natural theology[60], which is founded on a chain of logical necessities that reflects the ratio of the world (since it starts from ratio inferior in order, through syllogisms, to ascend to the level of God), the Greek Christianity is focused on a direct relationship with God, rejecting the Thomistic argument that the reason of this world is a necessary mediator between God and man, and, therefore, the Greek Christianity endows man with those symbols and significations that allow him to reign over needs and nature.

In *Genesis* 2:19–20, we read: "Now the Lord God had formed out of the ground all the wild animals and all the birds in the sky. He brought them to the man to see what he would name them; and whatever the man called each living creature, that was its name. So the man gave names to all the livestock, the birds in the sky and all the wild animals". The previous text means that, for so long as man is directly united with the Divine Logos, i.e. with the ultimate source of significance of the beings and things in the world, man's logos is free from natural necessities and, in addition, man's logos can be imposed on nature, since it is human consciousness that assigns significance to the world and not vice versa.

The Thomistic attempt to ascend to God through a series of syllogisms that start from ratio inferior and culminate in ratio superior keeps man necessarily dependent on the ratio of the world, instead of offering him the spiritual freedom that is described in the above Biblical text and is pursued by the Greek Christianity. Thus, Thomism stresses necessities, which reflect the inanimate (impersonal) nature's mode of life, whereas the Greek Christianity stresses freedom, which, according to the Bible, is God's mode of life, and, for this reason, the Greek Christianity rejects the Machiavellian motto that "the end justifies the means".

Throughout the Middle Ages, due to its rationalism, the Roman Church became an effective trainer in socio–political organization, ethics and logic. But also, due to its rationalism, the Roman Church succumbed to the lure of secular power and subordinated Christ's

---

60   Karl Barth (1886–1968) has pointedly observed that the linking of Christian thought about God with this supposed general knowledge is a fateful error, because important characteristics are imparted by what man thinks he knows of himself (Karl Barth, Church Dogmatics —A Selection, trans. and ed. G.W. Bromiley, Edinburgh: T. & T. Clark, 1961).

Gospel of freedom to historical and mainly political necessities, thus eventually legitimating authoritarianism.

The first significant renewal of learning in the West came when Charlemagne (King of Franks from 768 and Emperor of the Romans from 800 to his death in 814), advised by the grammarian Peter of Pisa and the English scholar and ecclesiastic Alcuin of York, attracted the scholars of England and Ireland, and by decree in 787 A.D. established schools in every abbey in his empire. These schools, from which the name *scholasticism* is derived, became important medieval educational centers. The 13th and early 14th centuries are generally seen as the high period of scholasticism, and Thomas Aquinas is the preeminent representative of scholasticism.

Charlemagne was an illiterate barbarian, who wanted to impose his authority on the Roman Empire, and, therefore, he used his network of schools as an instrument of cultural and political subversion. Thus, the Caroligian Franks attempted to articulate a new doctrinal approach to Christianity and a new philosophical system, but, before starting their 'educational career', they had not equipped themselves with the necessary educational qualifications.

When the Carolingian Franks began their doctrinal career, they had complete knowledge of only one theological system, namely, Augustine of Hippo's theology, they were unable to undertake a methodical and critical study of Augustine's Neoplatonic approach to Christianity, and they had a very elementary knowledge of the classical Greek thought. However, the Carolingian Franks had such a great arrogance and ignorance that began their attack on the Roman Papacy by questioning the decision of Pope Hadrian I (ca. 700–795) to support the Seventh Ecumenical Council of 786/8. Charlemagne condemned the Seventh Ecumenical Council at his own Council of Frankfurt in 794 in the very presence of Pope Hadrian's legates. Moreover, when the Franks captured the Papacy during 1009–1046, they had already rejected not only the Seventh, but also the Eighth Ecumenical Council of 879–880, which had been supported conjointly by Pope John VIII (d. 882) of Elder Rome and Patriarch Photius (ca. 815 – ca. 897) of New Rome (Constantinople) as well as by the remaining Roman Patriarchates of Alexandria, Antioch and Jerusalem.

It must be mentioned that Pope Hadrian I rejected the heresies of the Carolingian Franks not only for the sake of truth but for political reasons, too. In fact, Pope Hadrian I was trying to defend the Papacy's "plenitudo potestatis". The authoritarian ethos and generally the secularism of Pope Hadrian I were revealed in his reply to an Epistle of Empress Irene and her son: in that letter, Pope Hadrian I wrote about the Patriarch of Constantinople: "We are very much surprised to see that in your letter you give to Tarasius the title of ecumenical Patriarch. The Patriarch of Constantinople would not have even the second rank without the consent of our See"[61].

The Roman Emperors, from Constantine the Great (reigned 306–337) to the last Roman Emperor Constantine XII (reigned 1449–1453), accepted Christianity as the official cure of the sicknesses of religious despotism and of religious wars, and not as one more form of religion, but, following the example of the secularized Papacy, the elite of the Franks used Christianity as an instrument for the conduct of cultural diplomacy and power politics. Thus, in 809, a local Council of Charlemagne's bishops in Aachen, changed the Nicene Creed and introduced the term 'Filioque' (Latin for 'and from the Son'). According to the original Nicene Creed, the Holy Spirit proceeds "from the Father", and the term 'proceeds' signifies a kind of personal relationship, and not an authoritarian hierarchy, but, with the introduction of the Filioque, the Holy Spirit proceeds "from the Father and the Son", and, thus, the Holy Trinity reduces to an authoritarian Neoplatonic hierarchical structure. Pope Leo III intervened, forbidding the use of the Filioque, and engraving the Creed of the whole Church (without the Filioque) on silver plates, placing them on the wall of St. Peter's in Rome[62].

However, like Pope Hadrian I, Pope Leo III, apart from defending the orthodox version of the Nicene Creed, was also trying to preserve the Papacy's "plenitudo potestatis". Thus, finally, Pope Leo III did not hesitate to crown Charlemagne "Emperor of the Romans". In

---

61 Quoted in Abbé Guettée, The Papacy, New York: Carleton, 1866, p. 258ff.

62 The Eighth Ecumenical Council (879–880) anathematised any who altered the Nicene–Constantinopolitan Creed, thus condemning the Filioque. However, in the 11th century, the Church of Rome repudiated the Eighth Ecumenical Council, retroactively regarding the robber council of 869–870 to be ecumenical.

this way, Pope Leo III managed to overcome a number of serious personal and political problems. Tom Holland has explained the personal crisis and the selfish political agenda of Pope Leo III and the famous Coronation of Charlemagne on Christmas Day, 800, as follows: "Even though his election had been unanimous, Leo had enemies...On 25 April...he was set upon by a gang of heavies...Leo summoned Charlemagne to his duty: to stir himself in defense of the Pope"[63]. In fact, in the early winter of 800, Charlemagne approached the gates of Rome, and the proceedings against Leo formally opened on 1 December. Papal officials managed to convince Charlemagne that their master could in fact only be judged by God. Charlemagne, accepting this rhetoric, duly pronounced the Pope acquitted. Two days after the Pope's acquittal, Charlemagne attended Christmas Mass in the shrine of St. Peter in the Vatican. During that Christmas Mass, Pope Leo III placed a crown on Charlemagne's bare head, and the congregation hailed the Frankish king as 'Augustus' —the honorific of the ancient Caesars.

Charlemagne's biographer Einhard[64] argues that Charlemagne was not intending to become part of Pope Leo's political plans. In particular, in his book *The Life of Charlemagne*, 28, Einhard writes the following: "Charles accordingly went to Rome, to set in order the affairs of the Church...It was then that he received the titles of Emperor and Augustus [25 December 800], to which he at first had such an aversion that he declared that he would not have set foot in the Church the day that they were conferred".

There is evidence that, in later years, Charlemagne drew back from too sharp a confrontation with the Byzantine (Eastern Roman) Empire, dropping the phrase "of the Romans" while retaining the title "Emperor", and he dropped his idea of attacking the Byzantine province of Sicily. Furthermore, Charlemagne proposed marriage to the Byzantine Empress Irene, hoping "thus to unite the Eastern and Western provinces", as the chronicler Theophanes[65] put it, not under his sole rule —since he must have realized that it was impossible for him to become the Emperor of all the Romans— but perhaps on

---

63 Tom Holland, Millennium, London: Abacus Books, 2009, pp. 30–32.

64 Einhard (ca. 775–840) was a dedicated servant and a biographer of Charlemagne. See: Einhard, The Life of Charlemagne, trans. S.E. Turner, New York: Harper & Brothers, 1880.

65 Quoted in A.A. Vasiliev, A History of the Byzantine Empire, Milwaukee: University of Wisconsin Press, 1958, p. 268.

the model of the dual monarchy of the 5th century Roman Empire. Finally, all these plans collapsed with Irene's overthrow in 802.

The study of Aristotle's *Logic* was an arduous task even in the ancient era. In his *Topica*, I, 1, the Roman philosopher and statesman Cicero (106–143 B.C.) mentions that Aristotle "was not known to the rhetorician, inasmuch as he is not much known even to philosophers, except to a very few", because "the obscurity of the subject" deterred them from Aristotle's books. This "obscurity" created a need for the publication of explanatory comments on and introductory textbooks in Aristotle's philosophy. One such textbook was Cicero's *Topica* (Cicero wrote *Topica* for the benefit of his friend Gaius Trebatius Testa). Another such textbook was Porphyry's *Introduction to the Logical Categories of Aristotle* (known simply as the *Introduction*).

Porphyry (ca. 234 – ca. 305 A.D.) was a Syrian student of Plotinus. In 268, he experienced a major depressive episode, and he wanted to commit suicide. His teacher deterred him from committing suicide. As we read in Porphyry's book *On the Life of Plotinus*, 11, Plotinus told Porphyry that the tendency to commit suicide does not spring "from reason but from mere melancholy" and advised Porphyry "to leave Rome". Porphyry obeyed and left for Sicily, where, in 270, he learned about Plotinus's death. A few years after Plotinus's death, Porphyry returned to Rome and became the head of Plotinus's school there. During his stay in Sicily, Porophyry wrote his *Introduction*.

The publication of Porphyry's *Introduction* was an amazing success in both the West and the East. In the 6th century, the Roman philosopher Boethius translated Porphyry's *Introduction* in Latin, and, in the same century, the Syrian theologian Sergius of Resaina translated this famous book in the Syrian language. Moreover, in the 8th century, Porphyry's *Introduction* was translated in the Armenian language, and, in the 10th century, it was translated in Arabic. In both the Western Roman Empire and the Arab Empire, Porphyry's *Introduction* was the first systematic educational textbook in logic.

In his *Introduction*, Porphyry studies Aristotle's teachings about "what genus, difference, species, property, and accident are", and, in the first chapter of his *Introduction*, Porphyry goes on by stating the following problem: whether genera and species "subsist (in the nature of things) or in mere conceptions only; whether also if subsistent, they are bodies or incorporeal, and whether they are separate from, or in, sensibles, and subsist about these". However, Porphyry does not offer an answer to the previous problem, which he himself posed, and, instead, he argued that an answer to the previous problem "requires another more extensive investigation", thus limiting the scope of his *Introduction*.

Why did Porphyry omit to tackle the above problem in his *Introduction*? The answer to this question can be found in the Neoplatonic thesis that Aristotle was a Platonist; this thesis was widely held in the Hellenistic era. Furthermore, Porphyry wrote a book entitled *On the One School of Plato and Aristotle*. Thus, Porphyry did not want to focus his research work on the analysis of a subject on which the views of Plato and Aristotle were not identical to each other.

Let us examine more closely the issue that was silenced by Porphyry. In his *Phaedo*, 100c–e, Plato formulates his theory of ideas as follows: "if a person says to me that the bloom of colour, or form, or any such thing is a source of beauty, I leave all that, which is only confusing to me, and…hold and am assured in my own mind that nothing makes a thing beautiful but the presence and participation of beauty"; and he goes on as follows: "I stoutly contend that by beauty all beautiful things become beautiful…this principle will never be overthrown…by beauty beautiful things become beautiful".

In *Phaedo*, 100a, Plato makes his point clear as follows: "However, this was the method which I adopted: I first assumed some principle which I judged to be the strongest, and then I affirmed as true whatever seemed to agree with this, whether relating to the cause or to anything else; and that which disagreed I regarded as untrue".

In his *Timaeus*, 27d–28a, Plato argues that we must make the following distinction: "What is that which is Existent always and has no Becoming? And what is that which is Becoming always and never is Existent?…the one of these is apprehensible by thought with the aid of reasoning…whereas the other is an object of opinion with the aid of unreasoning sensation".

On the other hand, Aristotle argues that Socrates never claimed that universals (genera and species) are self–subsistent. In particular, qualifying Plato's thesis about the nature of universals, Aristotle writes in his *Metaphysics*, 1078b, 27–34: "There are two innovationswhich, may fairly be ascribed to Socrates: inductive reasoning and general definition...whereas Socrates regarded neither universals nor definitions as existing in separation, the others gave them a separate existence, and to these universals and definitions of existing things they gave the name of ideas".

In *Metaphysics*, 1071a, 17–22, Aristotle clarifies his own thesis as follows: "we must observe that some causes can be stated universally, but others cannot. The proximate principles of all things are the proximate actual individual and another individual which exists potentially. Therefore the proximate principles are not universal". Moreover, in the same section of his *Metaphysics*, Aristotle, goes on as follows: "it is the particular that is the principle of particulars; 'man' in general is the principle of 'man' in general, but there is no such person as 'man', whereas Peleus is the principle of Achilles and your father of you".

In *Metaphysics*, 1038b, Aristotle exposes his qualified Platonism as follows: "The universal also is thought by some to be in the truest sense a cause and a principle...it seems impossible that any universal term can be substance". Aristotle explains his thesis as follows: First of all, "the substance of an individual is the substance which is peculiar to it and belongs to nothing else; whereas the universal is common; for by universal we mean that which by nature appertains to several things". Thus, Aristotle is concerned with the following question "Of what particular, then, will the universal be the substance?", and he gives the following answer to that question: "Either of all or of none. But it cannot be the substance of all; while, if it is to be the substance of one, the rest also will be that one; because things whose substance is one have also one essence and are themselves one".

Second, Aristotle is concerned with the following argument: "substance means that which is not predicated of a subject, whereas the universal is always predicated of some subject. But perhaps although the universal cannot be substance in the sense that essence is, it can be present in the essence, as 'animal' can be present in 'man' and 'horse'". He counters the previous argument as follows: "Again, it is impossible and absurd that the individual or substance, if it is composed of anything, should be composed not of substances nor of the individual, but of a quality; for then non–substance or quality will be prior to substance or the individual. Which is impossible".

The above issues were never addressed by Porphyry. However, it should be mentioned that, in his dialogues *Timaeus* and *Sophist*,

Plato, under the influence of Aristotle's ontology, argues that reality consists of both beings (ideas) and non-beings (phenomena) as well as also of almost-beings and almost-non-beings.

In fact, in his early works, Plato was strongly influenced by Parmenides's ontology, according to which being is a totality, and being and non-being can never be reduced to each other. However, Aristotle, in his *Metaphysics*, distinguishes between 'potentiality' (potential being) and 'actuality' (actual being). The previous distinction presupposes a state of becoming, since a being is increasingly actualized and imposes itself on reality in accordance with an innate archetypal form, which is called entelechy by Aristotle; entelechy is the program of the actualization of a being, and it remains unchanged irrespective of the partial changes that the being under consideration undergoes. According to Aristotle, being is the simplest mental presence, but it is not absolutely simple. Aristotle construes being as a resultant whose components are categories that constitute a system; these categories are substance, form, the relation between substance and form, time and space, and they are qualities that can be identified with and attributed to being. Thus, Aristotle transcends Parmenides's dualism between being and non-being, and he proposes a more dynamic ontology. In his dialogue *Sophist*, Plato, under the influence of Aristotle's thought, abandoned Parmenides's dualism, and he argued that being and non-being are the extreme terms of an ontological series whose intermediate terms are the non-being of being and the being of non-being.

BOETHIUS'S CONTRIBUTION TO MEDIEVAL PHILOSOPHICAL EDUCATION

In his *Commentary on Porphyry's Introduction*, I, 158–161, Boethius pays particular attention to the problem of the nature of universals: "Porphyry bears in mind that it is an introduction he is writing, so he keeps to the style of a textbook. This is why he says he avoids the tangles of deeper questions and limits himself to a few reasonable conjectures about the simple ones". Boethius mentions that these deeper questions that Porphyry promises not to discuss in his *Introduction* are the following: (i) "Everything comprehended by the mind is either based in the real world, in which case the mind conceptualizes it and represents it to itself intellectually, or else it is not, in which case the mind represents it to itself through an empty image". (ii) "If genus and species are said to be immaterial, we come down to another urgent problem demanding a solution: do they exist immanently in bodies themselves, or might they also exist as immaterial substances over and above bodies?"[66]

In his *Commentary on Porphyry's Introduction*, I, 165–166, Boethius accepts that "it must not be thought that a concept is false simply because it is not an exact representation of its objects...someone who does this by compounding *is* deceived (e.g. when they think centaurs exist because they have joined a horse and a human)", but he argues that "someone who does it by analyzing, abstracting, and taking them out of the things in which they exist, not only is not deceived, but is the only person who can discover what is genuinely true". However, in the previous 'Platonic' thesis, Boethius fails to bear in mind the difference between a concept (which is a product of abstraction and hence can be known through analysis and syllogism) and a Platonic idea (which transcends the intellect and can be known through participation in its reality, and therefore, apart from logic, it calls for an erotic epistemology).

By failing to understand the difference between abstract knowledge and participation in Platonic ideas, Boethius cannot understand the original essence of Platonic philosophy. Thus, in his *Commentary on Porphyry's Introduction*, I, 166–167, he argues as follows: "In one sense, genera and species do actually exist, but in another sense they are conceived: they are indeed immaterial, but they exist in sensible things in conjunction with sensible characteristics; on the other hand, they are conceived as self–subsistent, and not as having their being in other things".

Boethius, according to his understanding of Plato's philosophy, maintains that our mind needs to transcend the fallacies that are caused by "compounding" ("per compositionem") and, through abstraction, to contemplate the pure species. Finally, he goes on as follows: "I do not consider it fitting for me to judge between the opinions of these two [Plato and Aristotle], for that is in the province of deeper philosophy".

---

66 Chadwick correctly has pointed out that Boethius did not elaborate enough on the concept of incorporeality; see: Henry Chadwick, Boethius, Oxford: Oxford University Press, 1981.

PHILOSOPHICAL REALISM

In the 9th century A.D., Johannes Scotus Eriugena, an Irish theologian, Neoplatonist philosopher and poet, initiated Western philosophy[67] with his book *De divisione naturae* (On the division of nature). According to Eriugena, 'nature' is the "universitas rerum", i.e. the "totality of all things", and it includes both the things that are ("ea quae sunt") as well as those that are not ("ea quae non sunt"). In addition, he argues that nature (as the totality of all things) may be divided into a set of four 'species' or 'divisions' ("divisiones") that retain their unity with their source, and these four divisions of nature taken together are to be understood as God.

Eriugena notes that 'nature' translates the Greek term 'physis', and 'physis' was often used interchangeably with 'ousia', or essence/ being. In the context of Eriugena's philosophy, the meaning of 'nature' is restricted to the act whereby essence is generated, whereas the term 'ousia' (essence/being) suggests something unchanging. According to Eriugena's philosophy, the four dialectical divisions ('species') of nature are the following: (i) Nature that both creates and is not created: this species is understood by human consciousness as the cause of all things. (ii) Nature that both creates and is created: this species is understood by human consciousness as the tank of the archetypes of all things. (iii) Nature that both is created and does not create: this species is understood by human consciousness as the set of all the things that are generated in space and time (i.e. it refers to the natural world). (iv) Nature that both does not create and is not created: this species is understood by human consciousness as the end of the universe's itinerary and as the return of all things to their source, i.e. to God. In the context of Eriugena's thought, God is the beginning, middle and end of all things.

According to Eriugena, Nature as God is the uncreated creating principle ("natura creans"), and God (Nature) created the world according to the eternal patterns (archetypes) in His mind (Logos), which Eriugena identified with the term intelligence. As Eriugena put it, Nature as Logos is a created creator. However, Eriugena explains, because the eternal patterns (archetypes) of the world are not external to God, but they exist inside God's intelligence, they are created only in the sense that they are *logically*

---

67   Augustine of Hippo and Boethius are considered members of the Roman world.

posterior to God's Logos, but they are not *temporally* posterior to God's Logos.

Therefore, according to Eriugena, universals not only exist, but also they pre–exist, i.e. universals are the archetypes of the particulars. For instance, the existence of the concept of man is prior to the existence of myself as a particular human being.

Moreover, in the 9th century A.D., Fredegisius, in his *Letter on Nothing and Darkness,* argues that to every name or term there corresponds a reality. Thus, according to Fredegisius, in the assertion that 'God created the world from nothing', 'nothingness' must refer to something definite, i.e. to some reality, and not to absolute zero. In the same spirit, the Dominican monk Remigius of Auxere (ca. 841–908), in his commentaries on the *Opuscula Sacra* and on the works of Boethius and Martianus Capella, argued that the species is "partitio substantialis" of the genus and that the species, e.g. 'man', is the substantial unity of many individuals: "homo est multorum hominum substantialis unitas". Fredrick Copleston has pointed out that the previous statement, "if understood as meaning that the plurality of individual men have a common substance which is numerically one, has as its natural consequence the conclusion that individual men differ only accidentally from one another"[68].

The above mentioned scholars, namely Johannes Scotus Eriugena, Fredegisius and Remigius of Auxere are characteristic representatives of philosophical realism. In the context of philosophical realism, God is part of Nature —even though He is the uncreated part of Nature, He is still part of Nature. In other words, since God contains the universals (archetypes of the world), He is part of Nature. Thus, from the viewpoint of the medieval philosophical realism, God is the ultimate general concept, which contains everything.

Anselm of Canterbury[69] (ca. 1033–1109), in his book *Proslogion,* 2, did not hesitate to put forward the following syllogism, which Immanuel Kant called "the ontological proof of the existence of God": "Everyone should admit that *something than which nothing greater can be thought of* exists", as a concept in one's mind, "since he understands this phrase when he hears it, and whatever is

---

68 Frederick Copleston, A History of Philosophy, Vol. 2: Augustine to Scotus, Kent: Burns & Oates, 1999, p. 141.

69 In 1093, Anselm was enthroned as Archbishop of Canterbury. In the Roman Catholic Church, he is considered a saint, and, in 1720, he was named a Doctor of the Church by the same Church.

understood exists at least in the understanding (or mind)". But Anselm of Canterbury continues his syllogism as follows: "*Something than which nothing greater can be thought of* cannot exist only (as a concept) in the mind because, in addition to existing (as a concept) in the mind, it can also be thought of as existing in reality (that is, objectively), which is greater (than existing only as an idea in the mind)". Hence, according to Anselm of Canterbury, "if *something than which nothing greater can be thought of* exists only as an idea in the mind, then 'that than which something greater *cannot* be thought of' is 'that than which something greater *can* be thought of', which is impossible (because it is a contradiction)". According to the previous syllogism, *something than which nothing greater can be thought of* must exist, not only as a concept in the mind, but in reality.

Like the other medieval representatives of philosophical realism, Anselm of Canterbury was not only philosophizing as a logician, in the sense that he assumed that the logical and real orders are exactly parallel, but also he did not hesitate to consider human intellect an ontologically sufficient foundation for the proof of God's existence. Like the other medieval representatives of philosophical realism, Anselm of Canterbury adapted God to his intellect's requirements and then he asserted that he understood God.

Moreover, in the 13th century, after the rediscovery of Aristotelianism by the West, Thomas Aquinas developed a new synthesis between Aristotelianism and Christianity. As I have already mentioned, Aquinas's synthesis is based on the rationalist thesis that God's will is determined by the ideas that are contained in God's mind. In the context of Thomas Aquinas's philosophy, 'ideas' are logically self–subsistent entities and lead to a confusion between God's pure mind and His wills.

The aforementioned theories of philosophical realism imply that general concepts (universals) constitute the authentic reality, whereas individuals belong to the world of imperfect phenomena. In other words, the 'human being' as a general concept is more real than myself as an individual. Hence, one's life and relation with the world are, or must be, subject to rules and axioms that are superior to any significance one may have as an individual. For, since the universal not only exists, but it is also the authentic form of existence, the behavior of the individual must conform to the commands of the universal. In other words, every individual's ego must yield to the universal. In the context of the previous arguments, the duty of an individual is to learn the commands of the universal and to try to comply with those commands, since they are more real than the individual itself. Thus, an individual's life is meaningful only if and to the extent that it complies with the commands of the universal. In other words, an individual is real to the extent that it negates its existential otherness for the sake of the universal.

From the aforementioned theories of philosophical realism, it follows that society, as a system of relations, must be structured in such a way as to serve its universal, which is the 'kingdom of God' (the most general concept of society). Hence, political institutions and structures must be homologous to their paradisiacal archetypes. The previous homology between society and God's kingdom implies who has the capability and the obligation to expose and impose the commands of the universal: that person is no one else but the Pope. This is the essence of the medieval West's philosophical realism.

Philosophical realism was a medium whereby the Vatican attempted to consolidate its authority. Due to philosophical realism, the Pope managed to impose his "plenitudo potestatis", i.e. his overlordship. According to philosophical realism, which is based on a misunderstanding of the classical Greek ontology and on the legalistic ethos of the classical Roman thought, the Pope had the right to behave like his archetype, i.e. God. Thus, gradually, the medieval Western man realized that the most effective way of fighting the Papacy's authoritarianism was the refutation of philosophical realism.

Throughout the Middle Ages, several sovereigns fought against the Pope, thinking that they could control or destroy the Papacy's secular power simply by subjugating the Papal State. However, the civil class, the bourgeois, realized that the Papacy's authority could be controlled only if the cultural underpinnings of the Papacy's authority —namely, philosophical realism— could be challenged and refuted. Therefore, the bourgeois used nominalism as a medium whereby they could counter the Papacy's authoritarianism. Moreover, the University of Paris played a protagonist role in the medieval philosophical controversies, and it became a major cultural opponent of the Papacy.

The largest school of the University of Paris was the so–called school of arts, where students studied the "trivium" (i.e. grammar, rhetoric, and logic) and the "quadrivium" (music, arithmetic, geometry, and astronomy). Every student was obliged to study the trivium and the quadrivium before pursuing further studies in theology, medicine or law. The graduates of the school of arts were called "artistes", and most of them were children of members of the bourgeoisie and of minor landowners. Many *artistes* had radical views and were causing riots. In 1210 and in 1229, major riots took place at the University of Paris, and, eventually, on 13 April 1231, after two years of negotiations, Pope Gregory IX issued the Bull "Parens scientiarum", which guaranteed the University of Paris independence from local authority, whether ecclesiastical or secular, placing it directly under Papal patronage. Moreover, in 1251, new fierce riots took place at the University of Paris, and they were settled in 1261, when it was decided that the University of Paris would continue allowing monks to become members of its faculty, but no monk would be allowed to teach at the school of arts, which thus was given the right to maintain a liberal intellectual environment.

NOMINALISM

In the medieval West, the major opponent of philosophical realism was nominalism. The most demanding problem in the history of Western medieval philosophy was that of the nature of the universals: Do concepts (i.e. 'genera' and 'species') exist in nature ('subsistentia'), or are they mere abstractions ('nuda intellecta')? Are they, or are they not, things? As I mentioned earlier in this chapter, the realists replied to the previous question in the affirmative. A different reply to the previous question was given in the 11th century by Roscelin[70], a monk of Compiègne. Roscelin's reply is known as 'nominalism', and it can be summarized as follows: "universalia sunt nomina", i.e. the universals (general concepts) are names. Universals are not things, but they are merely words ("flatus vocis"), which are used for taxonomic purposes[71]. Only individuals exist. Universals are not substances, but only words. There exist particular individuals, such as me, you, etc., but there is no such thing as 'society'.

Realists understand 'society' as 'universitas', i.e. as a universal,

---

70 Of his writings there exists only a letter addressed to Abelard.

71 By the term 'taxonomy', I refer to the science of classification or the result of it. A taxonomic scheme is a particular classification ('the taxonomy of...') arranged in a hierarchical structure or classification scheme.

whereas nominalists understand 'society' as 'societas', i.e. as a partnership of individuals. Realism leads to a society where the individual is subjected to (and annihilated in) the general organic unity of the universal. In the context of philosophical realism, society is founded on a rigid hierarchical structure, and it tries to preserve established social relations and structures, which serve the species, the 'universitas'. On the contrary, for nominalism, 'I exist' means that I am unique and that I experience and actualize my existential otherness. Furthermore, in the context of nominalism, society (as 'societas, i.e. as a partnership of individuals) is founded on mutual consent, i.e. on a social contract. Thus, nominalism is the philosophical underpinning of the modern civil society.

In the 13th century, the work of William of Occam, an English Franciscan friar and philosopher, played a major role in the history of nominalism. He denied the real existence of metaphysical universals, and he argued that only individuals exist, rather than supra–individual universals, and that universals are the products of abstraction from individuals by the human intellect and do not exist independently of the human intellect.[72]

As I have already mentioned, Thomas Aquinas and the other representatives of philosophical realism dramatically reduced God's (and eventually man's) freedom, since they interpreted the Platonic term idea as a logically self–subsistent entity and they argued that God's will is determined by the ideas that are contained in God's mind. In order to restore and safeguard God's (and man's) freedom, Occam (like the other nominalists in general) indiscriminately rejected the reality of the universals, and he argued that the universals are merely expressions of the individual's conscious states. Thus, Occam's philosophy consists in a metaphysically grounded individualism, since it negates the reality of the universals and affirms only the reality of the individual.

Nominalism offers outlet to the spiritually and politically oppressed individual of the medieval bourgeoisie, and it paves the way to the humanism of modern philosophy and to social–contract theory. The nominalists' theory of God's freedom gives primacy to individual will, which, in turn, leads to the creation of a society that is founded on a contract between individual wills. Thus, there is an

---

72 For more details about Occam's arguments, see: F.E. Baird and W. Kaufman, From Plato to Derrida, New Jersey: Pearson Prentice Hall, 2008.

important yet elusive relationship among nominalism, Friedrich Nietzsche's "will for power" and Martin Heidegger's method of seeing an entity as "present–at–hand" (in seeing an entity as present–at–hand, the beholder is concerned only with the bare facts of a thing or a concept). Nominalists were so eager to fight the totalitarianism of the medieval representatives of philosophical realism that they became oblivious of the risk that, without any supra–individual values, freedom of individual leads to an egopathic personality and to self–defeating and self–destructive forms of civil society and liberal democracy.

At the political level, nominalism emphasizes the principle of discretion and spiritually underpins the bourgeoisie's claims to political authority. The medieval bourgeois class promoted the principle of discretion on the basis of the arguments that were put forward by Aristotle in his *Politics*, 1276b–1277a. In particular, Aristotle writes in *Politics*, 1276b–1277a: "the goodness of a good citizen would not be one and the same as the goodness of a good man; for all ought to possess the goodness of the good citizen... but it is impossible that all should possess the goodness of a good man". Thus, in contrast to the realists' totalitarian thought, we should discard political clichés and we should understand that human beings have different aspects that should be evaluated individually.

Furthermore, the medieval bourgeois class resorted to Aristotle's *Politics* in order to find arguments that they could help the defenders of bourgeois society prove that the citizens' assembly is more infallible than the Pope and nobler than the feudal nobility. In particular, Aristotle writes in *Politics*, 1281a–b: "the political fellowship must therefore be deemed to exist for the sake of noble actions, not merely for living in common...the general public is a better judge".

The above quotes from Aristotle's *Politics* easily explain why the bourgeois class felt that Aristotelianism was expressing its values, why, in 1210, the Provincial Synod of Sens, which included the Bishop of Paris as a member (at the time Peter of Nemours), prohibited the teaching of Aristotle's works with the exception of Aristotle's logic and ethics, and why Pope Gregory IX ordered that Aristotle's works prohibited in 1210 not be used until they could be examined by a theological commission to remove any errors. Finally, in 1366, the Legates of Pope Urban V required that all candidates for the Licentiate of Arts at Paris had knowledge of all the known works of Aristotle.

The fierce ideological war between the Papacy and the bourgeoisie during the Middle Ages determined the manner in which Platonism and Aristotelianism were interpreted by the Western Europeans. The fact that the Papal Church attempted to found its philosophical realism on Plato's philosophy and the fact that the bourgeois class attempted to substitute Aristotelianism for the Papacy's philosophical realism determined the destiny of Platonism and Aristotelianism in the West. The West interpreted Platonism and Aristotelianism as if they were representing two spiritually different worlds, and, therefore, the West's interpretation of Platonism and Aristotelianism was alien to the Greek spirit. In the context of the Greek culture, Platonism and Aristotelianism do not represent two spiritually different worlds, but they represent one and the same world.

It goes without saying that ancient Greeks were fully aware of the fact that, in classical Athens, there were two different schools —namely, the 'Academy', which was founded by Plato, and the 'Lyceum', whose foundation was attributed to Aristotle— but the Greeks never treated those two schools as if they were philosophical opponents of one another. For instance, as we read in Diogenes Laertius's *Lives of Eminent Philosophers*, IV, 67, Aristotle was the pioneer of the "peripatetic Platonists".

In ancient Greece, the students of Aristotle were identifying themselves as Platonists and were being identified as Platonists by the supporters of other philosophical systems. In Plato's work (especially in the later Plato), the ideas are present in things, and the things participate in the ideas, aspiring to them as their goal, and Aristotle proceeds with an elaboration on Plato's philosophy in order to defend his theses that the soul is united with the body and that the soul is the entelechy (i.e. the end and completion) of the body. According to Plotinus, who was the most important Hellenistic philosopher, Plato is the root and the trunk of the 'tree' of Greek philosophy, and there is no incompatibility between Platonism and Aristotelianism, Aristotle's philosophy being a supplement to and an interpretative comment on Plato's work. Plotinus's view on the relation between Platonism and Aristotelianism was emphasized by the Byzantine scholars John Philoponus[73], Stephanus[74], David[75] and Elias[76]. Furthermore, the Greek Church Fathers believe that Plato and Aristotle are essentially in agreement with one another and differ from one another only with respect to their methods.

THE GENEALOGY OF A MISUNDERSTANDING AND THE GREEK TRADITION OF INTERPRETING CLASSICAL GREEK PHILOSOPHY

Even though the Western medieval scholars were claiming that their philosophical systems were founded on the classical Greek philosophy, their direct access to the original classical Greek philosophical texts was limited, and they were based on inaccurate Latin translations of classical Greek philosophical texts and on introductory textbooks. Thus, the medieval West interpreted classical Greek philosophy in a manner that served the medieval West's own historical needs and goals.

In the years of Augustine of Hippo and Boethius and throughout the Middle Ages, the West considered the Greek metaphysical term 'ousia' (essence) a universal, i.e. a general concept. Thus, in contrast to the Greek philosophical tradition, the West argued that Plato's 'ideas' were logically self–subsistent entities. But the classical Greek philosophers never identified the 'intellect' with the 'mind', and they never restricted knowledge within the boundaries of the intellect. In other words, the classical Greek philosophy never attempted to isolate the power of knowing from the powers of feeling and will, and it never subjected the latter to the first.

In the context of classical Greek philosophy, cognition does not produce knowledge by itself (whenever cognition produces

---

73   John Philoponus (490–570 A.D.) wrote commentaries on Aristotle's works, and Galileo Galilei cited Philoponus substantially in his works.

74   Stephanus of Byzantium was the author of an important geographical dictionary entitled Ethnica (6th century A.D.).

75   David was a 6th century Byzantine Christian Neoplatonist scholar and commentator on Aristotle and Porphyry. He also wrote an introduction to philosophy entitled Prolegomena.

76   Elias was a 6th century Byzantine Christian Neoplatonist scholar and commentator on Aristotle and Porphyry. In his preface to Aristotle's Categories, Elias argues that an ideal commentator "should be both commentator and scholar at the same time. It is the task of the commentator to unravel obscurities in the text; it is the task of the scholar to judge what is true and what is false, or what is sterile and what is productive" (quoted in N.G. Wilson, Scholars of Byzantium, London: Duckworth, 1983, p. 47).

knowledge by itself, that knowledge is considered imagination), but it is viewed as a process whereby the mind receives and processes sense–data. In particular, in Plato's *Timaeus*, 45d, the soul, like the body, is characterized by "that sensation which we now term 'seeing'"; and, in Aristotle's *On Sense and the Sensible*, 438b10, the soul operates as the centre of sensation. Hence, the classical Greek philosophy of vision is focused on an external light that allows one to see an image without the mediation of any subject's mental representations. Since, according to Plato's and Aristotle's theories of the vision of light, an image can be seen independently of (and prior to) the images formed in the mind, it follows that, in the context of classical Greek philosophy, knowledge is obtained by the transition of the mind from its own world to the external reality of an idea, and not by the transfer of an idea into the mind, where it would give rise to a representational theory of the entire object of vision through a combination of concepts. In other words, in the context of classical Greek philosophy, knowledge is obtained through pure experience, i.e. without the mediation of any mental representations, and, therefore, it is based on a vision that is prior to conceptual thinking.

In the context of Plato's philosophy, cognition is not based on bodily sensations, but this does not mean that it is based on representations created by a subjective mind; instead, according to Plato's philosophy, cognition is based on a peculiar mental *sensation*. Thus, according to Plato, the mind does not reproduce an external object through a visualization–conceptualization process, nor does it create mental models of an external object, but it *participates* in the transcendental idea of an external object, and, therefore, it knows an external object due to the experience of the light of the corresponding idea. It is this dependence of knowledge on the light of the idea that protected Platonism from lapsing into the problems of the nominalists' individualistic subjectivism without, on the other hand, following the path of medieval Western philosophical realism. Moreover, in Plato's *Republic*, those artists who, through their art, transform truth into a mental representation are exiled from Plato's ideal republic.

Thomas Aquinas and generally the medieval Western scholars ignored that, when Plato created the term idea, which is one of the most controversial philosophical terms, he simultaneously asserted that vision is the most representative sense of human mental life. Thus, the medieval West ignored that, in the context of Plato's philosophy, knowledge, i.e. consciousness's relation with truth, is primarily a spiritual *experience*, and, for this reason, it primarily consists in a psychological state and only secondarily in the discovery of causal relations. As Plato himself argues in his *Theaetetus*, 184d, the unity of the 'idea' as vision makes psychological unity possible: "it would be strange indeed...if there are many senses ensconced within us, as if we were so many wooden horses of Troy, and they do not all unite in one power, whether we should call it soul or something else, by which we perceive through these as instruments the objects of perception".

By contrast, European rationalism reduces the entire knowledge process to the formulation of causal relations, and additionally it attempts even to know God through causal relations. Plato's theory of ideas proposes a different way of knowing: an individual participates in the idea of human being due to psychological relations between human individuals, i.e. due to an experience of humanity, and not because one can logically conceive the notion of humanity. Thus, Plato's theory of ideas is founded on a simultaneously active and passive participation[77] of the spirit in social relations, and not on logical necessities.

Because, in the context of classical Greek philosophy, truth is not representational (i.e. it does not depend on mental images), the classical Greek philosophers do not identify the intellect with the mind. In particular, in his *Republic*, 511d–e, Plato argues as follows: "I think you call the mental habit of geometers and their like mind or understanding and not reason because you regard understanding as something intermediate between opinion and reason...and arrange them in a proportion, considering that they participate in clearness and precision in the same degree as their objects partake of truth and reality". Therefore, in contrast to Thomas Aquinas's philosophy, classical Greek philosophy does not subject action and will to the coercive logical authority of general concepts.

---

77   There are two general forms of 'participation' —the one is passive, and the other is active. The passive form of participation refers to those elements that beings have inherited from their common source and continue preserving them. Thus, this form of participation points to the dependence of beings on their source and/or on one another. The active form of participation refers to the beings' attempt to create a situation that will allow them to transcend their current situation. Thus, this form of participation points to identification within the framework of common activities ('identification' is a process whereby a being assimilates an aspect, property, or attribute of another being and is transformed wholly or partially).

Classical Greek philosophy does not subject action and will to the coercive logical authority of general concepts, because, according to classical Greek philosophy, the image of a thing exists as an energy of the given thing's essence, i.e. it is determined by (and it is an emanation of) the given thing's essence, and it is not created by the perceptive mind. Hence, according to classical Greek philosophy, the essence of the mind is not a self–regulating logical system.

By contrast, medieval Western philosophy was dominated by the view that the essence of the mind is a self–regulating logical system, and, therefore, in the context of Latin theology, God is perceived as pure energy. Within God as pure energy, essence, energy, will, knowledge and power are identified with one another, and the archetypal reasons (logoi) of God coercively pervade the totality of the cosmos, so that, according to Latin theology, even the evil is perceived as one of God's reasons (logoi). The previous view is unacceptable by both the classical Greek philosophy and the Greek Patristic thought, because, according to the classical Greek philosophy and the Greek Patristic thought, God is absolutely good and absolutely free from any essential determination, and the source of evil is merely man's own freedom of choice.

According to the medieval West's philosophical realism in general and according to Thomas Aquinas's philosophy in particular, the Creation is a temporal manifestation of the archetypal reasons (logoi) of God, and man knows the archetypal reasons (logoi) of God through the reasons of man's own intellect. Therefore, the medieval West's philosophical realism in general and Thomas Aquinas's philosophy in particular imply the following conclusions: the same reason (logos) pervades both God and the whole of nature; both God's freedom and man's freedom obey the same, all–pervading reason (universal logos); both God's will and man's will are subject to the same, all–pervading reason (universal logos). According to the previous philosophical path, necessity takes precedence over freedom, and, for this reason, as I have already mentioned, philosophical realism became an intellectual weapon whereby the Vatican attempted to impose and consolidate its authority over its subjects, and, later, philosophical realism became an intellectual weapon whereby rationalist university professors attempted to become the new (secular) authoritarian spiritual elite of Western Europe. Things become radically different, and freedom takes precedence over necessity, if one accepts the Greek philosophical tradition about sensation and knowledge.

The Greek Church Fathers adopted the classical Greek philosophers' views about sensation and knowledge, and, therefore, through classical Greek philosophy, they managed to understand and express God's absolute freedom of action by emphasizing that God's reasons (logoi) are realizations and manifestations of God's free *will* and are distinct from God's totally transcendental (and hence totally unknowable) essence. In other words, as the Greek Church Fathers from Dionysius the Areopagite to John of Damascus and later the Hesychasts teach, God is not determined by any laws, i.e. He is not determined by His nature, and His mode of existence is freedom.

3

THE RISE OF BOURGEOIS SOCIETY AND THE CULTURE OF MODERNITY

I N the 11th century A.D., the creation of towns and the development of international trade overturned the feudal system by giving rise to a new socio–political system. Moreover, the townspeople made serious attempts in order to codify and standardize customary socio–political practices, and they developed a corporate view of society practically organized by the guild system and culturally underpinned by Roman law. Thus, in the 11th and the 12th centuries, we begin to see the first fully–fledged theories of popular sovereignty[78]. For instance, John of Salisbury, in his book *The Policraticus* (1156–9), argues that 'aequitas' (equality) is the application by man of his own capacity for reason and right and that the good ruler must be a man of the state and an image of natural equality. In the words of John of Salisbury: "Between a tyrant and a prince there is this single or chief difference, that the latter obeys the law and rules the people by its dictates, accounting himself as but their servant"[79].

Henry de Bracton, in his book *De legibus et consuetudinibus angliae* (ca. 1239), stated that the royal 'voluntas' (will) is primarily concerned

---

78 Quentin Skinner, The Foundations of Modern Political Thought, 2 Vols, Cambridge: Cambridge University Press, 1970; Walter Ullmann, Principles of Government and Politics in the Middle Ages, London: Methuen, 1961.

79 Included in John Dickinson (ed. and trans.), The Statesman's Book of John of Salisbury, New York: Knopf, 1927, Book IV, ch. i.

with adjudication rather than with legislation[80]. According to Henry de Bracton, laws are promulgated through a co–operative process, and, therefore, the law of the land is not dictated by the royal will but is truly 'common'. Moreover, Marsilius of Padua, in his book *Defensor Pacis* (1324), a landmark in the history of civil political thought, argued that "the legislator, or first and proper efficient cause of law, is the people or whole body of citizens, or a prevailing part of it, commanding and deciding by its own choice or will in a general assembly and in set terms"[81].

Towns helped create new institutions: a more egalitarian judicial system, relatively stable policing and military institutions (as opposed to the notoriously unstable feudal armies, which usually were breaking up after their terms of service were up), a new tax system (by the end of the Middle Ages, monarchs were gaining the right to tax their subjects directly, and, in the 13th century, parliaments gained the right to rule on any proposed changes in taxation), etc. Gradually, towns became free republics, and the members of several different professions were organized into guilds[82]. By the late Middle Ages, guild membership and citizenship went hand in hand. For instance, in Florence, membership in a guild was a requirement of citizenship. Moreover, the Concordat of Worms (1122), which was a compromise arranged in 1122 between Pope Callistus II and Holy Roman Emperor Henry V settling the "investiture dispute", promoted the civil ethos of the townspeople[83], and, in the same year, in Cologne, a rebellion against the local archbishop–feudal lord broke out.

---

80   See: C.J. Nederman, "Bracton on Kingship Revisited", History of Political Thought, Vol. 5, 1984, pp. 63–77.

81   Included in Alan Gewirth (ed. and trans.), Marsilius of Padua, the Defender of the Peace, New York: Harper and Row Publishers, 1956, Book I, ch. xii.

82   The guild system created rules that governed taxation, established electoral processes and gave rise to new authorities and offices. The members of the guilds were pledged to assist one another in sickness or distress and to express solidarity to one another in danger. Moreover, some of the guilds maintained schools for the instruction of the children of the members; remnants of such schools exist in England to this very day, e.g. Corpus Christi at Cambridge.

83   The king was recognized as having the right to invest bishops with secular authority in the territories they governed (however, not with holy authority), and, therefore, bishops owed allegiance in worldly affairs both to the pope and to the king, since they were obliged to affirm the right of the secular authority (the king) to call upon them for military support.

Towns were attracting more and more people not so much for the pursuit of financial gain as for the pursuit of freedom. Serfs could earn their living by cultivating the land, but they could not enjoy enough freedom. Henri Pirenne[84] has pointed out that the quest for freedom was the strongest motive of the people who were leaving their agricultural jobs in order to live in a town. For instance, in the Middle Ages, many Germans used to say "Stadtluft macht frei" (i.e. "city air makes you free"). Carlo M. Cipolla[85] argues that, like the first European immigrants to America, the liberated serfs were moving to towns in order to have more opportunities for social and economic success than those supplied by the traditional and closed agricultural societies.

The townspeople —namely, liberated serfs, tradesmen, impoverished aristocrats and various other opportunists and fugitives from the feudal system— built their own walls around their towns, and, thus, they became permanent inhabitants of those towns and were called 'bourgeois' or 'burgenses', which literally means 'of a walled town'. Some of them managed to excel in their professions and to participate in the king's council. Additionally, members of the bourgeoisie often created secret societies, whose purpose was the protection of the community's interest. As we read in the *Annales Beneventani*, in 1003–1005, after the rebellions of the citizens of Benevento against their local prince, Landulf V, "facta est communitas prima", i.e. "the first commune is made". The first reference to a secret society organized by the bourgeoisie is found in the *History of Milan*, which was written in the 11th century by the historiographer Arnulfus of Milan: Arnulfus of Milan writes that, among the participants in the rebellion that took place in Milan in 980 against the local archbishop was the union of the bourgeois, and he characterizes this union as a "coniuratio" (i.e. "conspiracy") because its members were bound by mutual oaths.

The civil institutional framework abolished the feudal monolithic social pyramid and promoted a higher degree of social homogeneity. Within the framework of the bourgeois system, social stratification is based on social and economic success and is open to criticism

---

84 Henri Pirenne, Medieval Cities —Their Origins and the Revival of Trade, trans. F.D. Halsey, Princeton: Princeton University Press, 1952.

85 C.M. Cipolla, Before the Industrial Revolution —European Society and Economy 1000–1700, 3rd edition, trans. C. Woodall, New York: W.W. Norton & Company, 1993.

by the citizens. Moreover, it should be stressed that, in the late Middle Ages and the Renaissance, the concept of economic success was broader than that of the accumulation of economic wealth, because the medieval bourgeois understood economic success as the objectivation of the bourgeois ethos, i.e. of the bourgeois value system. In the late Middle Ages and the Renaissance, the transition from a rural society to an urban one was primarily a cultural question, because the transformation of a peasant into a bourgeois presupposed and depended on the adoption of a new system of morality and a new code of social conduct.

The medieval bourgeois saw their civilization as the manifestation of great spiritual principles in the political sphere. Thus, for instance, according to Marsilius of Padua, the city is a "perfect community" or one able to supply all that is needed for a good life. Moreover, Albertus Magnus, the major instructor of Thomas Aquinas, had admitted that a town can supply security (munitio), mental refinement and elegance (urbanitas), unity (unitas) and liberty (libertas), and, through this prism, he had attempted to explain why the Evangelist Matthew used the term town in order to refer to the community of the Church Fathers (in particular, in *Matthew* 5:14, we read: "A town built on a hill cannot be hidden"). However, the emergence of bourgeois society goes hand in hand with the emergence of a new and pervasive form of domination and stratification.

Bourgeois society pursued its emancipation from the political and spiritual despotism of the Papacy and from feudalism by asserting that bourgeois society itself is the exclusive source of the legitimacy of political authority. But, by rejecting any transcendental source of legitimacy of political authority, bourgeois society gave rise to a new kind of authoritarianism. In the context of bourgeois society, the 'social system' operates as an autonomous and absolute authority, since it is the source of the legitimacy of its power. In other words, the intrinsic 'logic' of the bourgeoisie imposes itself as an unavoidable nexus of necessities[86]. Furthermore, the morality of the bourgeoisie is identified with the bourgeoisie's own logic.

---

86 Thus, as Karl Marx pointed out in his Critique of Hegel's Philosophy of Right (1843), in the context of bourgeois society, the democratic element is admitted only as a formal element, since the state organism is merely a formalism of the state (Karl Marx, Critique of Hegel's Philosophy of Right, trans. A. Jolin and J. O'Malley, Cambridge: Cambridge University Press, 1982).

Bourgeois society is based on the autonomy of the signifier from the reality of the signified. Adam Smith's principle of sympathy and Immanuel Kant's categorical imperative are characteristic examples of this philosophical attitude: neither the value of sympathy nor the value of good will is any more a measure of the moral character of human relations, but, instead, the value of sympathy according to Adam Smith's moral theory and the value of good will according to Kant's moral theory are themselves subject to measurement. In other words, in Adam Smith's and in Kant's moral theories, value is not a signifier, but it is a signified that is derived from an objective process that is a closed logical system.

Bourgeois society, following the rationalist tradition of the Western spirituality, and especially nominalism, substituted the principle of logical consistency for the principle of personal participation as the foundation of knowledge. In other words, bourgeois society is one of the different possible consequences of rationalism. Bourgeois society has used the major weapon of the Church of Rome —namely, *ratio*— in order to counter the authoritarianism of the Church of Rome and to establish its own, more subtle, authoritarian system.

The moral theories of Adam Smith, who is the father of modern political economy, and of Immanuel Kant, who is the paradigmatic representative of the European Enlightenment, show that the coercive force of ratio underpins bourgeois political economy (for more details, see chapter 6). On the contrary, the Greek Church Fathers' morality is founded on and stems from love.

For the Greek Church Fathers and especially for the Hesychasts, love is neither a moral sentiment nor a categorical imperative, but it is a mode of life. Love as a moral sentiment is an emotion endowed with a subjective evaluation of things and beings according to the utility that one gains from his relationship with them. This means that, when one manifests the moral sentiment of love, he loves protected behind the fortress of his ego and, more than that, he pursues a program of satisfying his ego. Hence, ultimately, the moral sentiment of love that one expresses towards the object of his love returns to himself. On the other hand, if love is not a moral sentiment but a mode of life, then one loves, and, more specifically, he is psychologically transparent, open and benevolent to everybody, because this is the way he exists. When love is a mode of life, one loves in the same way that he breathes, i.e. without calculating practical results and utilities. Love is God's mode of being and the New Law of Christ (*John*, 13:34–35).

According to the New Testament and according to the Greek Church Fathers, God loves us neither because He expects or needs us to do something good for Him (since He is perfectly self–sufficient) nor because He is obliged to do so (since He is perfectly free), but because He exists as a communion of love (among the Three Persons of the Holy Trinity) and calls all His creatures to live in the same way. Similarly, a Christian loves God neither because he wants to receive something from God, nor because he wants to do something good for God (after all, God *is* the absolute Good), nor because he is obliged to do so, but because he wants to become like God and participate in the divine blissfulness. In the context of the Greek Patristic tradition, love means the choice of a certain mode of life, and, therefore, it is a post–moral attitude. Thus, the Orthodox Christian soul does not separate truth and love. In his "Twentieth Hymn on Faith", Ephraim the Syrian[87], one of the most influential 4th century Christian hymnographers and theologians, writes: "Truth and Love are wings that cannot be separated,/ for Truth cannot fly without Love,/ nor can Love soar aloft without Truth".

As I have already mentioned, the bourgeoisie has used nominalism as a weapon against the cultural underpinnings of the Papacy and of feudalism in order to create its own civilization. But even though nominalism can be used as a philosophical weapon against philosophical realism, which underpins both the religious system of the Papacy and the feudal political system, nominalism does not and cannot refute the rationalist core of philosophical realism. With respect to their commitment to rationalism, nominalism and realism are the two sides of the same coin. Therefore, both nominalism and realism can be used for the justification of spiritual and political despotism: realism can be used for the justification of spiritual and political despotism by the Papacy, the feudal political system and, generally, by communitarian political ideologies, whereas nominalism can be used for the justification of spiritual and political despotism by the bourgeoisie and, generally, by individualistic political ideologies. Organizational fetishism, bureaucratic and

---

87 He is venerated by Christians throughout the world as a saint. The best known of his writings is the "Prayer of Saint Ephraim", which is recited at every service during Great Lent and other fasting periods in Eastern Christianity.

technocratic management and the transformation of the human being into a technical means for economic growth are characteristic aspects of the kind of spiritual and political despotism that was established by the bourgeoisie and especially by the liberal oligarchy in the context of modernity.

ORGANIZATIONAL FETISHISM: THE AUTHORITARIAN FACE OF BOURGEOIS SOCIETY

Bourgeois society is a society culturally founded on technical means and on the transformation of man himself into a technical means, in the sense that bourgeois society seeks mechanical ('technocratic') solutions to man's problems. Thus, bourgeois society is founded on the subjection of faith to discursive reason and on the subjection of inspiration to formal organization. It is exactly this mechanical approach to the problems of human life that is rejected by both the Greek philosophy and the theological tradition of the Greek and generally the Eastern Orthodox Church Fathers. As I have already mentioned in this book, the Greek philosophical tradition emphasizes the unity between every being and its 'telos', i.e. its spiritual significance, and, therefore, it refuses to treat the beings and things in this world like 'objects', i.e. separated from a spiritual hierarchy in which they are embedded. From this viewpoint, as I argued in chapters 1 and 2, the classical Greek philosophers' theory of knowledge is different from the West's rationalism.

The Greek spiritual tradition treats every being and thing in this world as a bearer of a transcendental meaning —namely, either as a partaker of the world of ideas (in case of Platonism and Aristotelianism) or as a partaker of the Energies of God (in case of the Hesychasts). Thus, in the context of the Greek spiritual tradition, a scholar does not merely try to apply discursive reason to the world, but he also tries to *feel*, through intuition, the significance, the purpose, of the world. On the other hand, the legacy of the West's rationalism, which culturally underpins bourgeois society, treats every being and thing in this world as an 'object' that must be placed in a system of formal organization, i.e. it must be disciplined. In the context of the Western rationalism, technical means are analyzed into other technical means *ad infinitum*, thus giving rise to analytical science (as a science of technical means), which yields technical power, but it can yield neither knowledge of the spiritual significance, or ultimate purpose, of the world and of life in general, nor awareness of man's spiritual identity and freedom. An analytical scientist can indefinitely continue analyzing a thing without exactly knowing what that thing *is*, i.e. without being able to tackle ontological questions. Therefore, bourgeois society's wealth is primarily material, i.e. 'industrial' or 'financial'.

Furthermore, the Greek philosophers' and the Greek Church Fathers' approach to work is substantially different from the bourgeoisie's approach to work. The members of bourgeois society are —at least at an archetypal level— laborious because the concept of necessity occupies the dominant position in their minds, and, therefore, their lives are determined by attempts to cope with necessities. On the other hand, the members of the Greek spiritual tradition are idle because the concept of theory —which, in the Greek philosophical context, means contemplation of the world's purpose (teleology)— occupies the dominant position in their minds, and, as Aristotle has put it, idleness might, if properly cultivated, become the leisure that is a necessary presupposition for the cultivation of political and contemplative virtues. Thus, the Greek spiritual tradition —both during the pre–Christian and the Christian eras— never treated the economy as an autonomous value, but it always emphasized that the economy is inextricably linked to morality, society and politics. On the other hand, bourgeois society is founded on capitalism, which treats the economy as an autonomous value. Thus, in the context of bourgeois society, work was transformed into a system of cultural barbarism, which has been eloquently described by Bob Black as follows: "Work is production enforced by economic or political means, by the carrot or the stick. (The carrot is just the stick by other means.) But not all creation is work. Work is never done for its own sake, it's done on account of some product or output that the worker (or, more often, somebody else) gets out of it"[88].

In the context of bourgeois society, the labour force is led towards a spiritual state that is characterized by what Cornelius Castoriadis has called "insignificance"[89], because bourgeois society stresses

---

88   Bob Black, "The Abolition of work", in B. Black, The Abolition of Work and Other Essays, Port Townsend, WA: Loompanics Unlimited, 1985. Moreover, the complete essay is available on the internet at the following address: http://www.zpub.com/notes/black–work.html

89   Cornelius Castoriadis, The Imaginary Institution of Society, London: Polity Press, 1987 (originally published in 1975 by Éditions du Seuil).

conformity to the established formal system of organization and the substitution of discipline for discretion, and also it produces a 'citizen' who is detached from the life of the 'city' by unemployment, which leads to disintegration, and by precariousness, which leads to submission.

THE NEGATION OF CLASSICAL PHILOSOPHY AND
CHRISTIANITY BY CAPITALISM

In his book *A Contribution to the Critique of Political Economy*[90],Karl Marx correctly pointed out that the primary formation of capital was not due to the ownership of land or to the medieval guilds, but it was due to the wealth that was accumulated through usury and commerce. The accumulation of such wealth became possible in the 15th century, when the Papal Church adopted the view of the scholastic theologians that money bears a secret, innate virtue due to which it can multiply by itself. This new 'theological' view —which, deviating from Platonism and the teachings of the first Church Fathers[91], introduced the concept of money as an end in itself and offered moral legitimacy to the profession of usury— created the necessary spiritual presuppositions of capitalism, and these spiritual underpinnings of capitalism were enhanced by the Puritan movement[92]. Capitalism appeared in the historical foreground as a peculiar form of trade organized by the Fugger family in Germany. The Fugger family was a historically prominent group of European bankers who were members of the fifteenth– and sixteenth–century mercantile patriciate of Augsburg.

'Money' was already in existence in the ancient and the medieval societies of Europe, but it could not be transformed into 'capital' because financial wealth as such had no value in the minds of those people, who were creating *personal* relations with the land and with their trades. In order for such an economic regime to change, the landowner had to give priority to the exchange–value of his revenue over the use–value of his revenue. This change became possible

---

90 Karl Marx, A Contribution to the Critique of Political Economy, trans. N.I. Stone, New York: International Library Publishing, 1904 (originally published in 1859).

91 For instance, Basil the Great speaks of usury as not just making the poor poorer but depriving them of their freedom, and Gregory of Nyssa states that usury is a sin and a kind of perversion, since it draws gain from inanimate things.

92 Max Weber, The Protestant Ethic and the Spirit of Capitalism, New York: Dover, 2003.

as a consequence of the spiritual value that was assigned to the financial wealth in the 15th century. As a conclusion, the genesis of capitalism was due to the acknowledgement of a new dimension of money —namely, the exchange–value of money, next to the traditional use–value of money— which, in turn, was due to the fact that the scholastics abandoned Plato's anthropocentric economic legacy. The Platonic economic tradition does not treat money, or financial wealth, as an end in itself, i.e. as a bearer of an intrinsic value, but it treats money as a use–value for the sake of the human well–being.

In the *Laws*, 729a, and in the *Apology of Socrates*, 41e and 29d–e, Plato inveighs against excessive commercialism, which puts money before the human interest (well–being), thereby causing injustice, degenerate luxury, vicious extremes of wealth and poverty, and wars. Plato does not ignore the value of economic wealth, but he emphasizes that the human being must be the master of economic wealth and that economic wealth must not spiritually enslave the human being. Moreover, for Plato, economic wealth is good when it serves the well–being of the people. Hence, in the *Laws*, 743e and 870b, Plato emphasizes that it is not business that should be curbed, but bad business.

At this point, I should emphasize that there is a substantial difference between 'ownership' and 'capital'. Ownership is a legal relation, which exists in both pre–capitalist and capitalist societies. On the other hand, 'capital' —irrespective of whether it is private or public— is not the outcome of a specific type of ownership, but it is the outcome of the speculative employment of labour by the owners of capital (irrespective of whether the owners of capital are private entrepreneurs or the state).

When an economic system is based on the ownership of capital by private entrepreneurs, it is called 'market capitalism', and, when an economic system is based on the ownership of capital by the state, it is called 'state capitalism' (or 'bureaucratic socialism', e.g. the Soviet economic system, Maoism, etc.). At its most fundamental level, capitalism signifies a spiritual attitude: the treatment of financial wealth as a bearer of an intrinsic value and thus as an end in itself. This explains, for instance, why capitalist speculators trade in capital markets and money markets, through various speculative schemes and tools, instead of using money in order to acquire 'real–economy' assets, such as real estate, or build ship–vessels, factories, etc.

Market capitalism and, generally, Western liberalism are based on the concept of individual rights. Beyond their particular differences, all theories of individual rights treat the individual as a physical entity that belongs to a legal entity (i.e. the state). From this standpoint, the individual has inviolable rights to its work and to its property, which is the result of its work. Given that, in the context of the theories of individual rights, the individual is treated as a physical entity, it follows that the primary goal of the individual is its ontological, pre–social, self–sufficiency and that the primary existential challenge that the individual must tackle is the satisfaction of its own needs and wishes[93]. Thus, according to the theories of individual rights, the individual pursues to satisfy its needs and wishes through work and through property, which may be an outcome of work. In other words, the anthropological archetype that underpins the theories of individual rights is characterized by egoism and selfishness. Hence, the theories of individual rights give rise to a political economy that is primarily founded on the concept of 'right' and not on the concept of 'social service'.

By contrast, Plato points out that wealth is used wisely when it serves the goal of good life, which transcends man's material conditions, Aristotle gives primacy to distributive justice over individual rights, Jesus Christ states that "man's life does not consist in abundance of his possessions" (*Luke*, 12:15), and, in the first Christian Church, "all the believers were together and had everything in common" (*Acts*, 2:44). Thus, even though both classical Greek philosophy and Christianity promoted individual freedom and justified private property, they both gave primacy to the value of social service/offer over individual benefit.

Moreover, both classical Greek philosophy and Christianity give

---

93 Status–based theories of rights fix upon natural attributes of humans that give rise to rights. Instrumental theories describe rights as instruments by which the distribution of interests can be optimized. Contractual theories attempt to explain rights as means by which man can optimise his existential conditions. For instance, according to John Rawls, the role of the right of personal property "is to allow a sufficient material basis for a sense of personal independence and self–respect, both of which are essential for the development and exercise of the two moral powers" (John Rawls, Justice as Fairness —A Restatement, ed. E. Kelly, Cambridge, MA: Harvard University Press, 2001, p. 114). Additionally, T.M. Scanlon states that reasonable individuals "have reason to insist…on basic rights, which give them important forms of protection and control over their own lives" (T.M. Scanlon, "Rights, Goals, and Fairness", in J. Waldron (ed.), Theories of Rights, Oxford: Oxford University Press, 1984, pp. 137–152).

primacy to the morality of social life over the rules of economics. Basil the Great, one of the most influential early Church Fathers, in his sermon *To the Rich* (*Patrologia Graeca*, Vol. 31, 277C–304C), states that man's ultimate existential goal is deification and not economic success and that, if wealth is owned by a man, its only proper use is as a means to existential perfection (salvation). For Basil the Great, the previous statement means using wealth in accordance with Christ's commandment to love one's neighbor as oneself. In the same sermon, Basil the Great states that "it is right for those who are prudent in their reasoning to regard the use of money as a matter of stewardship, not of selfish enjoyment".

Individual rights as individual claims first cause social division and then give rise to a legal system whose purpose is to secure a minimum level of social cohesion ('order'), which primarily reflects and serves the interests and views of the social elite (i.e. of the politically and financially strongest individuals). Moreover, when morality is founded on the rights of the individual as a physical entity, it excites passions and it reduces freedom to the unleashing of passions. Basil the Great, in his sermon *To the Rich* (ibid), describes the moral decadence and violence that characterize the societies that are based on egoism as follows: "'The eye is not filled with seeing' (*Ecclesiastes* 1:8), and the money lover is not satisfied with getting. 'Hell does not say, Enough' (*Proverbs* 27:20, 30:16); neither does the covetous man ever say, Enough".

THE UTOPIAN CHARACTER OF RATIONALIST POLITICAL ECONOMY

The philosophical and ideological foundations of bourgeois society's political economy can be found in physiocracy, meaning 'rule of nature'. Physiocracy was particularly dominated by François Quesnay (1694–1774), Marquis de Mirabeau (1715–1789) and Anne–Robert–Jacques Turgot (1727–1781). According to the physiocrats, there was a 'natural order' that allowed human beings to live together. Within the framework of the physiocrats' political economy, the human being is merged with the natural world, and, therefore, the human being is merely a particular case of the manifestation of natural laws.

By characterizing the system of laissez–faire capitalism as 'natural', the physiocrats as well as those classical and neoclassical economists who followed their rationale attempted to present the logic that characterizes their economic theory as the only correct logic for the organization of social–economic life. The rationale of the physiocrats and of those classical and neoclassical economists who followed their path has been summarized and explained by Gunnar Myrdal as follows: "Like all their contemporaries, the Physiocrats tried to interpret the 'natural order' of human society... In the framework of the natural order events were viewed as causally connected. The interests of individuals gave direction and cohesion to economic life, just as the force of gravitation held the planetary system together"[94]. Due to the physiocrats, the concept of economic equilibrium is based on the natural sphere. Moreover, following the physiocrats' rationale, Adam Smith identified natural price and normal price, and the same did Alfred Marshall and J.B. Clark.

Adam Smith's most important contribution to economic analysis is his attempt to place the economic rationale of the physiocrats within a scientifically rigorous analytical setting by arguing that the market mechanism is a self–regulating 'natural' order and that the price system organizes the behavior of people in an automatic fashion[95]. In the half century after Adam Smith's seminal book *The Wealth of Nations* appeared, the law of diminishing returns was formulated by Thomas Malthus (1766–1834) and David Ricardo (1722–1823). For Ricardo, from whose thinking both neoclassical and modern economics derive, given that the total social product is limited by diminishing returns, "what was gained by one social class had to be taken away from another one"[96]. Following the intellectual legacy of David Ricardo, in the 1870s, W. Stanley Jevons (1835–1882) in England, Carl Menger (1840–1921) in Austria, and Léon Walras (1834–1910) in Switzerland, working independently from each other, founded modern ('neoclassical') economics.

The physiocrats, the classical economists, and the neoclassical economists follow a positivist epistemology, which has been summarized by J.E. Cairnes as follows: "Political Economy is a science in the same sense in which Astronomy, Dynamics,

---

94 Gunnar Myrdal, The Political Element in the Development of Economic Theory, London: Routledge & Kegan Paul, 1953, pp. 31–32.

95 P.A. Samuelson and W.D. Nordhaus, Economics, 14th edition, New York: McGraw–Hill, 1992, p. 376.

96 Ibid, p. 377.

Chemistry, Physiology are sciences"[97]. By giving prime importance to rational mastery as shaping the political and cultural arrangements in any given society, neoclassical economics, ultimately, marginalizes and methodically undermines individual liberty. The world of neoclassical economics —which is the 'orthodoxy' of modern political economy— marginalizes and methodically undermines individual autonomy, since, in the context of neoclassical economics, market economies are based on the postulation of laws that are deemed beyond critique (since they are assumed to be natural necessities).

The physiocrats' epistemology and ontology have strongly influenced Marxism, too. In addition, Marxism has preserved certain values and mentalities of liberalism. Thus, on 16 January 1861, Marx wrote to Lasalle: "Darwin's book is very important and serves me as a basis in natural science for the class struggle in history". Moreover, on 7 August 1866, Marx wrote to Engels about Pierre Trémaux's book *Origin and Transformations of Man and the Other Species*: "it represents a *very significant* advance over Darwin...Progress, which Darwin regards as purely accidental, is essential here on the basis of the stages of the earth's development... In its historical and political applications far more significant and pregnant than Darwin". Hence, on 17 March 1883, Frederick Engels said at the grave of Karl Marx: "Just as Darwin discovered the law of development of organic nature, so Marx discovered the law of development of human history".

Marx declared the overthrow of the capitalist system through the action of the working class. But he also argued that the proletariat revolution can be neither a form of spontaneous social explosion nor a conspiratorial act; the proletariat revolution, for Marx, can only be a conscious social movement within specific established relations of production. In other words, according to Marx, the proletariat revolution is not a form of self–action, but it is a historically necessary action whose outcome is naturally embedded in the institution of the bourgeois system and more specifically in capitalism. Thus, in their book *The Holy Family —or Critique of Critical Criticism* (1845), Marx and Engels stress that the organization of the proletariat (the "mass") accurately reflects the organization of the capitalist society.

---

97   J.E. Cairnes, The Character and Logical Method of Political Economy, London: Macmillan, 1888, p. 35.

Moreover, Marx repeated this argument in *The Communist Manifesto* (1848), where he argues that the proletariat is "the most authentic product" of the big industry.

Marx attempted to explain human history in terms of its conformity to universal rational laws[98]. Marx's failure to take man's freedom of will and subjectivity into account in his economic theories has rendered his critique of capitalism deficient. For instance, contrary to Marx's predictions and expectations, in the 20th century, the rate of exploitation (also called the rate of surplus value) was not rising continuously. Moreover, exactly due to the ability of humans to criticize, create and reform their reality in accordance with transhistorical values, i.e. due to the freedom of spirit, the rise in the workers' standard of living in advanced capitalist societies did not cause the collapse of capitalism (contrary to Marx's predictions and expectations), but it co–existed with the flourishing of capitalism.

The existence of values[99] causes the consciousness of existence, in the sense that, through values and due to values, the human being —as opposed to every other biological being— is not necessarily determined by the 'physical objectivity', but it can exist in a manner that shows that the human being can control and change the physical conditions of its existence, instead of being passively controlled by them. It goes without saying that the existence of the human being takes place in the physical realm (through natural functions of the nervous system[100]). But the fact that the human being is capable of decisively intervening in the fields of its natural energies and impulses implies that the thing that substantiates the personal mode of existence of the human being is not nature itself but it is

---

98   This element of Marxism was particularly stressed by Karl Kautsky, who, after the death of Engels, stood out as the most influential theorist of the Second International. Kautsky's conception of social evolution was always tied to that of natural evolution, and, thus, his analyses and critiques of capitalism are characterized by excessive emphasis on productive forces and objective necessity. See: L. Kolakowski, Main Currents of Marxism, 3 vols, Oxford: Oxford University Press, 1978.

99   According to R. Polin, by the term value, we mean "the centre of interest" towards which consciousness is directed whenever it is engaged in a practical activity (see: J.J. Kockelmans (ed.), Contemporary European Ethics, New York: Anchor Books, 1972).

100   John Searle has made the following observations: "Consciousness…is caused by neurobiological processes", but, simultaneously, "conscious mental states and processes have a special feature not possessed by other natural phenomena, namely, subjectivity. It is this feature of consciousness that makes its study so recalcitrant to the conventional methods of biological and psychological research" (John Searle, The Rediscovery of the Mind, Cambridge, Mass.: MIT Press, 1992, pp. 90, 93).

an 'existential otherness' towards the common nature of the human beings, and this existential otherness makes the human subject a unique existence. This existential otherness and this freedom from nature are the core of the personal substance of the human subject.

By ignoring the decisive role of spiritual freedom, Marx failed to recognize that the crisis of capitalism and of civil society in general is not a narrowly economic one, but it is connected to the manner in which social actors manage their freedom of will. Marx's theory of alienation[101] can explain neither the inner contradictions of capitalism nor social conflicts. If the producer were really alienated by the output of his work and if labour–power were really commodified, then the value of the commodified labour would be objectively determined, and, therefore, class struggle would be impossible. The very existence of class struggle and social conflict indicates that, on the one hand, the capitalists tend to transform labour–power into a commodity and, on the other hand, the commodification of the workers is impossible. Moreover, even though the capitalists tend to commodify the labour class, they expect from the labour class to be creative and even innovative, i.e. the capitalists need to creatively co–operate with the labour class in the production process, which is an obvious contradiction, since commodification contradicts creativity. The labour class's resistance to the capitalists' attempt to transform labour–power into a commodity transforms the price of labour–power into an object of tough negotiations and makes class struggle possible.

The antagonistic character of capitalist society indicates that human action is based on spiritual freedom, i.e. it presupposes a value system that transcends historical necessities. Therefore, the physiocrats' and Marx's thesis that social becoming is determined by economic laws that are essentially similar to natural laws is wrong. The human being cannot be fully transformed into a machine or a commodity, because there is an inextricable connection between creativity and freedom. In contrast to Marx's analysis of the revolutionary movement, it is exactly because man's consciousness *does not* mechanically reflect the conditions of material life of society that revolutions can occur. Moreover, the physiocrats' and Marx's

---

101 'Alienation' is associated with the removability or irremovability of property and of such immaterial possessions as liberties and rights and with the features that people are said to share by virtue of being citizens and / or human beings.

hopes that a rational re–organization of economic relations in accordance with natural–historical necessities can give permanent solutions to the economic problems are equivalent to the elimination of human creativity. If an organization is attracted only to the state of behavior that is called stability, then it will stop being creative; Cornelius Castoriadis explained this phenomenon as follows: "A factory in which the workers were really and totally mere cogs in the machine, blindly executing the orders of management, would come to a stop in a quarter of an hour"[102].

Both the capitalists' and the Marxists' hopes are utopian. What does the term utopian mean? Many people characterize something as utopian if it is founded upon or involves a noble yet chimerical ideal. However, this is not a sufficient definition of the term utopian, because it fails to account for the manner in which utopian actors are connected to their ideals. In essence, a utopia is a plan of action whose purpose is to rationally solve the major problems of social reality once and for all. Thus, the physiocratic economic models (including the equilibrium theory of laissez–faire capitalism) and Marx's communism are utopias because they claim to be proposals for man's *total* salvation *within* the limits and *according to* the terms of the reason of history. In other words, inherent in every utopia are a persistent tendency to give historical conditions primacy over man's spiritual freedom and a hope that, by changing historical conditions, man will enter into some kind of 'Promised Land'.

However, in the context of any rationalist theory of political economy, man's hope is inactive and sterile, since, in the context of rationalism, human creativity is essentially nullified. Historical becoming is a result of human creativity only if and to the extent that man tends to transcend himself and seeks the truth in true *being* and not in historical becoming itself. In other words, man is authentically creative if and to the extent that he has an existential vantage point from which he can understand and create history without being determined by historical necessities.

The cosmo–conceptions of physiocracy (which is the intellectual source of classical political economy) and Marxism are ideologies in the context of which, after the acceptance of the original axiomatic system, the logical consistency of the propositions that are deduced

---

102   Castoriadis, The Imaginary Institution of Society, p. 16.

from the original axiomatic system takes primacy over the meaning of the original axiomatic system itself. In other words, physiocracy and Marxism are poor imitations of natural–science theories, in which the content of an idea is subject to the logical application of the given idea. In general, modern economics is dominated by the argument that there are economic laws and that the primary aim of economics is the discovery of those laws. Thus, to a large extent, the modern scientific discipline of economics consists in the teaching of closed logical structures and self–fulfilling prophecies. The tyranny of logic is established when the meaning of a thing or being is subject to logical procedures from which all humans are urged to deduce , thus negating man's spiritual freedom. Thus, both physiocracy and Marxism subject man to rigid rational procedures that are characterized by intolerance towards human creativity. Both physiocracy and Marxism identify natural becoming with historical becoming. Hence, in the context of classical political economy and Marxism, man is essentially a victim of historical necessity, which contradicts Orthodox Christian anthropology.

As it has been pointed out by Henri Bergson[103], in rationalist societies, historical time tends to be identified with physical time, since there is no spiritual tradition capable of imposing the intentionality of human consciousness on time. In pre–rationalist, archaic societies, the intentionality of human consciousness was imposed on physical time through magico–religious rituals, which were allowing human communities to ritualistically transcend physical time and experience a return to the divine origin of time. All pre–rationalist, archaic societies pursued spiritual freedom through rituals. However, the civilization of classical Greece found a new way of pursuing spiritual freedom —namely, the creation of philosophical tradition. Instead of depending on the archaic habit of repeating rituals, the classical Greek philosophical schools created philosophical traditions. The term philosophical tradition means that an original, foundational truth is transmitted from one generation to another throughout history, and, therefore, historical time is different from physical time, since historical time is counted in spiritual capabilities whereas physical time is counted in coercive seconds.

---

103   Henri Bergson, Time and Free Will —An Essay on the Immediate Data of Consciousness, tr., F.L. Pogson, Montana: Kessinger Publishing Company, 1910.

As a result of the archaic habit of pursuing spiritual freedom and consciousness expansion through the precise repetition of the same ritualistic work, time tends to be fixated on concrete stages of man's spiritual development, and, therefore, such practices oppress the creativity of human consciousness. On the contrary, classical Greeks' attempt to pursue spiritual freedom and consciousness expansion through philosophical tradition encourages critical thinking. In the context of the classical Greek spirituality, a traditional truth, which is transmitted from one generation to another, is subject to continuous re–interpretation by different people and different generations. For the classical Greeks, tradition is not a set of concrete, 'sanctified' *answers* to problems of human life, but it is a set of existential–ontological *questions*, which oblige man to constantly seek and evaluate the ultimate meaning of his life and actions. Thus, in the context of the classical Greek spirituality, philosophical tradition is the ultimate social authority and gives rise to a hierarchical world of significations, or values, with which legislation and institutions must comply. According to the classical Greek political thought, the events of social life become meaningful through and due to their connection to a transcendental world of common significations, or values.

4

HESYCHASM

THE terms 'Hesychasm' and 'Hesychast' are derived from the Greek word for 'silence' or 'stillness' —namely, 'hesychia'. Thus, 'Hesychasm' ('hesychasmos') is the practice of silence, and the Hesychast ('ho hesychastes') one who follows this practice, striving thereby to achieve "interior stillness and freedom from passions" and to render his prayer "limpid purity"[104]. Furthermore, C.N. Tsirpanlis has written about Hesychasm as a practice that it is a "system of Christocentric mysticism…and [of] psychosomatic…practices — especially…perfect quietude of body and mind (to attain the vision of the Uncreated Light of God)— of Eastern ascetics (since the Fourth century Desert Fathers) known as the *hesychasts of Mt. Athos* (Greece)"[105].

The most important defender of the Hesychastic tradition is Gregory Palamas (1296–1359), who is venerated as a saint in the Eastern Orthodox Church. Hence, this type of monasticism is also called "Palamism", and it can be understood as a deep experience of communion and union with God through the "Jesus Prayer", or *Cardiake prosefche*. The "Jesus Prayer" exists in several forms: the most familiar formula is, "Lord Jesus Christ, Son of God, have mercy on me, a sinner", but it is sometimes shortened to "Lord Jesus Christ, have mercy on me", and Gregory Palamas himself was fond of a similar devotional entreaty, "Photison mou to skotos" [Enlighten my darkness].

---

104   C.N. Tsirpanlis, Introduction to Eastern Patristic thought and Orthodox Theology, Collegeville, MN: The Liturgical Press, 1991, p.7.

105   Ibid, p. 7.

Even though Hesychasm was a very old practice in the Greek East, the first analytical description of the Hesychasts' method of prayer in the Greek sources dates only from the late 13th century, in the work *On Vigilance and the Guarding of the Heart* by Nicephorus the Hesychast, a monk of Mount Athos. Moreover, there is a closely similar description in a work entitled *Method of Holy Prayer and Attentiveness*, which is attributed to Symeon the New Theologian (949–1022 A.D.), a Byzantine Christian monk and poet, who is venerated as a saint in Eastern Orthodox Church. In the previous texts, Nicephorus and Symeon the New Theologian describe the physical techniques that are used by Hesychasts as follows:

i. The aspirant is to sit with his head bowed, and, additionally, according to Symeon the New Theologian's *Method of Holy Prayer and Attentiveness*, the aspirant should rest his beard on his chest and direct his bodily eyes together with the mind towards the middle of his belly, that is towards his navel[106]. Other texts suggest that the aspirant's gaze should be fixed on the place of the heart.

ii. The aspirant's breathing rhythm is to be slowed down. In particular, Symeon the New Theologian's *Method of Holy Prayer and Attentiveness* gives the following advice: "Restrain the inhalation of your breath through the nose, so as not to breathe in and out at your ease"[107].

iii. As he controls his breathing, the Hesychast is at the same time to search inwardly for the place of the heart. In particular, Nicephorus writes that the Hesychast is to imagine his breath entering through the nostrils and then passing down within the lungs until it reaches the heart, and, in this way, he is to make his mind remain with the breath within the body, so that mind and heart are united[108].

---

106 Symeon the New Theologian, Method of Holy Prayer and Attentiveness, Greek text and French trans. I. Hausherr, "La méthode d'oraison hésychaste", Orientalia Christiana, Vol. IX, 2, No.36, Rome, 1927, p. 164.

107 Ibid, p. 164.

108 Nicephorus of Mount Athos, On Vigilance and the Guarding of the Heart, in Patrologia Graeca, Vol. 147. Moreover, see: E. Kadloubovsky and G.E.H. Palmer (trans. and eds), Writings from the Philokalia on Prayer of the Heart, London: Faber, 1951, pp. 22–34.

In the 14th century, Gregory of Sinai, who is also venerated as a saint in the Eastern Orthodox Church, taught Hesychasm to monks of Mount Athos, but he left Mount Athos, around 1335, spending his last years at Paroria, on the borders between the Byzantine Empire and Bulgaria, and thus creating an important spiritual communication channel between the Greek and the Slav worlds. The disciples of Gregory of Sinai were instrumental in propagating Hesychasm throughout Bulgaria, Serbia and Russia. In his spiritual teachings, which are contained in *Patrologia Graeca*, Vol. 150, Gregory of Sinai urges that the use of the Jesus Prayer (reciting it in the standard form: "Lord Jesus Christ, Son of God, have mercy on me, a sinner") should be so far as possible continuous, because it is an effective way of attaining image–free, or non–discursive, prayer. Additionally, Gregory of Sinai recommends Nicephorus's physical technique, explaining that this physical technique is an effective way of keeping guard of the heart and controlling the thoughts. However, Gregory of Sinai mentions that, while images and thoughts are to be excluded, not all feelings should be rejected: rightly practiced, the Jesus Prayer leads to a sense of joyful sorrow and to a feeling of spiritual warmth, which, according to the Hesychasts, make the aspirant capable of contemplating the divine light that, according to *Matthew*, 17:1ff, and *Mark*, 9:3ff, was manifested to the three disciples of Jesus Christ at Christ's transfiguration on Mount Tabor.

As the distinguished academic Dimitri Obolensky writes, "Byzantium, Bulgaria, Serbia, Romania and Russia were all affected by this new cosmopolitan movement [Hesychasm]", and, "through this 'Hesychast International', whose influence extended far beyond the ecclesiastical sphere, the different parts of the Byzantine Commonwealth were, during the last hundred years of its existence, linked to each other and to its centre and perhaps more closely than ever before"[109].

Hesychastic culture was transnational, providing a spiritual identity to all peoples, regardless of ethnic origin, and it promoted numerous new translations of Byzantine texts into Slavic languages. Thus, Hesychasm carried forth the ancient notion of 'ecumene' (i.e. common spiritual horizon), competing against the nationalist trends that had emerged in Byzantium since the era of Emperor Heraclius.

---

[109] Dimitri Obolensky, The Byzantine Commonwealth —Eastern Europe 500–1453, Crestwood, N.Y.: St. Vladimir's Seminary Press, 1971, p. 390.

In general, Hesychasm has important cultural–anthropological consequences, since it determines the manner in which the persons that endorse Hesychasm understand themselves and others.

Why is man's relationship with God so important? To answer the previous question, it is useful to reformulate it as follows: what is it that is at stake when man chooses his attitude towards the idea of God? The total rejection of the idea of God deprives man of the capability of looking at himself in a creative and trustworthy manner. Religion may be a man–made spiritual creation, but God Himself is not a man–made spiritual creation, and, therefore, neither the existence nor the in–existence of God can be scientifically established. However, God is the most, and, in fact, the only, trustworthy mirror in which man can look at his true self, since God is the absolute, transcendental unity. No other being or thing is *naturally* a total unity, since every being or thing in the world is characterized by contradictions and change. As Michel Foucault has pointed out, "nothing in man —not even his body— is sufficiently stable to serve as the basis for self–recognition or for understanding other men"[110]. Hence, without God, man is unable to look at himself in a creative and trustworthy manner. Hesychasm is a kind of relationship with God that helps man understand himself as a potential god.

THE HESYCHASTIC CONTROVERSY

Hesychasm was called in question and challenged during the decade 1337–1347, in what is known as the Hesychastic controversy. The attack on Hesychasm was launched by a learned Greek from South Italy, Barlaam the Calabrian (ca. 1290–1348), who was influenced by the 14th century rationalist schools of Western Europe. Barlaam was answered by a learned monk from Mount Athos, Gregory Palamas. Palamas's famous defense of the Hesychasts, *Hyper ton Hieros Hesychazonton* (In Defense of the Sacred Hesychasts), which was probably written between 1338 and 1341, is comprised of nine treatises in the form of questions and answers.

In order to understand the philosophical, symbolic and religious significance of Hesychasm, one must first of all bear in mind that Barlaam endorsed the Western thesis that the Greek philosophical

---

110   Michel Foucault, Language, Counter–Memory, Practice, ed. D.F. Bouchard, Ithaca, N.Y.: Cornell University Press; Oxford: Blackwell, 1977, p. 153.

term essence/being is a universal, i.e. a logically self–subsistent entity, and additionally he endorsed the West's tendency to identify the notion of mind with that of intellect. As I explained in chapter 2, the previous Western views are not in agreement with the Greek spirit. In contrast to the Western scholars' way of interpreting Platonism and Aristotelianism, the Greek Church Fathers adopted the Greek tradition of interpreting Platonism and Aristotelianism, which I exposed in chapter 2. Following the Greek philosophical tradition, the Greek Church Fathers have emphasized that God is absolutely free, since they have interpreted God's reasons (logoi) not as *essential* characteristics of God, but as *actions/energies* that are derived from God's will and are distinct from God's essence. In the context of the Greek Church Fathers' theology, God is not determined by His nature, and, in general, He is not subject to any logical necessity, and, therefore, in contrast to Thomas Aquinas's natural theology, the reason (logos) of the natural world is distinct from the reason (Logos) of God.

According to the tradition of the Greek Church Fathers in general and the teachings of Gregory Palamas in particular, God's 'energy' is different from God's 'essence', in the sense that God's energy is the life–force of God's essence, but the fullness God is present in God's energy according to God's own will. According to the Hesychasts, man can participate in God's energies —which are known as wisdom, love, providence, creativity, etc.— and man's ontological perfection, or deification, consists in man's participation in God's energies. However, the Hesychasts add, since God's energies are distinct from God's essence (even though God's energies are equally divine as God's essence), man's participation in God's *energies* implies that man participates in God, but simultaneously God's essence and hypostases (i.e. the three persons of the Trinity) remain totally transcendental and totally inaccessible to man, and, therefore, God's existence is characterized by absolute freedom.

Man's participation in God's energies should not be understood as a relation between an idea and its image, but as a free personal relation between God and man. If man's participation in God's energies consisted in a relation between an idea and its image, then man's freedom would be dramatically reduced, because, in that case, man's reasons (logoi) would be logically determined and subjected to God's reasons. On the contrary, in the context of Hesychasm, the knowledge of God and, hence, true theology consist in man's participation in God's energies, and man's participation in God's energies takes place if and to the extent that man is properly prepared in psychological terms. Thus, God's being is not a coercive universal. The relation between God and man is based on free will and not on logical necessity. It is the Western rationalism that —by treating the relation between God and man like a relation between a higher, more general concept and a lower, less general concept— mixes theology with logical necessity and coercion. For the Hesychasts, true theology is the personal experience of one's participation in God's energies, and the tradition of the Church Fathers is nothing else than a record of such experiences and their spiritual outcomes.

In contrast to the Western rationalist schools of philosophy and theology, the Hesychasts follow the Greek way of interpreting classical Greek philosophy, and, therefore, they keep in mind Plato's thesis that humans can attain a personal experience of the absolute good, but they cannot logically deduce the absolute good from a deterministic chain of syllogisms. Thus, Plato emphasizes that the knowledge of the absolute good presupposes not only the ability to give an account but also a psychic cleansing or cure. The metaphysical type of knowledge that corresponds to intelligence is what Plato has in his mind in *Phaedo*, 247c–e, where he describes the soul journeying in "that place beyond the heavens": "It is there that true being dwells, without colour or shape, that cannot be touched".

Additionally, in his *Republic*, 443d–e, Plato argues that one has cured his soul if he has "attained to self–mastery and beautiful order within himself, and…harmonized these three principles [the three parts of the soul: reason, the emotions, and the appetites]… linked and bound all three together and made himself a unit, one man instead of many, self–controlled and in unison". Sine, as we read in Plato's *Republic*, 585b, the purpose of our existence is our participation in the pure being (the Good) and our unification with the Good, psychic cleansing is a necessary presupposition for our transformation into the corresponding absolute principle; for, as Plato argues in *Phaedo*, 67b, "it cannot be that the impure attain the pure".

Following the teachings of Maximus the Confessor and the Greek Patristic consensus, Hesychasm emphasizes that there is absolute discontinuity between the uncreated essence of God and the essence of the world (the Creation). In other words, God and the world do not constitute a hierarchical universal unity. Such a hierarchical universal unity would contradict both the freedom of God and the freedom of man, since it would subject both God and man to a coercive, impersonal universal reason.

As I explained in chapter 1, Maximus the Confessor emphasized that God and man relate to each other through their wills, i.e. freely and personally, and not through their essences. Thus, man can attain the knowledge of God by obtaining the divine wisdom, i.e. by participating in the corresponding uncreated energy of God, which is distinct from the reason of the world. Therefore, Hesychasm is founded on the freedom of God and on the free actualization of man's full potential, which is deification, within God and through God. Gregory Palamas points out that spiritual knowledge comes, not through mere education, or worldly knowledge, but through the radiance that results from the cleansing of the mind (which, according to Hesychasm, resides in the heart) and the attainment of holiness and Apostolic virtue: "It is thus apparent that this radiance is above human intellect and knowledge"[111].

Timothy Ware (Bishop Kallistos of Diokleia), in his book, *The Orthodox Church*[112], summarized Gregory Palamas's teachings on the knowledge of God as follows: "we know the *energies* of God, but not His *essence*. This distinction between God's essence (ousia) and His energies goes back to the Cappadocian Fathers". Moreover, in the same book, Timothy Ware goes on as follows: "But however remote from us in His essence, yet in His energies God has revealed Himself to men. These energies...are God Himself in His action and revelation to the world. God exists complete and entire in each of His divine energies".

At this point, it is useful to add that the absence of any *essential* relationship between God and the natural world implies that there is no contradiction between the existence of God and any cosmological theory of the natural sciences. Physics is concerned with questions about the functions of the natural world. For instance, physics is

---

111   Gregoriou tou Palama —Hapanta ta Erga (Gregory Palamas —Complete Works), ed. P. Chrestou, Thessaloniki: Paterikai Ekdoseis "Gregorios ho Palamas", 1981–1986, Vol. 2, p. 258.

112   Timothy Ware (Bishop Kallistos of Diokleia), The Orthodox Church, Harmondsworth: Penguin Books, 1963, pp. 77–78.

concerned with questions of the following type[113]: What happened at or before the Big Bang? Was there really an initial singularity? What is the topology of space? Why is there an arrow of time; that is, why is the future so much different from the past? Are there non–local phenomena in quantum physics? Do the phenomena attributed to dark matter point not to some form of matter but actually to an extension of gravity? On other hand, the debate about the existence of God rises from a question whose nature is philosophical and not scientific —namely: *Why* does the natural world exist? Thus, if we understand God as the ultimate source of significance, or purpose, of the beings and things in the world, then God's existence means that the natural world is meaningful, and His existence does not contradict any theorem of the natural sciences. Therefore, no theorem of the natural sciences can prove or disprove the existence of God, as He is understood in the Bible. According to the Bible, God created the world only by His own free will, without any pre–existent 'raw materials', and, therefore, He is the transcendental positive void that generates the significance of all the beings and things in the world. Given that God did not use any pre–existent 'raw materials' in order to create the world, i.e. given that God's essence is totally unrelated to and totally distinct from the natural world, we cannot transform any theorems about the natural world into theological arguments. In other words, the discoveries of science do not reveal God's Logos Himself; instead, they reveal functions of beings and things that have been created by God[114], i.e. scientific theorems reveal results of God's *will*, but not God's *essence*.

Gregory of Nyssa, whose thought in a sense laid the foundations

---

113   See for instance: H. Price, Time's Arrow and Archimedes' Point —New Directions for a Physics of Time, Oxford: Oxford University Press, 1996, and S. Hawking and L. Mlodinow, A Brief History of Time, New York: Bantam, 2005.

114   In pantheism and in pagan theological systems, the nature of God is not totally distinct from the nature of the universe (e.g. the universe is considered to be an emanation from the Godhead). Thus, such beliefs identify the functions of God's mind with the functions of the natural world, and, therefore, belief in God becomes necessarily dependent upon a certain set of cosmological theorems. Hence, pantheistic and pagan religious beliefs try to control and to dominate scientific research because they are founded upon a particular cosmological paradigm, and any cosmological paradigm shift is a threat to the validity of their religious doctrines. On the other hand, in the context of Biblical theology, God (Creator) is totally distinct (and hence free) from the nature of the universe (Creation), and, therefore, no scientific theorem contradicts faith in God, simply because no scientific theorem can say anything essential about God.

for the classical Christian understanding of the cosmos, has pointed out how inadequate it is to understand the essence of the wind from its operation/work, which may be a sand dune. Furthermore, how do you understand the essence of a man who builds both a ship and a house by examining one or the other? By which of its works can we understand the essence of the sky? In the same way, how can the being of God be comprehended through His operations? Gregory of Nyssa insists that the essence of God remains inaccessible to us, both ontologically and epistemologically.

The earliest Church Fathers and generally the Hesychasts never felt that their faith in God could be threatened by any theorem of the natural sciences, because they understood God as the totally transcendental source of significance of all the beings and things in the world. From this perspective, every theorem of the natural sciences reveals a particular result of God's *will*, but it reveals nothing about God's *essence*. Nevertheless, in the Middle Ages, a conflict between religion and science was ignited because certain scholastic theologians, who were speculating about God's essence, used arguments of philosophical realism in order to defend their faith and, in this way, they attempted to show that it was possible to rationally, i.e. syllogistically, ascend from nature to God.

Those scholastic theologians founded their theology upon the confirmation of certain cosmological hypothetico–deductive systems, which were convenient for their theological arguments; in this way, they reduced God to a concept whose validity was vulnerable to the disproof of certain cosmological theorems and to the proof of new cosmological theorems. Hence, for many scholastics, faith in God became compatible only with certain scientific theorems and incompatible with others. For instance, the Roman Catholic Church felt obliged to oppose heliocentrism from 1616 to 1757! In other words, the naturalistic theology of certain representatives of the Roman Catholic Church, by deviating from the original Christian principle of the absolute transcendence of God's essence, gave rise to a kind of Christianity that prohibits and inhibits free scientific inquiry and progress. Thus, many Renaissance natural scientists reacted against the spiritual despotism of many Church authorities by indiscriminately discarding the Christian doctrine and espousing other approaches to religion that appeared to be friendlier to scientific research. On the other hand, from the Hesychasts' standpoint, the Orthodox Christian dogmatics leads to an understanding of God as the perfect archetype of the free person.

THE VISION AND KNOWLEDGE OF GOD AS UNCREATED LIGHT

Gregory Palamas teaches that, following the attainment of pure prayer, one becomes, through an intimate knowledge of, and encounter with, God within the heart, a true theologian. It is at this point in spiritual development that the spiritual aspirant for the first time begins to understand Scripture and its spirit. Furthermore, Gregory Palamas speaks even of physical reactions to pure prayer, referring to the joy of the heart at the coming of grace. But more importantly, pure prayer leads to the vision of God, Who manifests Himself in what Palamas calls "aktiston phos" (Uncreated Light), or "theia ellampsis" (Divine Radiation) of God. This Light, he maintains, was the same Light in which Christ appeared in Mt. Thabor at the Transfiguration[115]. It was also the Divine Light that Paul experienced on the road to Damascus, as a "pledge of [our] investiture therein"[116]. The mystical vision of Uncreated Light floods the mind with grace, such that the mind (nous) is totally cleansed and "liberated by the power of the Holy Spirit", as John Romanides writes, "from the influences of both the body and the discursive intellect"[117]. When the body is freed from the sin and controlled by the mind, which becomes its overseer, no longer do the physical and intellectual faculties exercise any influence whatsoever on the mental (noetic) faculty, but they are dominated by the mental faculty's unceasing prayer and are spiritually cleansed; this is why the Hesychasts emphasize that knowledge of God is grace (as opposed to an intellectual achievement of the individual) and that the mind is the tank of God's grace in man.

In his discussion of the vision and knowledge of God as Uncreated Light, Gregory Palamas explains the essence–energy distinction, in response to the accusations of Barlaam that, like the Messalian heretics, the Hesychasts claimed to achieve a physical vision of God by beholding what they considered His essence. Barlaam explained this as an apparition of light and the product of "created grace",

---

115 Gregoriou tou Palama —Hapanta, Vol. 8, p.158.

116 Ibid.

117 J.S. Romanides, "Notes on Palamite Controversy and Related Topics", Part II, The Greek Orthodox Theological Review, Vol. IX, Winter 1963–64, p.229.

in keeping with the Augustinian and Thomistic traditions, which prevailed in scholasticism. John Romanides has pointed out that, in contradistinction to the idea of knowing God through created apparitions of grace, the Hesychastic theology points out that, whereas "for Barlaam, knowledge of God is rational..., for Palamas knowledge of God is based on the supra–rational experience of the prophets, apostles, and saints; it transcends all rational knowledge"[118]. Whereas Barlaam espoused the principle "credo ut intelligam" of the post–Augustinian West, Gregory Palamas espoused the apophatic theology of the Greek Fathers.

Everywhere in his writings in defense of Hesychasm, Gregory Palamas makes it clear that the Hesychasts, unlike the Messalians, do not strive for a physical vision of the transcendent, unknowable Godhead (i.e. for a vision of the unseen *essence* of God); nor do they claim that the uncreated light of God is His unknowable essence. In the *Hagioritic Tome*, Palamas declares that the uncreated light, which the Hesychast sees when he comes to a knowledge of God, is a manifestation of the energies of God, which are perceived by the mind (the noetic faculty) and, indeed, by the senses, but only after the latter have been purified, transformed, and illuminated by the return of the spiritual mind to the heart, wherein the mind is illuminated by the divine grace. In Gregory Palamas's own words: "When they have achieved spiritual and supra–natural grace and power, those who have been so vouchsafed behold both sensibly and noetically that which is above all sense and intellect"[119].

Barlaam and his followers argued that, by the essence–energies distinction, Gregory Palamas had posited the existence of two Gods. Palamas's answer to this argument was that both God's essence and His energies are uncreated and that the distinction between them safeguards both the ability of man to achieve deification (since man can participate in God's uncreated energies, and thus man can literally know God) and God's absolute unity and unknowability (since God's uncreated essence remains totally inaccessible, and thus God is absolutely free from every natural and logical constraint). Through God's energies, we attain participation in the

---

118   J.S. Romanides, "Notes on Palamite Controversy and Related Topics", Part I, The Greek Orthodox Theological Review, Vol. VI, Winter 1960–61, p.191.

119   Gregoriou tou Palama —Hapanta, Vol. 3, p.510.

Divinity, while the Divinity's essence remains totally inaccessible and thus totally free. In other words, Gregory Palamas differentiates God's essence from the deifying energies, which, according to G.C. Papademetriou, those who have experienced deification recognize and know as the "'manifestations' and [uncreated] 'exteriorizations' of God"[120].

The essence–energies distinction is essential to the soteriology of the Orthodox Church and the teachings of the deification of man. As Christos Yannaras[121] has pointed out: "The West", like Barlaam, "rejected the distinction, desiring to protect the idea of simplicity in the divine essence", and thus, for the West, "the energies of God are either identified with the essence" of God (and hence they become inaccessible to man, since God and man are essentially distinct from each other) or with some "created result of the divine cause" (and hence they become accessible to man, but they do not literally offer deification of man, they do not lead to a literal personal relationship between God and man, since they are creations of God and not God Himself). Without the essence–energies distinction, man's deification, "even though supernatural", is thought to be "created…, as Western theologians have arbitrarily" held "since the ninth century"[122], and hence the knowledge of God by man becomes only indirect (and is often conditioned by intellectual power games).

In his theory of the vision of God as uncreated light, Gregory Palamas follows an ancient Greek philosophical tradition. In particular, from Plato's book *Phaedo* to Proclus's book *Alcibiades*, Greek philosophers propose a theory of vision that allows man to know the good and the truth without the mediation of intellectual images, i.e. the ancient Greek philosophical theory of vision allows man to know the good and the truth by *participating* in the good and the truth instead of intellectually reproducing the good and the truth. According to the ancient Greek philosophical theory of vision, this participation becomes possible because the light of man's eyes meets the sun's light under the necessary presupposition

---

120   G.C. Papademetriou, Introduction to Saint Gregory Palamas, New York: Philosophical Library, 1973, p. 43.

121   Christos Yannaras, "The Distinction Between Essence and Energies and Its Importance for Theology", St. Vladimir's Theological Quarterly, Vol. 19, no. 4, 1975, pp.242–243.

122   Ibid.

that man has cleansed his mind of all elements that contradict the transparency of light.

Gregory Palamas understands soul cleansing as a process that leads to psychological transparency. The goal of psychological transparency consists in the elimination of every impediment to divine energies' descent in man. From this standpoint, the subjection of the mind to 'ratio', i.e. the identification of the mind with the intellect, is a state of mental non–transparency. In other words, the subjection of the mind to 'ratio' implies that the mind is closed towards the uncreated divine grace and is restricted to created means of knowledge. Thus, Nicetas Stethatos, a very influential 11th century Hesychast, in his work *On the Soul*, explains that the tree of knowledge of good and evil, about which we read in *Genesis*, 2:9, is a metaphor of two spiritual paths, which are both available to man: according to the first path, which corresponds to the knowledge of good, man tries to empty his mind from every element that might be an impediment to divine energies' descent in him, and, thus, he tries to present his mind transparent and clean to God in order to be filled with God's uncreated energies; on the other hand, according to the second path, which corresponds to the knowledge of evil, man tries to distinguish good from evil by means of created 'ratio', i.e. without seeking his participation in the uncreated energies of God. That is why the Bible instructs us, "My thoughts are not your thoughts" (*Isaiah*, 55:8), and "Who has known the mind of the Lord?" (*Romans*, 11:34). In the same spirit, Gregory of Nyssa, in his *Commentary on Ecclesiastes*, writes on this point: "…human speech finds it impossible to express the reality which transcends all thought and all concept;…and he who obstinately tries to express it in words, unconsciously offends God". Thus, the Hesychasts strongly oppose theological rationalism and treat it as a repetition of Adam's error, which caused Adam's exile from the uncreated light of Paradise.

THE MIND–BODY PROBLEM ACCORDING TO GREGORY PALAMAS

In his *Hyper ton Hieros Hesychazonton* (In Defense of the Sacred Hesychasts), Gregory Palamas argues that Barlaam's argument against what the Hesychasts mean by "pure prayer", or prayer which is accomplished by concentrating the mind —which (according to the Hesychasts) is the "tameion" [repository] of the Holy Spirit—[123] in the heart, is based on a misunderstanding of the body. Barlaam and his followers, in arguing that the mind should be freed from the body in prayer, contradicted, in the view of Gregory Palamas, Paul's doctrine that the body is the temple of the Holy Spirit within man (1 Corinthians, 6:19). When the mind is cleansed of sin and passions, Palamas affirms, it functions in concord with the body, and one sees in himself "the grace promised to the pure in heart"[124].

Gregory Palamas, in the first triad of his sermons *Hyper ton Hieros Hesychazonton*, stresses that Hesychasm regards it "as evil for the mind to be concerned with the mindings of the flesh, and not wrong for the mind to be in the body, for the body is not evil". Thus, in the first triad of his sermons *Hyper ton Hieros Hesychazonton*, Gregory Palamas poses the following question: "We who carry as in vessels of clay, that is in our bodies, the light of the Father, in the person of Jesus Christ, in which we know the glory of the Holy Spirit—how can it dishonor our mind to duel in the inner sanctuary of the body?" In the second triad of his sermons *Hyper ton Hieros Hesychazonton*, Gregory Palamas gives the following answer to the previous question: "When spiritual joy comes to the body from the mind, it suffers no diminution by this communion with the body, but rather transfigures the body, spiritualizing it. For then, rejecting all evil desires of the flesh, it no longer weighs down the soul that rises up with it, the whole man becoming spirit".

Moreover, Gregory Palamas explains that the Hesychasts fight against the law of sin in order to banish it from the body and establish there the mind as an overseer. In particular, the Hesychasts lay down laws for every power of the soul and for every member of the body as is appropriate for it: to the senses they prescribe what they have to receive and in what measure, and this practice of spiritual law is called self–mastery; they bring the desiring part of the soul to that excellent state whose name is love; and they improve the intellectual part by banishing all that prevents the mind from soaring to God, and this part of the spiritual law is called 'nepsis'. Nepsis is a state of watchfulness or sobriety acquired following the Hesychasts' prayer techniques. Thus,

---

123 Philokalia ton Hieron Neptikon (Philokalia of the Holy Neptic Fathers), Athens: Ekdotikos Oikos "Aster", 1974–1976, Vol. 4, p.125.

124 Ibid, Vol. 4, p.125.

according to Gregory Palamas, both the mind and the body receive God's grace.

The theme of nepsis can also be found in the work of Evagrius Ponticus, who was a 4th century A.D. Hesychast and one of the first great teachers of mental prayer. In his work entitled *The Praktikos*, 48:29, Evagrius points out that the essential struggle of the monk is with his thoughts. Moreover, in his chapters *On Prayer*, Evagrius urges, "stand on guard and protect your mind from thoughts when you pray", and he adds, "do not let your eye be distracted during prayer, but detach yourself from concern...and give all your attention to the mind".

According to Hesychasm, the heart is the essence of the mind, and the mind is a power of the heart. As Gregory Palamas writes in the first triad of his sermons *Hyper ton Hieros Hesychazonton*, "the heart is the secret chamber of the mind and the prime physical organ of mental power". Gregory Palamas attacks the idea that man must drive his mind out of his body in order to attain spiritual visions as an erroneous belief and as a repetition of the mistake perpetrated by the Forebears of humanity in Paradise. In Paradise, the mind of the first created man was able to see God in a direct manner. In other words, 'Paradise' is that state of existence that is characterized by the unity between man and the source of significance of all the beings and things in the world. However, after the Fall, man's mind became dispersed upon creation, being continually engaged with creation, and not with the Divine Word as before. In other words, the Fall implies that man lost his direct contact with the Word.

In the first triad of his sermons *Hyper ton Hieros Hesychazonton*, Gregory Palamas writes that "after the Fall, our inner being naturally adapts itself to outward forms", and, in the second triad of his sermons *Hyper ton Hieros Hesychazonton*, Gregory Palamas adds that the aim of the Hesychast is to prevent his mind from "straying hither and thither" and for it to once again establish a direct relationship with God. Furthermore, in the first triad of his sermons *Hyper ton Hieros Hesychazonton*, Gregory Palamas says the following, quoting Basil the Great: "'For the mind', writes St. Basil, 'when not dispersed outwardly' —note that it goes out from itself, and, so having gone out, it must find a way to return inwards— 'returns to itself, and, through itself, ascends to God'".

Following Dionysius the Areopagite, Gregory Palamas speaks about two different movements of the mind by drawing a comparison with the eye: The mind is like the eye, in that it sees and observes visible things other than itself, and this, according to the terminology of Dionysius the Areopagite, is called the "direct movement" of the mind. The second movement of the mind is, according to the terminology of Dionysius the Areopagite, called the "circular movement" of the mind, and it occurs when the mind returns to itself. According to Gregory Palamas, the circular movement of the mind is the highest and most befitting activity of the mind. In the first triad of his sermons *Hyper ton Hieros Hesychazonton*, Gregory Palamas writes that, through the circular movement of the mind, the mind "even transcends itself and is united to God".

In order to understand the theses of Gregory Palamas, we must bear in mind the Greek Church Fathers' teachings about the human soul. According to the Greek Church Fathers, the human soul is not naturally immortal, but it becomes immortal due to God's grace, and, therefore, man is free to choose if the end of his life will be spiritual death or, alternatively, unification with God and, hence, eternal life in God. On the other hand, many Latin Church Fathers treat the human soul as if it were a naturally immortal entity, and, therefore, man's freedom to choose between life and death is eliminated in Latin theology. Thus, since the Latin Church Fathers believe that man is naturally obliged to live after death, they teach that God, functioning like a cosmic judge, distributes rewards and punishments to the souls of men according to the moral status and acts of each soul during its life on earth.

The Greek Church Fathers' theology and anthropology are based on the absolute distinction between the uncreated and the created. Thus, they stress that God alone is uncreated, and everything else, including the human soul, is created. In the context of the Greek Church Fathers' theology and anthropology, both life and death are manifestations of God's love and favor towards man. By the term death, the Greek Church Fathers understand existence in separation from God, Who, "is the way and the truth and the life" (*John*, 14:6), and, by the term life, the Greek Church Fathers understand existence in communion with God.

In the 2nd century A.D., Justin Philosopher and Martyr writes in his book *Dialogue with Trypho*, 4–6: "if the world is begotten, souls also are necessarily begotten... They are not, then, immortal?...No;

since the world has appeared to us to be begotten... If, then, it [the soul] is life, it would cause something else, and not itself, to live, even as motion would move something else than itself". In the same text, Justin Philosopher and Martyr continues as follows: "Now, that the soul lives, no one would deny. But if it lives, it lives not as being life, but as the partaker of life; but that which partakes of anything, is different from that of which it does partake. Now the soul partakes of life, since God wills it to live".

According to Hesychasm, the human soul is united with the body into a unified psycho–somatic nexus. In this context, the 'soul' can be understood as the personal bearer of the impersonal life–force, i.e. as an entity that is very close to what psychologists call 'personality' or 'personhood'. However, according to the Hesychasts, the mind is a power of the soul, but it is not an organic part of the soul, because the mind is derived from outside the soul.

The Hesychasts understand the mind as the tank, or repository, of divine grace in the human being, and not merely as 'ratio'. *Thus, it is very important to understand that, in the context of Hesychasm, the term mind should not be used interchangeably with the term intellect.* The knowledge that is based on the intellect is derived from a created source, but the knowledge that is based on God's grace is derived from the uncreated energies of God, i.e. directly from God. Moreover, according to the Hesychasts, the three aspects of soul, which are mentioned in the fourth book of Plato's *Republic* —namely, the appetitive aspect of soul (which is responsible for the base desires within people), the rational aspect of soul (intellect), and the spirited aspect of soul (which is the desires that love honor and victory and, in the just soul, it acts as the enforcer of the rational soul)— *are not organic parts (structural elements) of the soul, but they are the results of the exercise of freedom of will by man.*

Therefore, according to the Hesychasts, the essence of 'psychological illness' consists in the dispersion of man's mental energy upon the irrationality of the senses and the sensibles; this dispersion leads to the mind's captivity by the irrationality of the senses and the sensibles. Additionally, the Hesychasts maintain, the essence of 'psychotherapy' consists in the mind's liberation from the shackles of the senses and its return to the heart. In the sequel, I shall analyze the Hesychasts' theory of psychotherapy, which is based on the union between God's will and man's will, and, additionally, I shall argue that, for Hesychasm, there is a sharp distinction between the human *mind* and the human *intellect* and that Hesychastic psychotherapy is radically different from the West's medieval and modern schools of philosophical and scientific psychology.

HESYCHASTIC PSYCHOTHERAPY[125]

According to the Hesychasts, man's reason is a power of the soul (i.e. it is the rational aspect of the soul) and, hence, it is a human power, whereas the mind, being the tank of God's uncreated energies (grace) in man, is a divine gift. When man's reason is subject to the sensibles and passions, it tends to subjugate the mind and it darkens the mind. Thus, the Hesychasts, by following their psychosomatic and praying practices, attempt to bring the mind back to its normal position, which is the heart, in order to be able, in a state of mental cleanness, to receive the light of God's truth, which leads to the deification of man. The Hesychasts do not pursue to project the mind outside the body, since they do not treat the body like a mortal prison of an immortal psychical substance, but they pursue to keep the mind inside the body —through what Dionysius the Areopagite called the "circular movement" of the mind— since the purpose of the mind is to oversee the entire psychosomatic substance of man and to eliminate all those rational and all those passionate elements of the soul that could impede the descent of God's grace in the mind.

---

125 In the context of contemporary Christian Orthodox bibliography, one can find two influential books that attempt to draw from the writings of the Greek Church Fathers and from various Orthodox theological writers what they call "Orthodox psychotherapy". These two books are the following: Bishop of Nafpaktos Hierotheos, Orthodox Psychotherapy, trans. Esther Williams, Levadia, Greece: Birth of the Theotokos Monastery, 1994; Archbishop Chrysostomos, A Guide to Orthodox Psychotherapy, Lanham: University Press of America, 2007. The previous two books are thought-provoking and intellectually challenging, they touch on the interface between science and religion, and they have promoted a dialogue between theology and the so–called "mental health professions". Even though the previous two books are academically rigorous and informative, they have not analyzed the difference between the philosophical background of the Greek Church Fathers and the philosophical background of the Latin Church Fathers, and, in general, they have not addressed the impact of Greek philosophy on Christian theology. As I argued in chapters 1 and 2 of this book, this is a very important issue in order to understand the destiny of Christianity (and of 'spirituality' in general) in the West and the East. Additionally, the previous two books have not touched on the difference between the terms mind (nous) and intellect in the context of Hesychasm. As I argue in this book, in order to understand the Hesychasts' approach to psychotherapy and the potential of a dialogue between Hesychastic psychotherapy and Western psychology, we must study the Hesychasts' theses about the structure of the human psyche and their way of understanding the terms mind and intellect.

Thus, according to the Hesychasts, the essence of psychotherapy is the safeguarding of the divine grace, which was given to man as mind, or freedom of the soul.

For the Hesychasts, the mind does not have any organs, but it is an image of God. In other words, as I have already mentioned, according to the Hesychasts, the three aspects of soul —namely, the appetitive aspect of soul, the rational aspect of soul, and the spirited aspect of soul (passion)— are not organic parts (structural elements) of the soul, but they are the results of the exercise of freedom of will by man. Thus, since the mind does not have any organs, it is not naturally urged to move outside itself guided by material passions or attracted to the objects of the senses. The Hesychast's mind, instead of being concerned with or determined by the objects of the senses, leaves the objects of the senses in order to return to the heart, where it cleans itself, i.e. it is liberated from rational and instinctive commands, and it imposes its authority on the entire psychosomatic substance of man, and, eventually, having become the greatest manifestation of man's freedom of will, it is united with God's free will.

Hesychastic psychotherapy is substantially different from modern psychology. In the context of modern psychology, whose founders are René Descartes (1596–1650) and Wilhelm Wundt (1832–1920), man's soul was identified with man's consciousness (i.e. with thought and will), and, therefore, psychology —which, according to the Hesychasts and the classical Greek philosophers, was a theory of knowledge and truth— became a theory of consciousness and was combined with the methodical study of the nervous system. In particular, according to Wundt, "the exact description of consciousness [Bewusstsein] is the sole aim of experimental psychology"[126], and, furthermore, Wundt argues that "all experimental methods of psychology appeal to physiology for support, since they can never ignore the physiological stimuli [Einwirkungen] upon the organism or its physiological reactions"[127]. However, it soon became clear that the power of consciousness and the nervous system cannot explain the totality of psychological phenomena, and, therefore, depth psychology was added to the previous theories of modern psychology. The term depth psychology

---

126   See: E.B. Titchener, "Wilhelm Wundt", American Journal of Psychology, Vol. 32, 1921, p. 164.

127   Wilhelm Wundt, Logik, Vol. 3, Stuttgart: Enke, 1921, p. 219.

was coined by the Swiss psychiatrist Eugen Bleuler (1857–1939) to refer to psychological methods of therapy and research that seek the deep layers underlying behavioral and cognitive processes, i.e. they take the unconscious into account[128]. Some of the greatest pioneers of depth psychology were Pierre Janet, William James, Sigmund Freud, and Carl Jung.

In the context of depth psychology, scientific psychology attempts to analyze the layers of the soul that are not conscious and are formed by wishes and desires that are repressed by social norms and by reason and common sense, which are adaptation mechanisms to external reality. Thus, for psychoanalysts, the essence of psychopathology consists in painful explosions of censored and forbidden impulses or in more permanent symbolic manifestations of censored and forbidden impulses[129]. Psychoanalysts maintain that the analysis of censored and forbidden impulses and taboos leads to the revival of symbolically structured traumatic events and to the identification of those traumatic events' real dimensions, thus leading the patient to a balanced reconciliation with himself and with his environment. Through psychoanalysis, one becomes consciously aware of his unconscious, in the sense that consciousness assimilates repressed elements of the soul by establishing correspondences between symbolical elements and elements that belong to the external reality (i.e. to the world). Hence, psychoanalysis takes place according to the criteria and the expediencies of the ego[130],

---

128   See: David Hothersall, History of Psychology, 4th edition, New York: McGraw–Hill, 2004.

129   Freud considered that there was "reason to assume that there is a primal repression, a first phase of repression, which consists in the psychical (ideational) representative of the instinct being denied entrance into the conscious", as well as a "second stage of repression, repression proper, which affects mental derivatives of the repressed representative: distinguished what he called a first stage of 'primal repression' from 'the case of repression proper' ('after–pressure')" (Sigmund Freud, On Metapsychology, The Pelican Freud Library, Harmondsworth: Pelican, 1975–1986, Vol. 11, pp. 147, 184). Lacan gave particular emphasis to the role of the signifier in repression —"the primal repressed is a signifier"— examining how the symptom is "constituted on the basis of primal repression, of the fall, of the Unterdrückung, of the binary signifier...the necessary fall of this first signifier" (Jacques Lacan, The Four Fundamental Concepts of Psycho–Analysis, trans. Alan Sheridan, New York: W.W. Norton, 1978, p. 235ff.).

130   According to Freud's structural model of the soul, 'id', 'ego' and 'super–ego' are the three parts of the psychic apparatus: the id comprises the unorganized and unconscious part of the personality structure that contains the basic drives, and it acts according to the 'pleasure principle'; the ego comprises that organized part of the personality structure that includes defensive, perceptual, intellectual–cognitive, and executive functions, and it acts according to the 'reality principle'; the

whose reality, however, is not necessarily something different from a socially legitimized and established fantasy. The goal of psychoanalysis is not man's participation in a transcendental truth, which could offer the unity of the soul. Instead, psychoanalysis recognizes no such truth, assumes that man's soul is naturally and, hence, necessarily characterized by contradictions, and it simply attempts to fortify the ego against unconscious pressures and against explosions of repressed memories. In other words, the purpose of psychoanalysis is to offer psychological balance by giving rise to a self–sufficient ego–driven soul and to protect social cohesion against the destructive power of uncontrolled impulses.

Throughout history, men have instincts, and, to some extent, society represses human instincts in order to maintain its cohesion, while attempting to counterbalance social pressure with worship systems, rituals, celebrations, holidays, processes of self–actualization through work, etc. Even though modern psychology has analyzed the previous phenomena, it has not paid enough attention to role that the relationship between the individual and the community plays for the psychological cure of the individual. In the ancient Greek and the Byzantine societies, man existed through, within and due to his polis or community, and he was an organic element of the community. By contrast, as I mentioned in chapter 3, within the context of bourgeois society and modernity, man is a member of a partnership that is primarily motivated by the pursuit of survival, and he understands 'socialization', or 'communion', as a moral or a legal norm, and not as an ontological characteristic of the human being. Thus, from the standpoint of the Greek philosophy and Hesychasm, the modern man's psychological problems are primarily due to the fact that his soul lost its communal/relational character.

In the context of the ancient Greek and Byzantine societies as well as in the context of a Hesychastic collective, man's soul unites people together by understanding itself and the others as participants in the same universal truth (e.g. in Plato's world of

super–ego comprises that organized part of the personality structure, mainly but not entirely unconscious, that includes the individual's ego ideals, spiritual goals, and the psychic agency (called moral consciousness) that criticizes and prohibits one's drives, fantasies, feelings, and actions. Freud argues that the ego serves the external work, the super–ego and the id, and its task is to find a balance between primitive drives and reality and simultaneously to satisfy the id and the super–ego.

ideas, in the ethos of the polis, in the divine grace, etc.), whereas, in the context of bourgeois society and modernity, man's soul is identified with individual consciousness due to rationalism. The fact that rationalism attempted to transform the soul, from an energy of social life (the essence of personhood), into an organ of rational thought caused an enormous repression of the world of impulses, and this enormous repression of the world of impulses, in turn, caused a reaction that was expressed through an indiscriminate, occasionally nihilistic, attempt to justify and morally legitimate individual impulses[131]. Thus, due to rationalism (and as a response to rationalism), man developed a second, underground soul, which is in continuous conflict with the socially recognized and legitimate soul. In other words, due to rationalism, man incurred a spiritual fragmentation into conscious and unconscious psychic worlds. This tragic phenomenon was inconceivable for ancient Greeks, Byzantines and generally for the members of pre–modern societies, because, in those societies, the individual soul was substantiating and manifesting, through its own unity, the unity between the human being and the city. Therefore, for ancient Greeks, Byzantines and generally for the members of pre–modern societies, the essence of psychopathology consists in the expulsion of man from society as an existential state, i.e. in man's lapse into the misery and selfishness of a life in separation from the social whole, and not in the conflict between conscious and unconscious psychical worlds.

Modern Western civilization is founded on a human being whose soul is dominated by either ratio or by irrational passions —depending on each one's personality type— and it excludes

---

131   Marquis de Sade's novel Philosophy in the Bedroom (1795) expressed this situation in a dramatic and eloquent manner (see: Marquis de Sade, Justine, Philosophy in the Bedroom and Other Writings, London: Arrow Books, 1965). According to Dolmancé, who is the most cynical and dominant of the characters in de Sade's novel Philosophy in the Bedroom, morality, compassion, religion and modesty are all absurd notions that stand in the way of the sole aim of human existence: pleasure. However, this simple and straightforward moral criterion, known as 'hedonism', has two important defects. First of all, in the context of hedonism, consciousness constantly seeks pleasurable experiences that, by their own nature, do not last enough. Thus, a hedonistic consciousness searches for lasting pleasure in experiences that, by their own nature, do not last enough, and, for this reason, ultimately, consciousness experiences pain instead of pleasure. The second defect of hedonism is that, since different pleasures may contradict each other, it becomes extremely difficult, or rather impossible, for consciousness to evaluate all pleasures in a consistent manner. Whereas rationalism creates a monolithic consciousness and causes enormous repression, hedonism leads to a fragmented and disorientated consciousness, i.e., eventually, both rationalism and hedonism are psychologically painful options.

unselfishness. The modern Western man's soul finds the ultimate pleasure in outbursts of uncontrolled hedonism and in the exercise of coercive power. But, in this way, instead of obtaining psychological cure, the modern Western man becomes even more psychologically ill. Psychoanalysis cannot offer a real cure to such a person, because psychoanalysis considers man's inner fragmentation a natural and inescapable characteristic of the human being, and, therefore, it eventually makes man's spiritual fragmentation even deeper. Nor can a rationalist priest or spiritual guide offer real cure to such a person, because moralistic and legalistic recipes for the good life cannot offer psychic unity to a person whose soul is fragmented and practically obedient only to the commands of desire.

From Augustine of Hippo onwards, the dominant thesis of the Western scholars and of the Western Church with respect to the structure of man's soul is that individual reason (ratio) and irrational desire are organic parts —and not merely powers (as the Hesychasts maintain)— of the soul, thus leading to the spiritual fragmentation of man[132]. In the context of the Western spirituality, will is determined by reason and desire, and, therefore, man is spiritually fragmented into two psychic parts —the one is conscious and reason–driven and the other is unconscious and desire–driven. By contrast, according to the Hesychasts, will is a free power of the spirit, i.e. a free power of the mind, and the mind is distinct from the intellect, since the mind ('nous') is the tank of divine grace in man and the intellect ('dianoia') is the rational aspect (power) of the human soul.

If will is an organ of consciousness, then man's choices aim to offer him self–assurance and exclude freedom of will, which presupposes the capability of expressing self–denial, i.e. freedom of will depends on a creative transcendence of the ego. In order for a human being to be free, the human mind must be free to choose between good and evil, and this choice must be made by using one's power of will. But, if man's will is an organ of consciousness (i.e. if it is determined by reason), or if it is determined by irrational forces (instincts), then man's freedom is an illusion. Scholasticism

---

132 This psychological view affects many aspects of everyday life, too. The Western man is very familiar with the idea of simultaneously living multiple lives. For instance, he may have a very different behavioral code and value–system in his job from the behavioral code and value–system that he has in his private life, or he may be in love with another person than the one to whom he is married, etc.

and the modern theories of scientific psychology are predicated on the assumptions that man's soul is naturally fragmented into a conscious and reason–driven part and an unconscious and desire–driven part and that will is an organ of consciousness. Thus, not only is the aim of Hesychastic psychotherapy different from that of scholastic and modern psychological theories, but also Hesychasm and the Western (medieval and modern) schools of psychology are predicated on much different assumptions about the constituent components of the psychosomatic structure of man.

In the second triad of his sermons *Hyper ton Hieros Hesychazonton*, Gregory Palamas argues that, "among God's gifts some are natural; they are granted indiscriminately to all...Others are supernatural and full of mystery. These latter gifts I hold to be higher than the former", and continues as follows: "philosophy is one of the natural gifts of God, as are also the discoveries of human reason, the sciences".

The idea of soul on which scholasticism and modern scientific psychology are based is incompatible with Hesychastic psychotherapy not only because the Western (medieval and modern) schools of psychology reduce will to an organ of ratio, but also because they reject the Hesychastic principle that the mind is distinct from the intellect. Gregory Palamas has stressed the distinction between the mind and the intellect, because this distinction is a necessary presupposition of spiritual freedom, in the sense that, if man empties his mind from all rational and all irrational elements, which impede the descent of God's grace in it, then the mind can be filled with God's grace, which means that then the human being can be deified and, thus, the human being can experience the freedom that characterizes God's mode of existence.

Reason (ratio), desire and passion are innate powers of the soul, and, therefore, they are natural channels of knowledge, whereas the mind is a place of supra–rational wisdom. According to the Hesychasts, reason is concerned with the world of the senses, its aim being to organize sense–data into a rational whole. In particular, in the European Enlightenment, Immanuel Kant defined reason as a pre–existent (a priori) structure within the framework of which there exist various functions of categories, which, when they are adequately activated, can connect isolated segments of sensation (i.e. empirical data) into a whole, and, therefore, they allow consciousness to formulate synthetic statements[133] and transcend sense–data. On the other hand, according to the Hesychasts, the mind is concerned with the Divine Reason (Logos). Thus, if the mind is identified with the intellect, the mind is concerned with sense–data and with the organization of segments of sensation into a rational whole, instead of being exclusively directed towards the Divine Reason. Gregory Palamas upheld supra–rational knowledge against Barlaam's rationalism and against the West's rationalist theological tradition.

In the context of Hesychasm, the mind is the power of enlightened discernment, urging the soul to direct its attention to certain elements–stimuli and to ward off others, and, in this context, the mind does not operate according to human criteria, but it is a divine psychic power. The Hesychasts teach that nature is beyond good and evil, because good and evil are matters of personal decision and not of natural necessity, and, therefore, the choice between good and evil cannot depend on speculation about the nature of beings and things. According to Hesychasm, for the mind, the good is a state in which the mind is free from emotional disturbance and totally open and available to receive God's grace, whereas the evil is a state in which the mind is passionately related to and concerned with sensation. Since reason is concerned with the objects of the senses, the intellect does not have free will. It is only the mind that has free will, since it desires the supra–rational good, i.e. to participate in the Divinity. The mind can obtain the supra–rational good only if it is cleansed from the passions of the senses. This can be achieved through repentance, which means the return of the mind to the heart and an experience of a mental sensation that liberates the mind from its dependence on bodily sensation. By the term 'mental sensation', the Hesychasts refer to a passionless sensation of the cleansed mind, which is free from the influence of the images of the external world, and, as I shall explain in the sequel, it is different from the Oriental practice of meditation.

If the distinction between the mind and the intellect is eliminated, the soul reduces to the operation of the nervous system and to critical thought, and, therefore, it loses its freedom of will. Thus,

---

133 According to Kant, 'analytic statements' are true by definition, i.e. the negation of any analytic statement results in a contradiction or inconsistency (the theorems of mathematics and logic are characteristic examples of analytic statements), whereas the truth value of 'synthetic statements' can be determined only by relying upon experience.

if the distinction between the mind and the intellect is eliminated, the soul is not any more guided by the mind, which is the bearer of the supra–rational truth, towards the Divinity, but it is guided by reason towards a truth that is founded on perception, which isolates man from the Divinity and makes him ego–centric. Without the distinction between the mind and the intellect, the therapy of man's mind is impossible, and then moral codes, scientific psychology and psychiatry appear to be the only possible paths to psychic health. But, without the distinction between the mind and the intellect, freedom of will is impossible, because freedom of will is meaningful only if one can make *passionless* choices and not if one can merely make choices. If one is determined by his repressed desires, by his instincts and/or by logical necessities, then the very fact that he can make choices does not mean that he has free will. Free will presupposes the ability to make *passionless* choices.

THE PASSIONATE PART OF THE SOUL ACCORDING TO HESYCHASM

In the second triad of his sermons *Hyper ton Hieros Hesychazonton*, Gregory Palamas refutes Barlaam's arguments against the Hesychastic practice. In particular, Barlaam —based on Augustine's ascetic theory about a naturally immortal soul clothed in a mortal body— argues that the passionate part of the soul must be deadened in order to stop influencing the body. Thus, Barlaam teaches that the soul is a perfect gift from God, and, in prayer, it must be totally detached from sensation. According to Barlaam, the soul enters a state of spiritual darkness whenever it enjoys the powers of its passionate part and of the body. In other words, Barlaam considers sinful passion a result of the passionate part of the soul, and, therefore, he teaches that the passionate part of the soul must be completely deadened.

Gregory Palamas counter–argues that, if one follows the teachings of Barlaam, then prayer becomes a fantasy whose content is an idol of the soul (i.e. an idealistic, romanticized abstraction of the soul). For Gregory Palamas, prayer is not simply a mental action directed to God, but also it is an act of heart purification, in which both the soul and the body participate. If the soul suffers by passions, which are outcomes of the senses, then ascetic bodily practices help one fight negative and destructive passions and reinforce prayer. With regard to the practical life of the Hesychast, it must be mentioned that at its root is a regimen of ascetic pursuits that help to cleanse the essence of the mind and to purify the body, which comes to serve the soul. Thus ruled, the body is not an evil thing, but a thing of good, since it becomes a spiritual instrument. In other words, in Hesychasm, the transformation of man is not limited to the transformation and alteration of the soul alone, since man is soul and body together; the body must also take part in the journey to deification, because it too will be glorified. If one limits the struggle to his soul alone and does not extend it to the body as well, he can stumble into rupture, with traumatic consequences. This is the goal of such therapeutic methods of the Hesychasts as fasting, vigils, etc.

It must be stressed that, in Hesychasm, the ascetic practice is not undertaken in the spirit of a contemptuous disdain for the world. When the Hesychasts speak of the folly and vanity of the world and disdain for it, they are speaking of the untransformed world and the experiences of the untransformed human being. Asceticism is restorative, liberating man from his submission to the commands of undifferentiated instincts and physical necessities. It is, as Fr. Georges Florovsky has pointed out[134], not something that "blinds creativity". Rather, Florovsky has said, "it liberates it, because it asserts it as an aim in itself. Above all —creativity of one's self... Ascesis does not consist of prohibitions. It is activity, a 'working out' of one's own self. It is dynamic...[T]hrough the ascetic trial, the very vision of the world is changed and renewed".

The Hesychasts, following the Greek Patristic tradition, argue that no divine gift —not even man's soul— is *actually* perfect; God's gifts to man are only *potentially* perfect, and it is up to man's own will to transform their potential perfection into actual perfection. Hesychasm rejects every kind of prayer that reduces to an idealistic attempt to transcend the body, and also it rejects every kind of prayer that is separated from action.

Gregory Palamas stresses that, through the soul, God's grace is extended throughout the body and that God's gifts to man are activated through the body. Thus, in contrast to Barlaam's teaching that apathy consists in the deadening of the passionate part of the soul, Gregory Palamas argues that the virtue of apathy consists in the re–orientation of the passionate part of the soul from evil to

---

134   Georges Florovsky, Christianity and Culture, Vol. 2, in The Collected Works of Georges Florovsky, 2nd printing, Belmont, MA: Nordland Publishing Company, 1974, pp.127–128.

good. In addition, Gregory Palamas points out that we love through the passionate part of the soul, and, therefore, if one deadens the passionate part of his soul, he is unable to observe Christ's Law, which is to love God and one's fellow humans.

According to Hesychasm, the essence of psychopathology is the loss of the soul's power of communion, where 'communion' means the act of participating in another being. By losing the link between God's Spirit and the mind, i.e. by losing the power of participating in God, man's life and behavior are determined by the powers of egocentric satisfaction, which may be either rational or emotional. However, reason (ratio) does not have the power of communion. In contrast to Thomas Aquinas's and generally in contrast to the scholastics' teaching that man can know God through reason (and, more specifically, through ratio superior, which, according to Thomas Aquinas, is enriched by God's 'supernatural' intervention), Hesychasm stresses that reason —irrespective of whether reason is 'ratio inferior' or 'ratio superior'— does not have the mind's power of communion, because of the following two reasons: (i) Reason is based on a sharp distinction between subject and object, and, therefore, even though it can lead to a unified perception of the object of knowledge, it cannot unite the subject, i.e. the knower, with the object of knowledge. Hence, reason naturally keeps God and man separated from each other. Hesychasm has ontological significance, which means that the concerns of rationalism are inappropriate for understanding God, since they posit the interpretive or observing subject as in some way prior to its participation in God's energies. The Hesychasts stress the importance of the embeddedness of the mind in God's energies; humans know God within and through their participation in God's energies. (ii) Furthermore, in every manifestation of desire, the object of desire is simultaneously a thing and a telos–purpose, which is related to the notions of good and evil. If the significance of an object of desire is not related to the notions of good and evil, then it is determined only by instincts, and, therefore, the soul loses its freedom. A soul is free only if it can choose between good and evil independently from biological and ego–driven necessities.

Thus, a man is not free if he does not *feel* that he is free, i.e. if he does not understand the 'good' as a universal value, which transcends every necessity and simultaneously can be participated by man. A selfish conception of the 'good' is intimately connected to an unfree soul, and a soul that is not free is ill. If the good is supra–rational, then it plays the role of the universal significance of the beings and things in the world, and then man's participation in the good does not necessarily presuppose accurate analytical knowledge, but it necessarily presupposes a clean intention.

The Hesychast's goal is to liberate the mind from the influence of sense perceptions and not to eliminate reason. Thus, there is an elusive but critical difference between the methodology of Hesychasm and the methodology of Oriental schools of meditation. Since the Oriental schools of meditation identify the mind with the intellect, they understand inner silence as a state in which the intellect is detached from the world of the senses. On the contrary, the Hesychasts, by stressing the distinction between the mind and the intellect, maintain that the natural task of the intellect is to be concerned with the world of the senses in order to endow the world of the senses with a rational order that expresses the intentionality of the mind, whilst the natural task of the mind is to be directed towards God and receive God's uncreated energy. Therefore, it is the mind, and not the intellect, that must be detached from the world of the senses in order to operate as a pure vessel of God's grace. Hence, due to the detachment of the intellect from the world of the senses, meditation leads to yogic sleep (since the intellect cannot function without its active engagement in the world of the senses), whereas Hesychastic practices lead to an experience of participation in God's uncreated energies without any experience of sleep.

HESYCHASM, CHURCH FREEDOM AND THE 15TH CANON OF THE FIRST–AND–SECOND COUNCIL

By early Spring 1341, it was clear that the dispute between Gregory Palamas and Barlaam would need to be resolved by conciliar means. Six patriarchal councils were held in Constantinople between 1341 and 1351 to consider the issues[135]. The dispute over Hesychasm came before a Synod held in Constantinople on 10 June 1341 and presided over by Emperor Andronicus III. This Synod lasted only one day, and it vindicated Gregory Palamas. However, Emperor Andronicus III died just five days after the Synod ended, and thus Barlaam

---

135   See: Gerald O' Collins and E.G. Farrugia, A Concise Dictionary of Theology, New Jersey: Paulist Press, 2000, p. 186.

hoped for a second chance to present his case against Hesychasm. But Barlaam soon realized the futility of pursuing his cause, and left for Calabria, where he converted to the Roman Church and was appointed Bishop of Gerace. After Barlaam's departure, the theologian Gregory Akindynos continued the legacy of Barlaam's theology in Byzantium and became the chief critic of Palamas.

A council held in Constantinople in August 1341 condemned Akindynos, but Akindynos and his supporters gained a brief victory at a council held in 1344 that excommunicated Gregory Palamas for heresy. Moreover, Empress Anne and Patriarch John XIV had Gregory Palamas imprisoned. The Patriarch of Constantinople John XIV, surnamed Kalekas, was opponent of Hesychasm and of Gregory Palamas. Moreover, he was an active participant in the Byzantine civil war of 1341—1347 as a member of the regency for John V Palaeologos against John VI Kantakouzenos. The supporters of John VI Kantakouzenos were in favor of Hesychasm, whereas the supporters of John V Palaeologos were spiritually closer to the West[136]. In 1347, a new council —organized by Emperor John VI Kantakouzenos, who victoriously entered Constantinople— affirmed the resolutions of the Synod of 1341 and excommunicated Akindynos and his followers. The new Patriarch of Constantinople, Isidore, celebrated the triumph of 'Palamism' —i.e. of Hesychasm— by replacing the ecclesiastical hierarchy with 32 monks who were loyal friends of Gregory Palamas. Moreover, Patriarch Isidore ordained Gregory Palamas as Archbishop of Thessaloniki. On 15 August 1351, a decree of a Church Synod at Constantinople for the first time made the Hesychastic theological doctrines the exclusive "binding truth for the whole Orthodox Church"[137]. After Gregory Palamas's death, the controversies around Hesychasm continued until 1368, when the Patriarch of Constantinople, Philotheos, convened a last council on this matter, which proclaimed Gregory Palamas as a saint.

The Hesychastic controversy, the fact that Gregory Palamas and Maximus the Confessor were persecuted by the Orthodox

---

136   See: Steven Runciman, The Great Church in Captivity —A Study of the Patriarchate of Constantinople from the Eve of the Turkish Conquest to the Greek War of Independence, Cambridge: Cambridge University Press, 1986, p. 146.

137   Quoted in Edmund Fryde, The Early Palaeologian Renaissance (1261 — c. 1360), Leiden: Brill, 2000, p. 378.

Church authorities before eventually being canonized as saints of the Orthodox Church as well as several other similar events in Church history give rise to very important and thought–provoking questions about the structure and the identity of the Church. According to the Orthodox Church Tradition, the Church of Christ is a community of responsible persons, united in the Spirit of Christ, and not an authoritarian system. In particular, the *Apostolic Constitutions*, 10:19 (*Patrologia Graeca*, Vol. 1, 633) state the following: "I shall judge the bishop and the layperson. The sheep are rational and not irrational, so that no layman may ever say that, 'I am a sheep, and not a shepherd'…it is required that we flee from destructive shepherds".

The 15th canon of the First–and–Second Council[138] allows each person to separate from and break communion with any bishop who publicly preaches a heresy already "condemned by the holy councils or fathers". In particular, according to the previous canon:

> For those who separate from communion with their president because of some heresy condemned by the holy councils or fathers, when, that is, he publicly preaches heresy, and teaches it openly in the church, if such wall themselves off from communion with the above–mentioned bishop before conciliar examination not only are not subject to the penalty laid down by the canons, but are also worthy of the honor befitting the Orthodox. For they have condemned not bishops, but false–bishops and false–teachers, and they have not sundered the unity of the Church by a schism, but they have endeavored to protect the Church from schisms and divisions.

---

138 This council is given this title by Theodore Balsamon (a 12th century canonist of the Eastern Orthodox Church and Orthodox Patriarch of Antioch), John Zonaras (a 12th century Byzantine chronicler and theologian) and others. The First–and–Second Council was held in Constantinople and was assembled in the time of Emperor Michael, the son of Theophilus, and of Bardas Caesar, his uncle on his mother's side, in the year 861. It was attended by three hundred and eighteen Church Fathers. The reason why it is called the First–and–Second Council is, according to Balsamon, Zonaras and others as follows: There was held a first convention of this Council, and the Orthodox members won, and the heterodox (remnants of Iconoclasm) were defeated. But the heretics refused to have the records of this council preserved, and they made such a disturbance and fight that the first convention was dissolved without any definition and result being committed to writing. After some time had passed, a second convention of the same council was held, and again there was a discussion of the Orthodox participants with the heretics concerning the same subjects. This meeting's resolutions were written up. Thus, this council was called the First–and–Second, since it had held a first and a second convention.

When the above canon refers to 'councils' and 'fathers', it means Orthodox councils and Orthodox fathers. If a council makes a non–Orthodox resolution, then —irrespective of its composition and prestige— it is a false council, and it cannot be characterized as a regular Church Council. There have been many historical instances of councils at which non–Orthodox resolutions have been accepted —but the resolutions of these councils (known as 'robber councils') have not become part of the Orthodox Church's canons.

Maximus the Confessor, although he was only a simple monk, did not hesitate to cut off communion with every patriarch, metropolitan, archbishop and bishop in the East because of their having been infected with the heresy of Monotheletism. A precious document for Maximus's ecclesiology is a short letter that he wrote on 19 April 658 to Anastasius, his disciple and spiritual child, who was exiled apart from his master[139]. By then Maximus the Confessor and his few followers were on their own, since Rome, in the person of Pope Vitalian, had succumbed to imperial pressure and entered into communion with the other patriarchal sees. In the reply to the question, "What Church do you belong to? Constantinople? Rome? Antioch? Alexandria? Jerusalem? See, all of them are united, together with the provinces subject to them...", Maximus says he had spoken as follows: "The God of all pronounced that the Catholic [i.e. universal] Church was the correct and saving confession of the faith in him when he called Peter blessed because of the terms in which he had made proper confession to him".

Finally, the Sixth Ecumenical Council vindicated Maximus the Confessor and his few disciples and condemned for heresy four Patriarchs of Constantinople, one Pope of Rome, one Patriarch of Alexandria, two Patriarchs of Antioch and a multitude of other metropolitans, archbishops and bishops, admitting that, during all those years, that simple monk and his followers were recapitulating the historical manifestation of the true Christian Church, whereas all those notable bishops were wrong.

Furthermore, when the 15th canon of the First–and–Second Council refers to 'heresy', it means every deviation from Orthodox doctrine, and, thus, it does not refer only to those heresies which have already been explicitly qualified as such by previous Church

---

139 Quoted in Andrew Louth, "The Ecclesiology of Saint Maximos the Confessor", International Journal of the Study of the Christian Church, Vol. 4, 2004, pp. 109–120.

councils. In other words, Orthodoxy affirms not the councils as such but the common ethos of the fathers that participate in the Church councils and make the voice of Orthodoxy explicit, i.e. they pronounce (and do not create) truth. In addition, the personal pronouncement of the fathers as well as any resolutions of the councils of any rank are subject to checking by the collective mind of the universal Church, i.e. by the living Tradition of the Church. Only in the course of such a checking is the Orthodoxy of the conciliar resolutions and of the personal pronouncements of the fathers determined.

The Orthodox Church stresses conciliarity, in the sense that the criterion by which the decrees of the Church councils can be considered regular is that they agree with Orthodoxy, and not that they have been accepted by authorized persons. Thus, the Orthodox Church refuses to look on bishops as on professionals to whom the faithful must 'hand over' their faith for 'safe-keeping'. In 1848, the Orthodox Patriarchs of the East issued a *Reply* to Pope Pius IX, defending the Eastern Orthodox Church's synodal system of government and arguing as follows: "Among us, neither Patriarchs nor Councils were ever able to introduce innovations, because the defender of Religion is the very Body of the Church —that is, the people themselves, who desire to have their Religion eternally unchanged and identical to that of their Fathers".

In the light of Hesychasm, neither the Biblical truths nor the truths of the Tradition of the Church Fathers are objective facts. It would not be an exaggeration to argue that, in the light of Hesychasm and of the 15th canon of the First–and–Second Council, Christianity does not exist without Christians, i.e. Christianity is not independent of the Christian community, since Christianity consists in the *Christians' experiences* of Christ and of each other within the Body of Christ. Thus, the subjectivism that is latent in the 15th canon of the First–and–Second Council, in Hesychasm and even in the Gospels of the New Testament should not upset us. However, this subjectivism does not lead to arbitrary idealism, because the Christian subject is socialized through its participation in the Church community. The reality of the Church is the mystery[140]

---

140 As Gabriel Marcel has written in his book Being and Having, a 'problem' is something that bars the way and calls for a solution, whereas a 'mystery' is something in which one finds himself involved. Furthermore, Gabriel Marcel has pointed out that a 'problem' is in some way outside us and something

of participation in Christ and in the fellow Christians and of being participated by Christ and by the fellow Christians. Hence, since Church means 'participation', and 'participation' means (subjective) 'experience' (and not 'knowledge' of objective facts), the reality of the Church is subjective. Simultaneously, however, since the members of the Church participate in each other and in Christ, it follows that, in the context of the Church, there is no such thing as absolute individual, or pure subject, and, therefore, even though each member of the Church has its subjective experiences, there are symbols that have a common meaning for all the members of the Church, thus making the communication among all members of the Church possible and elucidating the identity of the Church as a social phenomenon.

In contrast to Søren Aabye Kierkegaard's existentialism, Hesychasm and the First–and–Second Council do not let the relationship between man and God become totally private. In Kierkegaard's philosophy[141], the relation between the ego and God is totally private, and, therefore, even though it can help us avoid the evils of conformist morality and assimilation into the crowd, it cannot save us from the evils of a sentimental religious life. The private character of the relationship between man and God in Kierkegaard's system implies the decision of man to live the passion of a relationship with an unsubstantiated romantic ideal and to call this relationship faith. Faith as romantic passion transforms the faithful person into a romantic knight who, like Cervantes's Don Quijote de la Mancha, lives a solitary life and is accountable only to God. Therefore, within the framework of a totally private relationship between man and God, man reproduces himself. On the contrary, Hesychasm and the 15th Canon of the First–and–Second Council create a communion of free persons, in the context of which the individual checks the whole and is checked by the whole. Thus, the Orthodox Church Fathers who decided, for

---

towards which we adopt an impersonal attitude, since it is an 'ob–jective' entity. On the other hand, Gabriel Marcel maintains, the 'mystery' of being brings us to the region of the 'metaproblematical' where it is necessary to transcend the subject–object dichotomy. For more details, see: Gabriel Marcel, Being and Having, trans. K. Farrer, Westminster: Dacre Press, 1949; Gabriel Marcel, The Mystery of Being, Vol. 1: Reflection and Mystery, trans. G.S. Fraser, and Vol. 2: Faith and Reality, trans. R. Hague, London: The Harvill Press, 1951.

141 See: Søren Kierkegaard, The Kierkegaard Reader, ed. J. Chamberlain and J. Rée, Oxford: Blackwell, 2001.

some period of time, to break off communion with certain Church authorities, did so not in order to create a new, separate Church, but in order, first of all, to actively denounce concrete heresies and thus to stimulate the Church members' sensitivity about the protection of Orthodoxy and, second, to force the universal Church to summon a council and reaffirm Orthodoxy. In other words, the Orthodox Church Fathers —even when they resist against Church authorities by breaking off communion— are always characterized by a deep social consciousness and never become romantic knights of faith.

Furthermore, Hesychasm rejects sectarianism and all kinds of legalistic religiousness. Hesychasm understands religion as God's revelation and as an invitation to live a true life, and, therefore, it contrasts this notion of religion with religion as a social institution and with religion as a psychological phenomenon. A Hesychast is a person that creatively undertakes his historical responsibilities, but his existential hopes are not exhausted in history. Thus, in the context of Hesychasm, the preservation of Orthodox Tradition does not mean the outer observance of formalistic and legalistic religious formulas. In the context of Hesychasm, the preservation of Orthodox Tradition primarily means the preservation of the understanding of Christianity as the mystery of man's participation in God. Thus, in the 10th century A.D., Symeon the New Theologian[142], a famous Hesychast and one of the most influential Doctors of the Eastern Orthodox Church, reacted against the attempt of the Theological School of Constantinople to articulate a rationalist method of exposing and defending the Orthodox Christian Faith.

In the 10th century A.D., rationalism was dominant in the West, and it started influencing Byzantium's academic theology, too. In the era of Symeon the New Theologian, those Byzantine theology professors who were influenced by the West's rationalism developed a 'technocratic' form of Orthodox Christian theology, which gives primacy to discursive reason and formalistic definitions of theological concepts and preserves the outer characteristics of genuine Orthodoxy, but it lacks an active bond with Orthodox

---

142 See: J.A. McGuckin (ed. and trans.), The Book of Mystical Chapters —Meditations on the Soul's Ascent, from the Desert Fathers and Other Early Christian Contemplatives, Boston, Mass.: Shambhala Publications, 2002; Symeon the New Theologian, Hymns of Divine Love, trans. G.A. Maloney, Denville, N.J.: Dimension Books, 1975.

spiritual *life*. Thus, even though those rationalist Byzantine theologians did not deviate from the dogma of the Orthodox Christian Church, their theological methodology was a serious threat to the essence of Orthodox Christianity, since their rationalist approach to Orthodoxy transformed the Church Fathers' message into a 'museum object', which could be analytically studied but it could not be transmitted as a *way of life*.

The 10th century rationalist Byzantine theologians interpreted the notion of sanctity not as the traditional purpose of Christian life but as a historical phenomenon of the past, and, therefore, they confined their contemporaries' spiritual life to the observance of Church rituals, systems of morality and dogmatically accurate beliefs. Symeon the New Theologian reacted against the previous theological trends, because he was primarily seeking the knowledge that deifies man and not the knowledge that merely satisfies intellectual curiosities. Thus, Symeon the New Theologian contrasted Hesychasm with a formal 'Orthodox Christian' religious system that was dogmatically and canonically correct but it could neither meet man's existential needs nor lead to the deification of man.

Symeon the New Theologian seeks *experiential* knowledge and emphasizes the *sensation* of God's light. Thus, in his poem "As soon as your mind has experienced", Symeon the New Theologian writes:

> "As soon as your mind has experienced/ what the scripture says:/ 'How gracious is the Lord',/ it will be so touched with that delight/that it will no longer want to leave the place of the heart".

Moreover, in his poem "What is this awesome mystery", Symeon the New Theologian writes:

> "What is this awesome mystery/ that is taking place within me?/ I can find no words to express it;/ my poor hand is unable to capture it/ in describing the praise and glory that belong/ to the One who is above all praise,/ and who transcends every word".

According to Symeon the New Theologian, God revealed Himself in the world of the senses, i.e. He was incarnated, in order to save man, and, therefore, man's salvation presupposes the continuous presence of God in man's life. If God is absent from man's everyday life, then man's salvation is impossible. For Symeon the New

Theologian, 'divine revelation' means that man knows God by participating in God and not merely by observing rules. Thus, in his poem "We awaken in Christ's body", Symeon the New Theologian writes:

"We awaken in Christ's body/ as Christ awakens our bodies,/ and my poor hand is Christ, He enters/ my foot, and is infinitely me./ I move my hand, and wonderfully/ my hand becomes Christ, becomes all of Him/ I move my foot, and at once/ He appears like a flash of lightning". In the same poem, Symeon the New Theologian goes on as follows: "For if we genuinely love Him,/ we wake up inside Christ's body/ where all our body, all over,/ every most hidden part of it,/ is realized in joy as Him,/ ... / he awakens as the Beloved/ in every last part of our body".

By the end of the 20th century, it became clear that the culture of Hesychasm is closely related to a peculiar form of post–modernism and particularly to post–modern hermeneutics, whereas the majority of the Eastern Orthodox Churches (even though they espouse the same doctrines as Hesychasm) were unable to manifest the Hesychastic ethos, because they had adopted secularism and they were oscillating between modernity[143] and a peculiar delirium of sentimental religiousness that is phobic towards man's spiritual development.

Hesychasm's attitude towards Christianity and social life in general is close to Gianni Vattimo's post–modern hermeneutics. Unlike Derrida's method of "deconstruction"[144], which is focused on the functional structures of a text, hermeneutics combines subjectivity with an attempt to arrive at an agreement or consensus as to what the text means, or is about. In particular, Vattimo formulates a post–modern hermeneutics in *The End of Modernity*[145], where he distinguishes himself from the French 'school' of post–

---

143 Habermas and Ben–Habib write about modernity: "The project of modernity formulated in the 18th century by the philosophers of the Enlightenment consisted in their efforts to develop objective science, universal morality and law, and autonomous art, according to their inner logic" (Jürgen Habermas and Seyla Ben–Habib, "Modernity versus Postmodernity", New German Critique, No. 22 (Special Issue on Modernism), 1981, p. 9).

144 According to Jacques Derrida's theory of deconstruction, texts collapse under their own weight once it is demonstrated that their 'truth content' is merely the "mobile army of metaphors" identified by Nietzsche. See: Christopher Norris, Derrida, London: Fontana, 1987.

145 Gianni Vattimo, The End of Modernity —Nihilism and Hermeneutics in Postmodern Culture, trans. J.R. Snyder, Baltimore: Johns Hopkins University Press, 1988.

modernism by studying post–modernity as a matter for ontological hermeneutics. Vattimo sees the heterogeneity and diversity in our experience of the world as a hermeneutical problem that should be tackled by developing a sense of continuity between the present and the past, and he argues that this continuity is to be a unity of meaning rather than the repetition of a functional structure and that the meaning is ontological. In other words, the present is meaningful because it transmits a culture (and not a functional structure) from the past to the future, and tradition is a creative relationship with an original truth and not an attempt to attach humanity to a particular form of social life in an immature or neurotic fashion.

Hesychasm implies that a person is creative neither because it creates new forms of social life nor because it aims at the fixation of humanity on a particular form of social life. For Hesychasm, the essence of creativity does not consist in the form of social life. For Hesychasm, the essence of creativity consists in the experience of an original truth, which, exactly because it is not subject to any rigid form, can be constantly re–interpreted, it enriches the sentimental world of the human being and it is a great inner source of inspiration and power.

THE MARGINALIZATION OF HESYCHASM IN THE GREEK EAST

The Ottoman rule was a 'black–out' period in the history of Hesychasm. Thus, the modern Greek theology, which was formed in the beginning of the 19th century (after the Greek revolution and the creation of the Greek State) "was entangled by a tragic adventure", as the distinguished Greek historian Panagiotes Chrestou[146] has pointedly argued. In particular, as Chrestou[147] has argued, the heart of the neohellenic theology was rooted in the Eastern Orthodox tradition, but the neohellenic theology was intellectually fed and conditioned by Protestantism (especially Puritanism and Pietism), and its argumentation derived from scholasticism (rationalist rhetoric).

In the 15th century, the development of the Hesychastic movement in Byzantium was violently interrupted by the Ottoman

---

146   P.K. Chrestou, "Neohellenic Theology at the Crossroads", The Greek Orthodox Theological Review, Vol. XXVIII, 1983, p. 51.

147   Ibid.

yoke, and, in the 19th century, the revival of Hesychasm in Greece was methodically undermined by several Protestant and Roman Catholic ideas and teachings, which influenced the newly created Greek state, whose national ideology was to a large extent structured by scholars who belonged to the school of German romanticism and by the royal Dynasty that was imposed on Greece by foreign powers as a means of foreign political and cultural control over the Greeks. However, in the 18th century, Greek monks attempted to revive the Hesychastic theology.

The *Philokalia* is a collection of Hesychastic texts. The Greek word philokalia means love of the beautiful/holy/exalted. The book *Philokalia* was first assembled at Mount Athos by Nicodemus of the Holy Mountain[148], a great 18th century theologian and teacher of the Orthodox Church, and Makarios of Corinth, a great 18th century mystic, writer and Metropolitan of Corinth. The first edition was published in Venice in 1782; a second was published in Athens in 1893, which included a prayer by Patriarch Kallistos; and a third was published in Athens between 1957 and 1963 by the Astir Publishing Company.

The zenith of the theology of Palamism, or Hesychasm, in Byzantium was followed by the fall of Byzantium to the Ottomans in 1453. After the end of the Roman Empire in 1453, the migration waves of Byzantine scholars and émigrés played a key role in the revival of Greek and Roman studies that led to the development of the Western Renaissance. These Byzantine émigrés were grammarians, humanists, poets, writers, printers, lecturers, musicians, astronomers, architects, academics, artists, scribes, philosophers, scientists, politicians and theologians, who brought to Western Europe the far greater preserved and accumulated knowledge of their own (Greek) civilization[149]. On the other hand, the Hesychastic renaissance that

---

148   However, not even Nicodemus of the Holy Mountain was immune to Western theological influences, since he edited Greek translations of Lorenzo Scupoli's book Combattimento Spirituale and J.P. Pinamonti's book Exercizi Spirituali. Moreover, under Western theological influences, Nicodemus of the Holy Mountain, in his books Pedalion (or 'Rudder') and Exomologetarion (or 'Manual of Confession'), reproduced Western notions of Church piety, Western legalistic and sadistic teachings about God's relation to humanity, and a form of Manichean moralism; for more details, see: Christos Yannaras, Orthodoxia kai Disi sti Neoteri Hellada (Orthodoxy and the West in Modern Greece), Athens: Domos, 1993 (in Greek).

149   N. G. Wilson, "From Byzantium to Italy: Greek Studies in the Italian Renaissance", The Sixteenth Century Journal, Vol. 25, Autumn, 1994, pp. 743–744; Deno John Geanakoplos, Constantinople and the

took place in Byzantium during the 14th and the 15th centuries, primarily due to Gregory Palamas, was violently interrupted by the Ottoman regime.

The Ottoman rule was a catastrophic experience for the Byzantine world in general and for Hesychasm in particular. Whereas the Arabo–Islamic world has rich philosophical, religious and scientific traditions, the Turkish nomads that conquered Constantinople in 1453 had an extremely poor culture and a very elementary and primitive understanding of civilization. Thus, the Shia Arabs of Egypt and the Persians detested the primitive and newly Islamized Sunni Turks[150].

The Latin Crusaders seized and looted Constantinople in 1204, under the pretense that they were fighting for the liberation of the Holy Land, and, thus, the Latin Crusaders paved the way for the fall of Constantinople to the Ottoman Turks[151]. Moreover, the Venetians who were living in Constantinople conducted insurgency campaigns against the Byzantines and played active role in the collapse of Byzantium and the victory of the Ottoman Turks over Byzantium. The most important strategic mistake of Byzantium was to trust the West and especially the Venetian financial oligarchy and surrender the commanding heights of the economy —trading and customs collection— to Western entrepreneurs and greedy oligarchs.

The Turkification of the Asia Minor was a gradual process that was taking place during a period of several centuries before the Fall of Constantinople in 1453. The Turks came in waves from Central Asia, crossing the Iranian plateaus, but their population was always significantly smaller than that of the local Byzantine a gricultural communities[152].

Throughout the history of the Ottoman Empire, the Turks were the ruling racial minority within their vast dominion, and they managed to maintain their race fresh by mating with non–Muslim women and by offering political and social privileges to all the subjects that adopted Islam, learned the Turkish language and were

---

West, Madison: University of Wisconsin Press, 1989.

150   John Bowle, A History of Europe, London: Heinemann, 1979.

151   Michael Grant, The Civilizations of Europe, London: Weidenfeld and Nicolson, 1965, p. 133; C.W. Previte–Orton, The Shorter Cambridge Medieval History, Cambridge: Cambridge University Press, 1952.

152   George S. Harris, Turkey —Coping with Crisis, Boulder, Colo.: Westview Press, 1985.

obedient to the Sultan's authority[153]. For instance, Ishak Pasha was a Greek who became Ottoman general and Grand Vizier during the reign of Mehmet II ("The Conqueror"), and several Ottoman Sultans (such as Ahmed I, Ahmed III, Bayezid II, Mustafa I, Mustafa II, Osman II, etc.) had Greek mothers.

The strength of the Ottoman Empire was due to the following facts[154]: it was geographically identical to the Byzantine Empire and, therefore, it had the geopolitical significance and power of the Byzantine Empire; the Ottoman Empire was founded on a system of public administration and military organization that the Turks had already borrowed from the Greeks before the capture of Constantinople by the Ottoman forces; the elite military forces of the Ottoman Empire were staffed by the boys of Christian Byzantines who were violently Turkified. However, as Robert Byron[155] has pointed out, the major difference between the Byzantine Empire and the Ottoman Empire was that, under the first, civilization was advancing, whereas, under the latter, civilization was shrinking. Moreover, Roger Portal[156] has pointed out that the Turks led the civilization of the Byzantine world to a dead point and, in several countries that had been seized by the Turks, the Ottoman rule caused the regression of civilization. In general, according to P.J. Marshall and Glyndwyr Williams[157], for the Turks, there is no middle ground between total oppression and excessive engagement with the harem and the eunuchs.

Additionally, it should be mentioned that, from the standpoint of the genuine Islam, the Ottoman Empire was a degenerate form of Caliphate, and it violated the Qur'an on several occasions. The barbarian hordes of the Ottoman Turks used Islam as an instrument for the pursuit of their imperialist agenda and were culturally unable to appreciate the true spiritual essence of the Caliphate, as it has been articulated and exposed by the prophet Muhammad and by his first three successors —namely, Abu Bakr, Umar ibn al–Khattab and Uthman ibn Affan.

---

153   Philip K. Hitti, History of the Arabs, London: Macmillan, 1970.

154   Robert Byron, The Byzantine Achievement, Mount Jackson, VA: Axios Press, 2010 (first published in 1929).

155   Ibid.

156   Roger Portal, The Slavs, London: Weidenfeld and Nicolson, 1965.

157   P.J. Marshall and Glyndwyr Williams, The Great Map of Mankind, London: J.M. Dent and Sons, 1982.

Sheikh Imran Nazar Hosein, in his seminal book *Jerusalem in the Qur'an*[158], emphasizes that the Qur'an, in sura Al–Maidah, 5:51, writes that, ultimately, Muslims will forge an alliance with the Rum, i.e. with the Eastern Orthodox Christians. The Qur'an distinguishes between those Christians who are not Rum and forge a Judeo–Christian alliance (i.e. primarily Western Christendom) and other Christians (Rum) about whom Allah says in sura Al–Maidah, 5:82: "and you will most surely find those who show the greatest love and affection for the believers (i.e. Muslims) to be those who say We are Christians". Western Christianity, which is not Rum, has already forged an alliance with the Zionists, and it was to that Zionist Judeo–Christian alliance that the Qur'an referred when it prohibited Muslims from ever maintaining friendship and alliance with such Jews and such Christians who, themselves, were friends and allies of each other (sura Al–Maidah, 5:51). Sheikh Imran Nazar Hosein has pointedly observed that the most formidable obstacle to such a Muslim–Orthodox Christian alliance being forged was the conduct of the Ottoman so–called Islamic Empire, which played a sinister role in seeking to ensure enduring Greek and Orthodox Christian bitterness and hatred for Islam.

The Ottoman rule inhibited the development of the Hesychastic spirituality in the Greek East for approximately four centuries. Moreover, after the liberation of the Greeks from the Ottoman rule in the 1830s, the development of the Hesychastic spirituality was inhibited by the Western patrons of the newly created Greek State.

Two persons that played a key role in the implementation of a policy of cultural and institutional Westernization in Greece were the Greek priest and scholar Theocletos Farmakides (1784–1860) and the German statesman and scholar Georg Ludwig von Maurer (1790–1872). In 1832, Otto, a royal prince of Bavaria, became the first King of Greece under the Convention of London, and he reigned until his deposition in 1862. Moreover, in 1832, a council of regency was nominated during Otto's minority, and Maurer was appointed a member. Maurer had an ambitious political and cultural program for the institution of the Greek State according to the principles and values of his contemporary Bavarian elite.

Theocletos Farmakides was an associate and a protégé of Maurer within the Church of Greece. Farmakides's mission was to organize

---

158   Sheikh Imran Nazar Hosein, Jerusalem in the Qur'an, New York: Masjid Dar–al–Qur'an, 2003.

the Church of Greece according to the ethos and the interests of the Bavarian rulers of Greece and to promote Western theological systems through the University of Athens. Thus, Theocletos Farmakides was appointed by Maurer as his adviser on Church Affairs and later as the Chief Secretary of the Holy Synod of the Church of Greece. In 1833, Farmakides assisted the Bavarian Regents acting for King Otto, who was a minor, to proceed with their plan to excise the Church of Greece from the Patriarchate of Constantinople and transform it into a "national Church" controlled by the state, according to Protestant ecclesiological systems. Indeed, in 1833, the Bavarian rulers of Greece declared the Church of Greece to be autocephalous, and placed it under the authority of a permanent five-member Synod of Bishops appointed by the King, who was made head of the Church of Greece, even though he was a heterodox. King Otto was a Roman Catholic, and Georg Ludwig von Maurer was a Protestant.

The policy of cultural subversion that was applied against the Greeks by the Bavarian Regents in the 1830s was more subtle than that of the Ottomans, because the Bavarians applied 'soft power'[159], i.e. they attempted to conquer the Greeks' hearts and minds in order to impose their Bavarian values and institutions on the newly established Greek State. Furthermore, whenever it was deemed necessary by the Bavarian Regents, 'hard power' was being applied, too. In particular, the Bavarian Regents destroyed many Greek Orthodox monasteries and besmirched many monuments and treasures of the Greek Orthodox spirituality. General Ioannis Makrygiannis (1797–1864), a leading figure of the Greek War of Independence (1821–1832), writes in his *Memoirs*[160] that the Bavarian rulers of Greece "totally destroyed the monasteries, and the poor monks, who had wasted themselves in the Struggle, are now dying of starvation, on the streets, whereas those monasteries were the first bastions of our Revolution".

As a result of the above-mentioned situation, the national Church of Greece, which was instituted in 1833, maintained the Orthodox

---

159   Joseph Nye Jr. coined the term 'soft power' in his book Bound to Lead —The Changing Nature of American Power, New York: Basic Books, 1991. The primary currencies of soft power are an actor's values, culture, policies and institutions as well as the extent to which these "primary currencies", as Nye calls them, are able to attract or repel other actors to "want what you want" (Joseph Nye Jr., Soft Power —The Means to Success in World Politics, New York: Public Affairs, 2004, p. 31).

160   Ioannis Makrygiannis, Apomnemoneumata (Memoirs), Athens: A. Karavia Publications (in Greek)

Christian doctrines and liturgical traditions, but, beyond these formal aspects of religious life, the rest of its being was immersed in Western concepts and values, such as nationalism, rationalist religious rhetoric, legalistic morality and Western forms of pietism. Thus, from the 19th century onwards, many members of the Greek Orthodox clergy and laity may follow canonical rites and comply with formal aspects of the Christian Orthodox Tradition in the context of certain Church practices, but, during the rest of the day, they are rationalists and they confuse the Western notion of intellect with the Hesychastic notion of *nous* (mind).

Furthermore, in the 19th century, in the context of broad geopolitical calculations, the Bavarian rulers of Greece, Great Britain and France were keen to avert the creation of a Greco–Russian spiritual and geostrategic alliance. For the Western patrons of the Greek State, Hesychasm was incompatible with their political, economic and societal plans for the Greek State. Thus, the Greek State was spiritually founded on values and institutions that were alien to the Hesychastic tradition.

In the 19th and the 20th centuries, in Greece, it became clear that, contra the Hesychasts' ethos and ecclesiology, the government reserved the right to transfer or retire bishops on the grounds of political suitability. For instance, the revolutionary government of Colonel Nicolas Plastiras did not find Archbishop Theokletos suitable to its purposes and it arbitrarily replaced him with Archimandrite Chrysostom Papadopoulos on 25 February 1923. Under these conditions, a general Synod of the Church of Greece was held on 24–30 December 1923, at which Plastiras, S. Gonatas (prime minister) and A. Stratigopoulos (minister of Religious Affairs and Education) were present. Colonel Plastiras clarified his agenda to the bishops: "The Revolutionary government…will reckon itself happy to see the rebirth of Church set in motion…Consequently, it would not have you limit yourselves to the ancestral Canons, but to proceed to radical measures"[161].

Plastiras wanted to integrate Greece deeply into the modern international capitalist system, and, therefore, he adopted the Gregorian calendar and, with the collaboration of Archbishop Chrysostom Papadopoulos, he managed to modify the religious

---

161 Archimandrite Theokletos A. Strangas, Ecclesias Ellados Istoria (History of the Church of Greece), Vol. 2, Athens, 1970, p. 1181 (in Greek).

calendar, too, in order to harmonize both the civil and the religious calendars of Greece with the Western calendar. When the new calendar was first imposed on Greece in 1924, virtually all of the clergy submitted, even though that decision was anti–canonical, because the Church of Greece, the Patriarchate of Constantinople and the Church of Romania implemented the new calendar without the assent of the other Orthodox Churches. Thus, these three local Churches, by introducing a new calendar into their jurisdictions' religious life, broke thereby the universal Orthodox Church's unity in the celebration of the feasts and divided the Orthodox Christians into two opposing parties on account of the calendar.

In the context of the Orthodox Christian Tradition, the Church calendar is not merely a system by means of which people measure time, but it is a symbolic system by means of which the members of the Orthodox Church experience and give witness to their spiritual unity, since all of them agree on the spiritual significance of each and every day. The purpose of the Church calendar being to underpin the spiritual unity of the Church, any change in the Church calendar is canonical if and only if it has been approved by the universal Orthodox Church.

As a result of the calendar schism of 1924, the Greek Orthodox Christians were divided into the New Calendarists and the Old Calendarists, the latter being those who adhere to the traditional liturgical calendar used by the Orthodox Church for the past 1600 years. Because of the confusion that prevailed in the 1920s in Church life, the local Orthodox Churches that adhered to the traditional liturgical calendar (e.g. the Orthodox Churches of Russia and the Patriarchate of Jerusalem) remained in ecclesiastical communion with the innovating Orthodox Churches of Greece, Constantinople and Romania, which had audaciously changed the Church calendar without taking into account the Church's conciliar decrees and anathemas. Thus, given that the majority of the local Orthodox Churches that are devoted to the traditional liturgical calendar and in general to the Orthodox Tradition have not cut the New Calendarists off from ecclesiastical communion, and for as long as there is no conciliar decision condemning the new calendar State Church of Greece for heresy, the new calendar Orthodox Churches, even though they have caused a serious problem in the universal Orthodox Church, have not fallen from Grace.

However, many old calendar communities have cut the New Calendarists off from ecclesiastical communion, and these 'radical' old calendar communities are known as zealots. Many old calendar zealots have gradually lapsed into an erroneous ecclesiology. In particular, many old calendar zealots, consciously or unconsciously, have adopted an ecclesiology that is founded on Western romanticism, Augustinianism and Kierkegaard's Christian existentialism. Thus, gradually, many Greek old calendar zealots were transformed from defenders of the Orthodox liturgical calendar into existentialist religious fighters.

Instead of resisting the anti–canonical Church calendar reformation for the sake of the Orthodox Christian Tradition, many old calendar zealots have adopted a sectarian and Manichaean ethos, and they are divided into several unstable communities (self–proclaimed "synods of Genuine/True Orthodox Christians") that fight against each other and create several schisms within the camp of the Old Calendarists. In short, the old calendar zealots correctly point out mistakes of new calendar bishops, but they interpret them in a heretical manner. Furthermore, since the Greek old calendar zealots started lapsing into multiple internal schisms and heresies from the 1940s onwards, many communities of old calendar zealots have ordained uncultured persons into the priesthood and have been manipulated by Greek intelligence agents who —acting according to NATO's geopolitical plans— aim at preventing the Greek–Orthodox traditionalist movement from forging a strategic spiritual and geopolitical alliance with the official Russian religious and political authorities.

In Orthodox tradition, ecclesiastical communion is not some formality, but a matter of substance: it is a sacred and deifying relationship. Thus, Basil the Great (4th century A.D.) emphasizes that communion with the heretics is inadmissible (*Patrologia Graeca*, Vol. 32, 937D–940A). However, the fact that, in the 1920s, the new calendar Churches followed an anti–canonical (schismatic) policy on the issue of the Church calendar but simultaneously they did not completely break off (since they have remained in communion with old calendar Churches) implies that the new calendar Churches are still members of the Body of the universal Orthodox Church, though ailing ones. According to the 15th Canon of the First–and–Second Council, when one breaks communion with the ailing part of the Church Body, he does so primarily in order to aid in the repentance and cure of the ailing member and in order to contribute to the convocation of a competent synodal body, whose purpose would be the proclamation of sound doctrine. Therefore, Old Calendarists are in principle allowed to break communion with innovating New Calendarists, but those traditionalist Orthodox Christians who decide to take this strict and extreme ecclesiological measure must do so in the spirit of Christian love, i.e. in order to offer pastoral/ spiritual care to the ailing part of the Church Body, and not because of a sectarian and Manichean ethos.

The domination of a sectarian and Manichaean ethos among the Greek old calendar zealots contributed to the humiliation of the original old calendar movement by the New Calendarists. Many old calendar zealots have tragically failed to understand the Orthodox approach to tradition, and they tend to endorse a form of traditionalism that has a strong affinity with the Hindus' rigid theories about stability, hierarchy and the caste system. In contrast to the caste system and generally in contrast to Asian systems of rigid traditionalism, the Orthodox Christian approach to tradition allows institutional change and encourages a progressive attitude to history, stressing, however, that every change must serve the goal of man's Christocentric deification and must take place through conciliar processes. In other words, the Orthodox Christian approach to tradition is concerned with the preservation of the Christians' ultimate purpose of action and with the processes of legitimized institutional change, and it does not seek to preserve any system of societal relations and customs as an end in itself. By simultaneously combining stability and change, the Orthodox Christian approach to tradition is intimately related to the principles of spiritual vigilance and personal moral responsibility.

In contrast to the new calendarists' innovative attitude and in contrast to the various sects of the old calendar zealots, the Patriarchate of Moscow, known also as the "Third Rome" of the world Orthodoxy, has followed a healthy traditionalist attitude, and, therefore, the Russian Orthodox Church has never encountered any disputes over the Church calendar.

FROM THE BYZANTINE PHILOKALIA TO THE RUSSIAN PHILOKALIA

Even though the Ottoman rule in Byzantium marked the end of

the Hesychastic renaissance in the Greek East and even though Hesychasm could not be easily transplanted in Western soil, due to the Hesychasts' opposition to scholasticism and Western rationalism, Hesychasm found fertile land in Russia, and it blossomed there after the fall of Byzantium. The Russian Hesychastic tradition is contained in the six volumes of the *Little Russian Philokalia*, which has been published by the St. Herman of Alaska Brotherhood. The six volumes of the previous book are devoted to the following Russian Hesychasts: Vol. 1: St. Seraphim of Sarov; Vol. 2: Abbott Nazarius of Valaam; Vol. 3: St. Herman of Alaska; Vol. 4: St. Paisius Velichkovsky; Vol. 5: Elder Theodore of Sanaxor; Vol. 6: Elder Zosima of Siberia.

Russia can be considered as the New Byzantium, and the Patriarchate of Moscow is widely known as the "Third Rome". By the 9th century A.D., in the region that, in the modern era, corresponds to the states of Bulgaria, Serbia and Romania, the foundation of the culture of the Slavs who lived there was Byzantine. In the region that, in the modern era, corresponds to the states of Russia and Ukraine, the dominant culture had three components: an inherited pre–Christian Pagan component and two acquired components derived from Christianity and Byzantium. Furthermore, it should be mentioned that, from the dawn of humanity, the Russian civilization has been a multicultural one, and Russia had extended political and commercial ties with Central Asian and Middle Eastern states as soon as the 9th century A.D. Thus, the Christocentric ecumenism and the multicultural character of the Byzantine Empire were particularly appealing to the Russians.

In the late 9th century A.D., Scandinavian warrior–traders, the Varangians, gradually took control of the major waterways from the Baltic to the Black Sea. This process began in about 860, when the people of Novgorod invited the Varangian Prince Rurik to become their ruler. In 882, Rurik's successor, Oleg, captured Kiev, where he was succeeded in about 912 by Rurik's son, Prince Igor. The Rurik dynasty survived as rulers of Russia until 1598.

By the 10th century A.D., the Russian city–states of Novgorod, Pskov, Smolensk, Suzdal, Kiev and Vladimir had been established on the basis of an elaborate Pagan culture and a prosperous trading system. The main trading partners of the Rus, as these people came to be known, were Byzantium and the Greeks who had been living for several centuries on the northern shores of the Black Sea.

Moreover, during this period, the Rus were being frequently attacked by nomadic Asian tribes, such as the Khazars, the Pechenegs and the Polovtsians.

From the beginning of the 9th century, the Russian world was increasingly exposed to Christianity. Patriarch Photius of Constantinople, in his "Encyclical to the Eastern Patriarchs" (866), writes that Greek Orthodox missionaries were active in Rus in the middle of the 9th century[162]. Additionally, as early as 846, the Arab geographer Ibn Khordabekh wrote in his *Book of Roads and Countries* about Rus–Christians who were trading with Byzantium and the Middle East[163]. It should be mentioned that Novgorod and other Russian merchant cities prospered without joining the initial capitalist movement, which was primarily a Western phenomenon, and this is another element that proves the cultural and political affinity between Russia and Byzantium.

In the second half of the 10th century, Prince Vladimir of Kiev united under his rule a large part of southern and central Rus, and he adopted Orthodox Christianity as the official religion of the Rus. The Russian Orthodox Church followed the Byzantine Orthodox pattern completely, and it creatively assimilated pre–Christian Russian folk traditions.

The adoption of Byzantine Christianity by the Rus played a key role in the development of Russian literature and marked the beginning of literacy after the adoption of the new alphabet. Two brothers from Thessaloniki, Cyril (826–869) and Methodius (815–885), created the alphabet for the Russian liturgical language, which was influenced by Greek linguistic models and was the common literary language of all the Christian Orthodox Slavs. Moreover, Byzantine art was another important cultural bridge between Byzantium and Russia throughout the Middle Ages.

In the 13th century, Alexander Nevsky (1219–1263), Prince of Novgorod, Grand Prince of Kiev and Grand Prince of Vladimir, played a key role in preventing the submission of Russia to the Roman Catholic Pope and the Germans. In 1193, Pope Celestine III declared the Northern Crusades, encouraging the Holy Roman

---

162 Ihor Shevchenko, Byzantium and the Slavs, Harvard Ukrainian Research Institute, 1991, pp. 95–100.

163 A.P. Novoseltsev, The Eastern Slavs and Russia in the 9th–10th Centuries, Moscow: Gosudarstvennoe Izdatel'stvo, 1965.

Empire (Germans) and the Kingdom of Sweden to advance eastward, into Latvia, Estonia and Lithuania. Within a decade, much of the region was under Teutonic control. Alexander Nevsky stood on the shores of Lake Peipus determined to halt the German knights' encroachment on 5 April 1242. Marching his army out onto the frozen water, Alexander Nevsky scored a major victory at the Battle of the Ice. Thus, he prevented the Teutonic Knights from entering Russia, and he hardened the dividing line between the Papacy and the Orthodox Christian Church. He was canonized by the Russian Orthodox Church in 1547, and his principal feast day is 23 November.

Russia has assimilated core elements of the Byzantine culture and of the Byzantine political and social institutions, and simultaneously it has maintained its multicultural and communal ethos. However, Western influences have been undermining the Hesychastic and generally Byzantine roots and orientation of the Orthodox Russian Church since the 13th century. In the 16th century, Patriarch Nikon of Moscow attempted to reform the liturgical ritual of the Orthodox Russian Church. The spiritual core of his reforms was Latinism, and, therefore, his attempt was countered by the people with the Old Believers schism. Moreover, endorsing the authoritarian ethos of the Papacy, Nikon called himself "the pastor of the whole world" and persistently developed the idea that "the priesthood is higher than the tsarship", thus introducing scholastic notions and problems in the Orthodox Russian Church and generally in the Russian society.

The movement of the Old Believers[164] in Russia reacted and resisted against the projects of spiritual Westernization that were promoted by Patriarch Nikon and then by Tsar Peter, Tsarina Catherine II and Tsar Alexander I. Thus, the so–called Old Rite of the Orthodox Russian Church was a form of Orthodox resistance against Protestantism and Roman Catholicism. But, under the influence of

---

164   However, it should be mentioned that certain denominations within the tradition of the Russian Old Believers finally lapsed into a mentality of 'exclusive' mysticism, which brings them closer to the existentialist model of a romantic knight of faith and to non–Christian mystical traditions. In the context of Hesychasm, the antithesis between the 'Church' and the 'mystic' is false. Thus, the Popovtsy ('with priests') were Old Believers who strove to maintain old traditions of the Russian Orthodox Church, whereas the Bespopovtsy ('priestless') were Old Believers who condemned all outward forms, rejected "the World", and, endorsing a sectarian and quasi–magical ethos, claimed that any priest or hierarch who has ever used the Nikonian Rites has forfeited apostolic succession.

three centuries of Polish pressure, by the 16th century, Ukraine had gone far ahead in the project of spiritual Westernization. Thus, when Tsar Alexis consolidated his authority over Moscow, Ukraine and Belarus, the state and the Church authorities of Russia encountered the following dilemma: should Moscow force its Byzantine Orthodox ethos on the South Russian Church, or should Moscow endorse the project of Latinisation and reform Church life on Kiev's lines? Tsar Alexis and Patriarch Nikon chose the latter course. Under Tsarina Sophia and Tsar Theodore, the Latino–Frankish influence in Moscow increased even more, especially after the conclusion of a "lasting peace" with Poland in 1686 and a military alliance with it against Turkey.

Weakened by the conflict between Latinism and the Old Believers, the Orthodox Russian Church gradually became incapable of leading the spiritual development of its people. Thus, ultimately, the Orthodox Russian Church succumbed to the despotism of Tsar Peter, who ruled the Tsardom of Russia and later the Russian Empire from 1682 until his death in 1725. Peter articulated his own answer to the cultural dilemmas and challenges of Russia: neither Latinism nor Moscow's Byzantine tradition, but German Protestantism and Renaissance post–Christian philosophy were the spiritual movements that he found most promising and more suitable for the development of human creativity.

The major spiritual force of resistance against the Westernization of Russia was the Optina Hermitage (or Pustinia). Paisius Velichkovsky (1722–1794), who is venerated as a saint by Orthodox Christians, was very influential in reviving Hesychasm in Russia, and his Hesychastic work found in Optina Monastery a 'headquarters' from which Hesychasm spread throughout Russia.

Ambrose of Optina, who was canonized in 1988 by the Local Council of the Russian Orthodox Church, was one of the most influential Elders of Optina Monastery. Ambrose was visited by many prominent figures of the Russian culture, such as Fyodor Dostoevsky, V.S. Solovyov, A.K. Tolstoy, M.P. Pogodin, N.N. Strachov, etc. Ambrose of Opitina spent seven years in the Orthodox East (as a member of the Russian Spiritual Mission in Jerusalem), came into personal spiritual contact with the elders of Mount Athos and conducted several theological debates with Roman Catholic and Protestant priests.

Seraphim of Sarov (d. 1833), is one of the most renowned Russian Hesychasts and, together with Sergius of Radonezh (d. 1392), he is one of the Russian Orthodox Church's most highly venerated saints. Seraphim of Sarov was deeply rooted in Byzantium's Hesychastic tradition, and his teaching that the purpose of Christian life is the attainment of the Spirit of God is derived from Palamism. Two of the most characteristic statements by Seraphim of Sarov are the following: "Acquire a peaceful spirit, and around you thousands will be saved", and: "A sign of spiritual life is the immersion of a person within himself and the hidden workings within his heart".

Furthermore, it should be mentioned that a significant problem that Orthodox Christianity has been encountering in Russia and generally in the Slavic world since the Middle Ages is the emergence of heresies that are due to the fact that several communities in those countries have come in touch with Orthodox Christianity without having assimilated the philosophical preliminaries to Orthodox Christian theology. As I have already mentioned in this book, the Greek philosophical education has played a key role in the development of Orthodox Christian theology. In Russia and generally in the Slavic world, on several occasions, Gnostic and occult traditions were mingled with Orthodox Christianity and gave rise to several heresies and superstitions; Bogomilism, Florensky's and Bulgakov's Sophiology (or Sophian doctrine), E.P. Blavatsky's Theosophy, the Khlysts, Rasputin's cult, certain Old Believers' communities and Russian political–spiritual groups that have endorsed Aleister Crowley's "Thelema" (since the era of George Raffalovich who financed *The Equinox* journal issued by Crowley and Marina Lavrova who was for a time the "Scarlet Woman" of the "Great Beast") are some characteristic examples of spiritual systems that are opposite to Orthodox Christianity and especially to Hesychasm.

The Russian Hesychastic tradition is a direct continuation of the Byzantine Hesychastic tradition, and, therefore, it should be differentiated from alternative mystical systems that have been developed in Eurasia. Inherent in the Hesychastic tradition is the Greek notion of *logos*. The Greek notion of *logos* is different from both the Western notion of *ratio* and the Oriental notion of the *transcendent*. Thus, the Greek philosophical education is a very important prerequisite for an accurate elucidation of Hesychasm. Without sufficient knowledge of Greek philosophy, Orthodox

Christian mysticism can be confused or mingled with the Western cultural movements of existentialism, symbolism and surrealism and with Oriental mystical traditions (e.g. yoga, Sufism, Blavatsky's Theosophy, etc.).

In the context of the Geco–Christian theology and especially in the context of Hesychasm, the Church community gives rise to and spiritually nurtures a universal soul, i.e. one that pertains to the whole Christian body. Thus, by the term 'universal soul', the Hesychasts do not mean the transcendent *per se*, but they mean the openness and the expansion of logos due to the other's presence. The classical Greek philosophers understand the soul as the link between the particular and the universal, and they give meaning to phenomena through the soul's participation in the 'idea', or 'genus'. The Greek Church Fathers adjusted the previous Greek philosophical tradition to the Gospel of Christ, and, therefore, according to the Greek Church Fathers, the 'universal' is the life of the Church, which is something totally different from faith as a psychological phenomenon. In contrast to other forms of mystical spirituality, the Hesychastic tradition does not emphasize the supra–rational *per se*, but the event of Church communion.

Within the Church community, the soul becomes aware of itself through the experience of communion, and communion becomes equivalent to truth. Outside the Church, the Divinity reduces to a cultural datum, which can help the soul to transcend the level of instinct and ascend to higher levels of being, but it cannot illuminate the soul. The experience of illumination is intimately related to the experience of communion.

BEYOND WESTERN AND ORIENTAL TRADITIONS:
THE PECULIAR PHENOMENON OF HESYCHASM

Hesychasm, as a spiritual tradition (theology and anthropology), is different from both the West (Euro–Atlantic area) and the Orient (Asian area), and it is a separate spiritual zone. In the sequel, I shall summarize the fundamental principles of the Western spirituality, the Oriental spirituality and the Hesychastic spirituality:

I. Oriental spirituality:
- Man and nature are one.
- The spiritual reality and the physical reality are one.

- Mind and body are one.
- Man should understand and experience his basic oneness with nature, the spiritual and the mental, rather than attempt to analyze, categorize, rationally organize and control, or consume the things of the world.
- Because of his oneness with all existence, man should feel 'at home' in any place around the world and with any person.
- Science and technology create an illusion of progress, because, due to science and technology, we do not experience the environment itself but rather a projection of it, created by us.
- Illumination involves achieving a sense of oneness with the entire cosmos, and it is a state where all dichotomies have been eliminated.
- Illumination is necessarily dependent on meditation.

II. Western spirituality
- Man has characteristics that substantially distinguish him from the natural realm and the spiritual realm.
- The human being is composed of three distinct elements: body, soul and spirit.
- There is a personal God who is over man.
- Man must control and manipulate nature in order to secure his survival.
- The Western culture emphasizes rational thought and an analytical approach to problem solving.
- Science and technology have given us a good life and underpin our hope for a better future.
- Action and competitiveness should be recognized as great merits and be rewarded.

III. Hesychasm:
- The human being is the crown of the Divine Creation and should act as the wise master of the universe, remaining in communion with the Divine Logos (*Genesis*, 1:24, 28, 2:15).
- Soul and body are not one, but they are united.
- The structure of man is bipartite and not tripartite, i.e. the body and the soul are united integrally, the soul being the 'telos' of the body, and the spirit is not a separate quality that is distinguishable from the soul. The Greek Church Fathers

emphasize that 'spirit' does not constitute a third element of man (i.e. a substance distinct from the soul), but it is a higher power of the soul *per se*, or it signifies the uncreated grace of the Holy Spirit, which is not an element of man but illuminates and deifies man.

- There is a personal God who can be participated by man in the context of a free person–to–person relationship.
- Man must be the illuminated king of the natural world, and this can be achieved if and to the extent that man is in communion with the Divine Logos, who is the source of the significance of the natural world.
- Science and technology are creations of the human spirit, and, if man acts with the awareness that he is the living image of God, science and technology are part of God's command to man to "subdue" the earth (*Genesis*, 1:28) and to establish a rational order on the earth (*Genesis*, 1:28, 2:19).
- Awareness of and commitment to the 'telos', or purpose, of being and communion with the Divine Logos should be recognized as the greatest merits of man.

5

THE METAPOLITICS OF HESYCHASM

A S I explained in the Introduction of this book, by the term culture, we mean the attempt of a human community to live meaningfully, i.e. to give meaning to the world and to its actions. Therefore, in the context of culture, every being and thing in this world is embedded in a symbolic system, i.e. it exists inextricably united with its 'telos', or purpose, or meaning. Peter Berger and Thomas Luckmann have pointed out that symbolic universes "integrate different provinces of meaning and encompass the institutional order in a symbolic totality"[165], and, in effect, all human activity occurs within a symbolic universe. According to Berger and Luckmann, "the symbolic universe is conceived of as the matrix of all socially objectivated and subjectively real meanings"[166] and it "links men with their predecessors and their successors in a meaningful totality serving to transcend the finitude of individual existence and bestowing meaning upon the individual's death"[167].

Furthermore, as I have already argued, myth —namely, the spiritual core of beings and things— is the major determining factor of civilization. By changing the mythological foundation of a civilization, one can change the manner in which the members of the given civilization see themselves and the world, and, eventually, he can change the given civilization itself.

---

165 P.L. Berger and T. Luckmann, The Social Construction of Reality —A Treatise in the Sociology of Knowledge, Garden City, N.Y.: Doubleday & Co., 1966, p. 88.
166 Ibid, p. 89.
167 Ibid, p. 95.

According to Christ, an action is meaningful if its 'telos', or purpose, is transcendental and not a practical issue *per se*. Thus, Christ always applies discretion and teaches and practices the Law of Love. The Jewish establishment (i.e. the Pharisees and the Sadducees) fought Christ, because it endorsed exactly the opposite attitude, as it is clearly shown in the following Biblical texts:

- *Matthew*, 12:10–12: The Pharisees rejected Christ's principle of discretion and Law of Love, and they placed their rules above human need. In contradistinction to the Jewish establishment, Christ taught that, if one's convictions do not allow him to help certain people, his convictions may not be in tune with the Divine Logos.

- *Matthew*, 23:5–7: Christ exposed the hypothetical attitudes of the Jewish religious leaders. The Pharisees' sentimental attachment to their leadership positions was stronger than their relationship with the Divinity.

- *Matthew*, 23:15: The Pharisees' disciples were attached to Pharisaism, not to God. Pharisaism gives primacy to history *per se* (i.e. historical goals, historical achievements and historical structures) over history's transcendental 'telos', and, therefore, it is a religion of deeds and of authoritarian structures, which press people to surpass others in what they can do and to comply with certain directives. Contra the Pharisees, who were emphasizing outward obedience at the expense of inner renewal, Christ taught that salvation is above all a mystery and it is based on man's participation in the Holy Spirit, i.e. in the uncreated energies of God. The religious systems that are based on self–motivation and self–control cause chronic guilt, apathy, depression and constant desire of approval. On the contrary, the spirituality that is based on one's participation in the Holy Spirit results in joy, thankfulness, service, forgiveness and love (*Colossians*, 2:11–15).

- *Matthew*, 16:1: The Pharisees and the Sadducees demanded "a sign from heaven". In other words, the

Pharisees and the Sadducees endorsed a rationalist attitude towards Christ's supra–rational work.

In philosophical terms, the antithesis between Christ and the Jewish establishment is due to the latter's decision to endorse attitudes that belong to the philosophical schools of rationalism and historicism. Furthermore, the fundamental agreement between classical Greek philosophy and Christ, as I explained in chapter 1, is due to Plato's and Aristotle's teachings about logos, hypostasis and eros (love).

BEYOND RATIONALISM AND HISTORICISM

Rationalism is founded on the distinction between the subject and the object, and it subordinates man's spiritual life to the intellect's logical necessities. Rationalism is an attempt to find common universal laws by ignoring unique qualitative differences of diverse human experiences. As a reaction to the traumatic consequences of rationalism and as an attempt to give voice to the particularity and to account for the unique diversity of historical contexts, the West, in the 18th and the 19th centuries, developed historicism, which stresses the importance of developing specific methods and theories appropriate to each unique historical context.

Thomas Pangle[168] has pointed out that historicism "is the embracing term for the various and diverse doctrines which have in common the teaching that humanity lacks a fixed nature and hence any universal or permanent norms", and, therefore, according to historicism, "mankind, in the most important respects and in regard to its deepest needs and highest norms, changes and differs fundamentally from one historical epoch or culture to another".

The origins of historicism can be found in German idealism and especially in the philosophy of G.W.F. Hegel. According to Hegel's historicist position, any human society and all human activities, such as science, art, or philosophy, are defined by their history, so that their essence can be sought only through understanding their history.

In the philosophical system of Hegel, 'spirit' is understood as

---

168   T.L. Pangle, "Introduction", in T.L. Pangle (ed.), The Rebirth of Classical Political Rationalism
—An Introduction to the Thought of Leo Strauss, Chicago: University of Chicago Press, 1989, p. xxix.

the highest essence of everything, and all else is considered mere appearance (*Schein*), as the self–projection of the idea into itself. Hegel calls spirit the ground (*Grund*) of appearance, and he argues that the more appearance expresses spirit (i.e. essence) the more it collapses into spirit. Finite things decline into the absolute idea and thereby reveal it. Thus, according to Hegel, 'being' is the idea that moves far away from itself, i.e. it gives rise to a contradiction, in order finally to return to itself enriched by its voyage.

Hegel transcended the subject (individual 'ego') of the earliest German idealism (Johann Gottlieb Fichte and Friedrich Wilhelm Joseph Schelling) in order to ascend to a quantitatively higher (bigger), and hence spiritually safer, subject —namely, the historical subject (i.e. the nation). In Hegelianism, reason (*Logos*) is the self–consciousness of the spirit, and thus it consists in the knowledge of a truth that is totally determined by historical becoming, since, in Hegelianism, the universal subject is history, and spirit is the reason of history. Hence, in Hegelianism, even though man has the power of knowing the historically constituted truth, he cannot be identified with history, but he exists alienated within a deterministic historical setting; therefore he is not true himself, i.e. he is not true as an individual. From this perspective, the life of the individual human being follows an itinerary that is determined by historical phenomena, independently of the individual's inner experiences. Thus, Hegel rejects the old Platonic, Aristotelian and Christian metaphysics, in the context of which man's soul has a personal relation to and an experience of the divine reality.

Hegel seems to ignore that history is meaningful only if it is not the realm of necessity, i.e. only if it can be rejected in the same way that a free subject can reject the idea of God. Furthermore, contra Hegel, historical action is creative if and to the extent that man tends to transcend himself (in order to arrive at a higher self, instead of returning to himself according to Hegel's dialectic) and seeks truth in being. On the contrary, Hegelianism turns out to be a peculiar kind of nihilism.

Historical action reduces to nihilism if and to the extent that man tends to transcend only established historical conditions and seeks truth in becoming. In the context of Hegelianism, time is linear[169], and, therefore, the significance of the transient present is determined by the need for continuous change in view of some deterministic end or an eternal becoming. Hence, in Hegelianism, the present as such is essentially nullified, i.e. insignificant.

With Hegel, modern Western philosophy becomes focused on the attempt to reveal the reality of the human being in its historical dimension. Thus, from Hegel's perspective, the foundation of philosophy is the integration of being in time as a historical experience, whereas, before Hegel, the foundation of philosophy was a trans–temporal absolute (e.g. Plato's idea, God, the medieval West's ratio, Kant's categorical imperative, etc.).

Before Hegel, freedom was understood as man's choice to be united with the unchangeable and absolute 'good'. Historicism in general and Hegelianism in particular signal a major philosophical shift, since they understand freedom as the attempt to achieve goals within the context of the natural world and history. Thus, the new purpose of philosophy is not to know the absolute truth but to comprehend the spiritual existence of the human being in the context of the metaphysics of historical life and to describe man's integration in time as the objective reality of civilization.

After Hegel, the most influential attempt to cultivate historicism and the philosophy of existence was due to Martin Heidegger[170]. The purpose of Heidegger's philosophy is to deconstruct the metaphysical foundations of the human subject, as it is understood in the context of modern Western philosophy. But Heidegger himself is organically integrated in Western philosophy. On the one hand, Heidegger disagrees with all his predecessors in the history of modern Western philosophy, he understands Being as otherness, i.e. as a principle without ontological substance, and he maintains that the Present exists as a structure and not as subjective consciousness.

---

169   When Hegel refers to "absolute knowledge", he endorses a linear concept of time, i.e. the time in which the subject "sees itself as a passing moment", and alienation–externalisation (Entäusserung) is disclosed as linear time itself. According to Hegel, the purpose of this succession is "the revelation of the depth of spirit" ("the absolute concept"), which is equivalent to "the raising up of its depth… the negativity of this withdrawn I". For Hegel, "time appears as the destiny and necessity of spirit that is not yet complete within itself, the necessity to enrich the share which self–consciousness has in consciousness, to set in motion the immediacy of the in–itself" (G.W.F. Hegel, Phenomenology of Spirit (originally published in 1807), trans. A.V. Miller, Delhi: Motilal Banarsidass, 1998, Paragraph 801).

170   Martin Heidegger, Being and Time, New York: Harper & Row, 1962.

On the other hand, Heidegger proposes a worldly and time–dependent method of transcending one's existential conditions, and, from this viewpoint, his philosophy is an organic part of the Western philosophical tradition.

From the Western Renaissance onwards, the entire Western philosophy has been motivated by the attempt to articulate a theory by means of which humanity could transcend its existential conditions through secular institutions and politics. The Cartesian thinking individual, the Kantian subject (i.e. a historical actor filled with reason and will), the Hegelian historicity of spirit, Kierkegaard's esotericity, Nietzsche's will to power, the phenomenological attempt to explain meaning that strips out reference to abstracting, historical or structural influences, as well as scientific objectivism and technology have a common goal: to help the Western subject transcend its existential conditions with worldly (as opposed to spiritual) means. Heidegger argues that all the previous attempts have been unsuccessful and that their stalemate is due to the fact that they understand Being as substance and that they confine truth to judgment. According to Heidegger, the previous stalemate can be overcome by understanding Being as otherness, which reveals the truth of a new possibility of existence through the experiencing ego's direct and unmediated awareness of the Present (*Dasein*).

Heidegger wants to strip out the ego only to the extent that it maintains residues of the consciousness of the external world, which are, even indirectly, elements of the transcendent. Heidegger attempts to purify the ego from the previous residues of consciousness according to a worldly method of transcending one's existential conditions, and, therefore, he argues that we should understand Being as otherness, or difference, and also that we should understand the human being as the presence of Being. According to Heidegger, the Present should be understood as the structure of existence, and not as the consciousness of existence, and, furthermore, for him, the Present is the event on which the understanding of Being is founded. In this way, Heidegger believes that he has managed to eliminate the thinking subject of Western metaphysics, whose paradigmatic representatives are Kant and Descartes. But, contra Heidegger, the subject cannot be eliminated in the previous way, because the subject, like the subconscious, participates in every philosophy whose purpose is to dispute the subject. In particular, in the context of Heidegger's philosophy, the subject is eliminated only to the extent that it is understood as a syllogistic, or representational, certainty, but the subject is restored immediately after one gives primacy to the 'sum'[171] (I am) over the 'ego' (I).

In the context of Cartesianism, the power of the subject is founded on the principle of "cogito ergo sum" (I think therefore I am). In the context of Heidegger's philosophy, the subjectivism of the Cartesian 'cogito' is substituted by the subjectivism of the Heideggerian 'sum'. The ego as individuality is the core of the reality of the manifestation of the Heideggerian Being in the Present (Dasein). It is exactly for the previous reason that Heidegger's philosophy (which, from a certain viewpoint, can be considered as a form of inverted Cartesianism) is an organic part of the modern Western philosophy and philosophically alien to Plato, Aristotle and the Byzantine spirituality.

In philosophy, there are three crucial questions: 'what', 'why' and 'how'. Heidegger does *what* modern Western philosophy does in general, that is, he attempts to propose a firm and safe method of transcending one's existential conditions with worldly means. With respect to the question 'why', we should mention that Heidegger, like Western modernity in general, has broken away from those ancient and medieval traditions in which the meaning of existence was as crystal clear as the harmony of the cosmos or the goodness of God. Heidegger, like modern Western philosophy in general, subscribes to the idea of a continually volatile historical reality, in which man is concerned only with the results of his action, and the meaning of existence reduces to a complex and strictly private issue. In other words, with respect to the questions 'what' and 'why', Heidegger's philosophy is organically integrated in modern Western philosophy. It is only with respect to the question 'how' that Heidegger's philosophy differs from the philosophical systems that were created by his predecessors in the history of modern Western philosophy.

In contrast to Heidegger's philosophy and in contrast to modern Western philosophy in general, Plato, Aristotle and the Hesychasts understand 'theory' as the entelechy of philosophy, and, as Aristotle writes in his *Metaphysics*, Λ:1–9, 'theory' (wisdom, or first philosophy) is not concerned with the learning, knowledge or discovery of truth,

---

171 The Latin term 'sum' is the first person (singular form) of the present tense of the verb 'esse' (to be).

but it is an active orientation of the mind towards a truth with which the mind is already familiar, i.e. it is an active orientation of the mind towards the divine reality. Thus, Aristotle equates pleasure with the energy of theory and not with the acquisition of knowledge. Furthermore, according to Aristotle's *Metaphysics*, chapter Λ, 'theory' is superior to 'knowledge', exactly due to the fact that the first is concerned with the divine reality, whereas the latter is exhausted in human reason. Thus, theory is founded on man's "mental eye" (and is related to spiritual intuition), whereas knowledge is founded on and derives from the subject, i.e. from a historical being filled with reason and will, and more precisely from a historical actor capable of acting on the basis of reason and will.

In *Metaphysics*, Λ, Aristotle never argues that God is a form at all, and he never suggests that God and sensible substances are anything but univocally substances. In *Metaphysics*, Λ, Aristotle understands God as energy, life, "nous" (mind) or "noesis" (mental energy), but, in Λ9, he emphasizes that God is a noesis that is simply noesis of the divine reality itself and of nothing else, which seems to yield no positive content to the description of God. Hence, in *Metaphysics*, Λ, Aristotle endorses apophatic theology, and he treats apophatic theology as the culmination of his ontology, thus paving the road to the apophatic theology of the Hesychasts. Additionally, in *Metaphysics*, Λ, Aristotle articulates a primitive form of the Hesychasts' thesis about the essence–energies distinction, by arguing that God is somehow a cause to the sensible world, but God seems to be directly a cause only to the outermost heaven, and everything else God produces is a consequence of the heavenly motions. Moreover, Aristotle maintains, God is an efficient cause only by being a final cause (the ultimate and transcendental source of significance of the beings and things in the world). The previous Aristotelian arguments about God's relation to the world are very similar to theses that have been put forward by Maximus the Confessor and Gregory Palamas.

Thus, Nietzsche's and Heidegger's attempt to deconstruct metaphysics is also an attempt to deconstruct Plato's and Aristotle's philosophy. Heidegger has not completely understood the metaphysical content of Plato's philosophy, and he erroneously attributes the subject/object dichotomy to Plato. In contrast to Heidegger's arguments, for Plato and Aristotle, truth is not a critical perception, but, as it is mentioned in Plato's *Phaedrus* (esp. 76–77), truth is the event of the soul's ecstatic movement towards the transcendental sphere of being. This is something very different from Heidegger's analysis of the subject/object dichotomy.

The subject/object dichotomy is something irrelevant to Plato's theory of philosophical vision, because, according to Plato, philosophical vision consists in the *participation* of the philosopher in the object of philosophical vision, i.e. it is based on 'looking at' and not on 'being conscious of'. Therefore, Plato, in his *Republic*, inveighs against 'mimesis', because it leads to an abstraction of truth from sensible data, whereas, for Plato and Aristotle, truth is communion with the transcendental sphere of being. There is no place for the subject in Plato's philosophy.

In chapters 2 and 4, I argued that the West's 'ratio' is substantially different from the Greek East's 'logos'. Moreover, in the light of the arguments that I put forward in chapter 4 and in the present chapter, Hesychasm and the classical Greek philosophy (Platonism and Aristotelianism) are opposite to historicism, too.

THE METAPOLITICS OF HESYCHASM

In this book, by the term metapolitics, I mean the relation between politics and metaphysics and particularly the relation between politics and man's existential goals. In other words, the study of metapolitics, consists in the task of identifying and studying the manner in which the people under investigation understand the relation between politics and their existential goals.

According to the Western schools of rationalism and historicism, according to certain Zionist movements and according to certain Islamic political theories, such as Wahabbism and the Muslim Brotherhood, that are based on the concept of *hakimiyya* (the sovereignty of God) and *hijra* (designating the flight of Muhammad from Mecca to Medina in 622 A.D.), politics has primacy over the pursuit of truth and it subordinates metaphysics to the pursuit of political goals. Thus, in the context of the previous Western, Zionist and Islamic systems, politics becomes an absolute principle and is autonomous from the spiritual aspects of human life. This has dramatic consequences for the quality of culture that the previous systems create. The transformation of politics into an absolute principle generates the following three political phenomena: (i) Theocracy: *the political system* coercively imposes conformity to a certain metaphysical system. For instance, certain Muslim communities teach that, outside the *hijra*, society is not only corrupt, but impious, and the sole manner of dealing with it is by direct political and military action. (ii) Absolute monarchy and metaphysically grounded political authoritarianism: in this case, *the political system* uses metaphysics as an ideological underpinning of the political establishment. (iii) Liberal democracy: in this case, *the political system* itself becomes a metaphysical principle, in the sense that politics imposes itself as a utilitarian end–in–itself.

Classical Greek political philosophy and Hesychasm are spiritually alien to theocracy, absolute monarchy and liberal democracy. In general, in the context of the Greek and Greco–Christian spirituality, politics is understood in an instrumental way, i.e. politics serves the citizens' existential goals. The ancient Greek polity was founded on an ontological (existential) request: the pursuit of the truth of life, and, for the ancient Greeks, truth means man's participation in, or experience of, the absolute Logos, and thus the transformation of a set of historical / natural entities into a meaningful world ('cosmos').

In his sermon *Contra usuarios* (i.e. Against financial speculators), Gregory of Nyssa, one of the most influential Greek Church Fathers and saints in both East and West, stresses that law must safeguard life in a harmonious polity. In general, according to the ethos of Hesychasm, politics is concerned with the basic needs of human life, and the most important issues of social life are of a spiritual–anthropological nature, and not of a political one.

On the other hand, Muslim fundamentalists' "holy war against the infidels", the inscription "In God we trust" on the U.S. Dollar and certain Zionists' teachings about the unique holiness of the Jewish race[172] subordinate spirituality to politics. There is a significant yet elusive spiritual affinity among several elements of Protestant ethics (especially those related to the spirit of capitalism[173]), Islamic fundamentalism (which has been strongly influenced by Western colonial powers) and Zionism, because all of them need and use God in one or more of the following ways: as the supreme guarantor of fairness in economic transactions; as the supreme guarantor of

---

172 Contra certain Zionist teachings, Rabbis of Halakhic Judaism teach that Jews were not inherently chosen. For instance, Rabbi Eliezer Berkovits maintains that "God never chose the Jews", but "any people whom God chose was to become the Jewish people"; see: Ira Bedzow, Halakhic Man, Authentic Jew —Modern Expressions of Orthodox Thought from Rabbi Joseph B. Soloveitchik and Rabbi Eliezer Berkovits, New York: Lambda Publishers, 2009.

173 Max Weber, The Protestant Ethic and the Spirit of Capitalism, New York: Dover, 2003.

a system of moral policing; as the supreme guarantor of processes and institutions by means of which the 'faithful' (to the rationality of the market according to Western capitalism or to Allah according to certain fundamentalist Islamic movements) can grab and enjoy the wealth of the 'infidels'; as the supreme guarantor of a particular political order and as the underwriter of an imperialist policy.

The Hesychast seeks to experience God's life and especially Christ's victory over death. This quest cannot be fulfilled through systems of morality nor through political institutions, since, according to the Bible, the pioneers and 'doctors' of this mystical experience, which is the essence of the Church, were thieves, prostitutes and prodigals. Jesus said to the crossed thief who repented: "Today you will be with mein paradise" (*Luke*, 23:43); this thief was neither baptized nor partook of the Lord's Supper. When Jesus was at the house of a Pharisee, said to a prostitute: "Your faith has saved you; go in peace" (*Luke*, 7:50). In the parable of the Prodigal Son, Jesus contrasted rational thinking in terms of "law, merit and reward" with God's "love and graciousness"[174], and he stressed that, when the prodigal son returned to his father, the latter treated him with a generosity far more than the prodigal son had a right to expect (*Luke*, 15:11–32).

Additionally, Jesus calls the Pharisees an evil "brood of vipers" (*Matthew*, 12:34), "hypocrites" (*Matthew*, 23:23) and "blind guides" (*Matthew*, 23:16,24), not because their ideas were evil, but because they politicized them in order to promote their own selfish purposes. Jesus charges the Pharisees with having committed blasphemy against the Spirit (*Matthew*, 12:31), because they took the Law that applies to the heart (i.e., the Law of the *Spirit*, according to *Romans*, 8:2–11) out of its proper context and forced it upon others through political lawmaking.

Thus, the political culture of Hesychasm is alien to both politicized theocracy and secularism, and instead it stresses the mystery of man's spiritual transformation (repentance), which makes everything new. For, if man changes, i.e. if he transcends himself, then the results of his historical action will change accordingly.

The metapolitics of Hesychasm is a safe path to the true 'open society', because Hesychasm rejects and actively condemns

---

174 See: A.J. Hultgren, The Parables of Jesus —A Commentary, Michigan: Wm. B. Eerdmans Publishing, 2002, pp. 70–82.

every attempt to sanctify any legal order or institution. From the Hesychastic perspective, society is constantly subject and open to improvement. The major goal and the first priority of a Hesychast is his participation in the absolute good, and this goal, being of a purely spiritual nature, can be achieved under any historical conditions. But once achieved, the previous goal transforms the consciousness of the human being and makes it a wise reformer of its existential conditions, because then a human being's criteria of action transcend biological and historical necessities.

From the viewpoint of Hesychasm, politics means unselfish care for and service to society through a wise use of such instruments as laws and institutions. Thus, from the viewpoint of Hesychasm, a policy-maker must be characterized by a vigilant mind in order to be able to continuously adapt laws and institutions to the well-being of society, instead of sanctifying certain laws and institutions and instead of creating totemic bureaucratic structures[175]. Moreover, the ethos of the Hesychastic collective implies that workers must directly participate in the management of the companies in which they work and that the government must be sincerely and systematically accountable to the citizens.

The communal/relational spirit of the Hesychastic collective leads to an 'ecclesiastical' form of management of political and economic affairs: for the Hesychasts, this form of management is neither a sphere of bureaucratic management of individuals by social architects nor a sphere of *a priori* rational organization; on the contrary, it entails the establishment of institutions for knowledge production and informed collective decision-making for every political and economic affair. In this context, the site for knowing, deliberating about and questioning the law is something that belongs to all (communal —"ta koina", in Greek). Therefore, each and every political and economic institution (including corporations of course) should operate according to the synodal tradition (known also as the principle of conciliarity) of the Orthodox Church. This means that, in the sphere of political and economic life, people should enjoy and give witness to the ontological freedom of the human being

---

175 For instance, in the 20th and the 21st centuries, the Eurozone and the International Monetary Fund attempt to transform certain political and economic Programs into political totems and to subjugate human life to 'sanctified' financial regimes, while NATO attempts to operate like a global Holy Inquisitor.

through institutions of self–government and collective decision–making. From this perspective, I argue in this book that the ethos of the Hesychastic collective is the most genuine and effective path to 'open society' and to a true liberalism, a liberal liberalism (*Acts*, 5).

John Chrysostom (ca. 347–407), a prominent Early Church Father and Archbishop of Constantinople, whom the Orthodox Church honors as a saint and counts among the Three Holy Hierarchs (together with Basil the Great and Gregory Nazianzus), writes in his work *Pros piston patera* (To a faithful father), 3, 14 (*Patrologia Graeca*, Vol. 47, 372–374): "what has turned the world upside down is that we think only the monk must live rigorously, while the rest are allowed to live a life of indolence". In his previous work, John Chrysostom stresses that "a man is not defined by whether he is a layman or a monk, but by the way he thinks". For instance, the father of the great Hesychast Gregory Palamas, Constantine, lived a Hesychastic life as a senator and member of the imperial court in Constantinople, and, in 2009, he was canonized by the Greek Orthodox Church and the Christian Orthodox Patriarchate of Constantinople.

THE HESYCHASTIC COLLECTIVE

According to the Hesychasts, their monastic collectives in particular and the Orthodox Church in general constitute a hierarchical communion of unselfishness and an image of the relationship among the Persons of the Holy Trinity, where the Father is the source of the Son and of the Holy Spirit, but He does not dominate over them. In the context of the Holy Trinity, the Son is begotten of the Father by an eternal generation, and the Holy Spirit proceeds from the Father by an eternal procession, but, notwithstanding this difference as to origin, the Persons are co–eternal and co–equal. Thus, the Hesychastic society is neither a matter of individuals coming together to advance their interests nor a matter of a general concept (abstraction of genus) that is coercively imposed on individuals, but it is a community founded on spiritual unity.

In the context of Hesychasm, social unity can be achieved through peoples' participation in the same truth, i.e. social unity is a consequence of a freely chosen spiritual attitude. By contrast, if a political power attempts to establish social unity merely by means of laws and institutions, social unity reduces to a system of inhuman totalitarianism, and then individualism and liberalism emerge as "the lesser evil". In contrast to totalitarianism and to liberal democracy, a Hesychastic collective is the embodiment of the communal spirit.

Thus, Hesychasm leads to a deeply antiauthoritarian ecclesiology. From the viewpoint of Eastern Orthodox mystical ecclesiology, ministry, or clergy, is in essence the representation, or ambassadorship, of the Eucharistic community. Ministry belongs to the whole community, and it is lifted up in one person, who is the representative of the community. Thus, in 2 *Peter*, 5, the entire community of the Church (i.e. both the laity and the ministry) is described as follows: "like living stones, are being built into a spiritual house to be a holy priesthood". Additionally, in 2 *Peter*, 9, the entire community of the Church (i.e. both the laity and the ministry) is described as follows: "you are a chosen people, a royal priesthood, a holy nation". The bishop, in particular, symbolizes the spiritual unity of the local Church that he represents. In contrast to feudal authority and privileges, apostolic succession is not an object that is transferred from one bishop to another. Apostolic succession is a mystery, and it is carried through the community, which is the guardian of the faith, and not through the episcopal office itself.

In his *Homily for Holy Pentecost*, John Chrysostom writes the following about the role of the priest in the Eucharist:

> ...he does not touch the offerings before he himself has begged for you the grace of the Lord and you cry in answer to him: "And with your spirit". By this reply you are also reminded that he who is there does nothing, and that the right offering of the gifts is not a work of human nature, but that the mystic sacrifice is brought about by the grace of the Holy Spirit and his hovering over all...If the spirit was not present there would be no Church assisting, but if the Church stands round it is clear that the Spirit is present.[176]

The Hesychasts understand the history of the Church in a supra-rational manner, i.e. as a mystery. Hesychasm is founded on classical Greek philosophical concepts (such as those of Logos and hypostasis), on the witness of Biblical Israel's Patriarchs and Prophets, on Jewish monastic traditions that existed during the second Temple period (including the Essenes and the Therapeutae),

---

176   John Chrysostom, Patrologia Graeca, Vol. 50, 458–459.

and primarily on the essence–energies distinction and the doctrine of man's deification.

According to Hesychasm, if the Church endorsed a rationalist attitude, i.e. if it obeyed necessities, then the Church would pursue either a biologically grounded unity or a politically grounded unity, and, in both cases, it would give rise to totalitarianism. For instance, Leninism is a characteristic example of a rationalist interpretation of the eschatological visions and the communitarian ethos of the Russian people, i.e. it is an attempt to use political means in order to achieve the level of social unity that the Church achieves through mystery.

The political autonomy of the human being presupposes that the meaning, or purpose, of being must never be identified with the practical end of a temporal plan. If the meaning, or purpose, of being is transcendental, then it inspires and guides historical action, but, exactly because it is transcendental and not a material goal, it endows historical action with a universal significance; history is an endless progressive process towards a transhistorical purpose. On the contrary, if the meaning, or purpose, of being is itself a material goal, then it reduces to a managerial method (and particularly to what Alain de Benoist has called "la gouvernance", or "micromanagement"), life loses its symbolic significance and is formalistically organized.

By refusing to recognize a transcendental meaning, or purpose, of being and by reducing the ultimate significance of politics to a political goal, liberalism transforms politics into an insignificant and hence self–destructive closed system, in which each and every historical goal is simply the means for the pursuit of another one according to a Sisyphean task. Thus, according to Alexander Dugin[177], as "managers and technocrats take the place of the politician who makes historical decisions" and as "masses of people are equated to a mass of identical objects", liberalism, or rather what Dugin calls "postliberal reality", ultimately "leads straight to the complete abolition of politics".

Similarly by refusing to recognize a transcendental meaning, or purpose, of being and by reducing the ultimate significance of politics to a political goal, fascism and national–socialism can transform crime into a legitimate political methodology and lead

---

177   Alexander Dugin, The Fourth Political Ideology, U.K.: Arktos Media Ltd., 2012, p. 20.

to phenomena of moral collapse such as those that were accurately described by Hannah Arendt in her book *Eichmann in Jerusalem*[178]. Fascist and national–socialist leaders are dangerous because, under their rule, it is extremely difficult to find higher values that would bind them. Hence, there is a very short distance between a Pharaoh and a "Führer" (such as Adolf Hitler) or a "Duce" (such as Benito Mussolini). Benjamin Franklin, who played a key role in the founding of the United States of America in the 18th century, has pointedly argued that "man will ultimately be governed by God or by tyrants", thus warning us against the transformation of historical institutions into political totems and against the transformation of political leaders into Pharaohs, or "Führers", or "Duces". In other words, through the previous statement, Benjamin Franklin warns us against political idolatry and against putting all our existential hopes in historical goals.

Christ has explicitly taught that autocracy and imperialism were part of the offers that Satan made to Christ during the forty days in which Satan tempted Jesus (*Matthew*, 4:1–11; *Mark*, 1:12,13; *Luke*, 4:1–13). The Bible warns us against the mortal potentates who have sold their soul to Satan in return for Earthly power. As God spoke in *Hosea*, 8:4: "They set up kings, but not by Me; They made princes, but I did not acknowledge them".

By transcending politics, Hesychasm can offer *criteria* for political decision–making and thus give a transcendental meaning to politics. From this viewpoint, the metapolitics of Hesychasm consists in a *symbolic* Republic, like Plato's Republic, whose purpose is not to be itself historically instituted, or objectified, but, by remaining a transcendental vision, to spiritually guide and inspire political action. In other words, in the political sphere, Hesychasm is the 'Archimedean point' from which the political reality can be utilized and restructured according to the intentionality of the man who has understood and experienced his theanthropic potential. Every alternative political thesis is equivalent to an ontological disgrace of man.

The political goal of Hesychasm is not to freeze historical becoming, i.e. its political goal is not to sanctify a set of concrete answers to political problems, and, therefore, Hesychasm is substantially different from theocracy and totalitarianism. The

---

178   Hannah Arendt, Eichmann in Jerusalem, London: Penguin Books, 2006.

political goal of Hesychasm is to make policy–making and political life meaningful through its theanthropic ideal. As we read in *1 Corinthians*, 7:23: "You were bought at a price; do not become slaves of men".

Vladimir Sergeyevich Solovyov[179], one of the most influential 19th century Russian philosophers, theologians and poets, introduced the notion of "Godmanhood" (Bogochelovechestvo), i.e. the incarnation of the divine idea in man, and, by following this deeply Hesychastic theanthropic ideal, he managed to Christianize Nietzsche's "Superman", by showing that Nietzsche's "Superman" expresses a yearning to transcend oneself and that this yearning can be satisfied through the mystical path of Hesychasm.

However, as I have already emphasized, the genuine Hesychastic tradition is deeply metapolitical, and it rejects every attempt to reduce it to a specific political system. Hesychasm implies and emphasizes that the ultimate purpose of historical action is transhistorical and generally that the ultimate purpose of praxis is not practical but transcendental. Hesychasm teaches us how to transcend ourselves in order to ascend to a higher ontological level and thus actualize our ontological potential. Hesychasm does not prescribe specific institutions, but it provides us with criteria for evaluating and choosing institutions. This is the essence of Hesychastic metapolitics.

Hesychastic metapolitics is the safest and most consistent path to the ideal of 'open society'. A society is open if it is willing to reflect on itself and be re–instituted by accepting new institutions. By emphasizing the freedom of spirit from political institutions and by refusing to accept any practical goal as the ultimate purpose of historical action, Hesychasm gives rise to a society without political totems and safeguards the openness and transparency of the social system. As we read in *2 Corinthians*, 3:17: "Now the Lord is the Spirit; and where the Spirit of the Lord is, there is freedom".

HESYCHASM AND THE PROBLEM OF VALUES

In contrast to animals, human beings communicate with each other and with the world in terms of and through values. Additionally,

---

179   Vladimir Solovyov, Divine Sophia —The Wisdom Writings of Vladimir Solovyov, ed. by Judith D. Kornblatt, New York: Cornell University Press, 2009.

when human action is a result of personal freedom and responsibility, it is based on and guided by values. By the term 'value', we mean the link between the consciousness of action and the object of action. Through values and due to values, man is aware that he is not necessarily determined by the 'natural objectivity', but he can control and change his existential conditions, instead of being passively controlled by them.

Louis Lavelle[180] has explained the difference between the terms 'value' and 'price' as follows: a price is a fact whereas a value is a judgment (a conscious act). Additionally, R. Polin[181] has argued that a value is the "centre of interest" towards which consciousness is oriented whenever it is engaged in action. Hence, values transcend action and simultaneously they are embedded in action, since values constitute the structure of action, and action confirms the existence of values.

According to the objectivist theories of value[182], since consciousness searches for values, it logically follows that consciousness is unable to provide its own self with values, and, therefore, the source of values transcends consciousness. Furthermore, Gabriel Marcel[183] has argued that each value is a particular mode of being, and it enriches the set of the basic modes of being that are studied in ontology.

In contrast to the objectivist theories of value, the subjectivist theories of value emphasize individuality or 'otherness'. Sartre[184] argues that one's personal freedom is the ultimate foundation of values and that no value system is mandatory. For Sartre, the human being is free because it is not a self (an "in-itself") but a presence–to-self (the transcendence or "nihilation" of one's self). Hence, we are "other" to ourselves, and, irrespective of what we are or what others ascribe to us, we are "in the manner of not being it". According to Sartre, we are responsible for our "world", we create our "world", as our existential horizon, and, therefore, our value system stems from our life–orienting fundamental "choice".

---

180   Louis Lavelle, Traité des Valeurs —Théorie Générale de la Valeur, Paris: PUF, 1951.

181   Kockelmans (ed.), Contemporary European Ethics.

182   R.W. Sellars, "The Spiritualism of Lavelle and Le Senne", Philosophy and Phenomenological Research, Vol. 11, 1951, pp. 386–393; René Le Senne, Le Mensenge et le Caractère, Paris: F. Alcan, 1930.

183   Gabriel Marcel, Man Against Mass Society, trans. G.S. Fraser, St Augustine's Press, 2007.

184   J.–P. Sartre, Being and Nothingness, trans. H.E. Barnes, New York: Washington Square Press, 1992 (originally published in French in 1943).

From the perspective of Hesychasm, communion is the source of values. The Hesychasts' approach to the problem of the source of values is different from both the objectivist theories of value and the subjectivist theories of value. According to Hesychasm, the human being is a 'person', i.e. an–existential–otherness–in–communion (or an–individual–in–a–relationship), and, therefore, a person is neither a mere individual (an otherness) nor an undifferentiated element of a system (a unit of a rational order). The 'person' is ontologically founded on communion, which means that —contra the subjectivist theories of value— there is no such thing as absolute individual, conceivable in itself, and simultaneously —contra the objectivist theories of value— the ontological category of communion is founded on a concrete and free person. The 'person' cannot exist without communion, and, therefore, the objectivist theories of value are right when they argue that consciousness is not an ontologically sufficient source of values. Simultaneously, communion should never deny or suppress the person and particularly the existential otherness that is inherent in the notion of personhood, and, therefore, the subjectivist theories of value are right when they recognize and declare the ontological significance of otherness. However, neither the objectivist theories of value nor the subjectivist theories of value can lead to a general theory of value, since neither of them has fully understood the notion of personhood. On the contrary, Hesychasm, by combining the classical Greek philosophical notion of 'hypostasis' with the Gospel of Christ, has tackled the problem of values through the notion of personhood, which gives rise to spiritual unity without negating individuality, or otherness.

ORTHODOX CHRISTIAN ESCHATOLOGY AND THE 'NEW WORLD ORDER'

On several occasions, in this book, I emphasized that, in the context of the philosophy of Plato and Aristotle and in the context of Hesychasm, every being and thing in the cosmos is constantly united with its 'telos', or purpose. Therefore, according to Hesychasm, Christian eschatology signifies the eternal and dynamic relationship between Christ, being the Logos of God (i.e. the source of significance of every being and thing in the cosmos), and the cosmos.

The Orthodox Christian eschatology emphasizes that the 'eschaton', i.e. the end of history, is "a new Heaven and a new Earth", as we read in *Revelation*, 21:1, and in 2 *Peter*, 3:13. The Incarnation of the Logos in the person of historical Christ inaugurated the 'Last Times' by revealing the Logos of God within history, and ever since then the historical manifestation of the Church (i.e. of the communion between God and man) has been constantly "growing" (*Ephesians*, 2:21–22 and 4:16); the divine "seed" is developing into a "great tree" in which the righteous will "abide" and find rest, according to *Luke*, 13:19.

Hesychasm rejects all those eschatological teachings which are dominated by the fear of Satan, by an anxiety of an imminent evil, by the fear of a judgmental God's 'forensic verdict', by the risk of sin, by a guilty conscience, and/or by the scholastics' moral rationalism. The previous gloomy eschatological teachings, which have been torturing the Western psyche since the Middle Ages and which have been rejected by Hesychasm, are reflected in several Western art movements, which express a psychology of fear, misery and corruption and look for an existential shelter in occultism or in the field of dreams. Characteristic examples of such Western art movements are the following: the so–called decadence art (Joris–Karl Huysmans, Hieronymus Bosch, Lucas Cranach, Pieter Bruegel, William Blake, etc.), the European symbolists' occult art (Gustave Moreau, Richard Dadd, Jean Delville, etc.), the surrealists' occult and nightmarish images (Austin Spare, Felix Labisse, Salvador Dali, Rene Magritte, etc.), the decadence and occult literary works of Edgar Allan Poe, Charles Baudelaire, Arthur Rimbaud, Paul Verlaine, Stéphane Mallarmé, Giosue Carducci, Gabriele D' Annunzio, Giovanni Pascoli, Guido Gozzano, Hermann Hesse, etc.

In contrast to the gloomy Western eschatological traditions, the metaphysics of Hesychasm implies that true Christians live out their sanctification and "renewal" in Christ and believe that every historical moment is the "last hour" (1 *John*, 2:18), in the sense that time is not merely a cosmological dimension, but it has a transcendental meaning. The "End" of history means the consummation of the work of salvation, the perfect attainment of the Kingdom of God, and the "gathering together" (2 *Thessalonians*, 2:1) in the "marriage of the Lamb" (*Revelation*, 19:7). This is the Christocentric vision of the 'New World Order'.

This Christocentric New World Order will come by way of eschatological tribulations; "for then shall be great tribulation" (*Matthew*, 24:21). But the living bearers of hope will realize that those "sorrows" (*Matthew*, 24:8) herald the birth of the New Creation, the "New Jerusalem" (*Revelation*, 3:12, 21:2).

The core issue of John's *Apocalypse* is the controversy about the meaning of being, i.e. about the ultimate source of significance of beings and things in the world. Christians insist that the meaning of being is transcendental, that is that God is the ultimate source of significance of beings and things in the world. The Antichrist is the archetype of the historical actors that do not live in communion with the ultimate source of significance of beings and things in the world, and, hence, they have lapsed into a state of spiritual insignificance, i.e. their mind (*nous*) has been deadened. For instance, the blasphemy of deifying the civil authority or the financial oligarchy is hinted at by Paul: the Antichrist will try to show "that he is God" (2 *Thessalonians*, 2:4). Additionally, Nicodemus of the Holy Mountain pointedly notices that "many Antichrists have appeared, all of whom are forerunners of the one who in and of himself and properly is, and is called, the Antichrist...heresiarchs took on the personality of him who is the Antichrist *per se*"[185].

Andrew of Caesarea (first half of the 6th century A.D.) was a Greek theological writer and Bishop of Caesarea in Cappadocia, and he is famous for his seminal *Commentary* on John's *Apocalypse*. According to Andrew of Caesarea, "Babylon the great" (*Revelation*, 17:5) is either "the confusion of [this] world and the turmoil of the present life"; or "the earthly kingdom in general, as though [existing] in a single body"; or "the capital city until the coming of the [ultimate] Antichrist"; or "that which bears the dominion of the worldly kingdom until the end of time"; or "that which rules in the time of the Persians, or the old Rome [regaining its ancient power], or the new [Rome, the seven kings and kingdoms having thus come to pass]" (*Patrologia Graeca*, Vol. 106, 345A, 372D, 376A, 377BCD, 380C, 381ABD, 396A, 392D).

Another eminent commentator of John's *Apocalypse* is Arethas of Caesarea, who became Archbishop of Caesarea in Cappadocia early in the 10th century, and he is the compiler of a Greek commentary on the *Apocalypse*, for which he made considerable use of the similar work of his predecessor, Andrew of Caesarea. Arethas's view is the

---

185 Nicodemus of the Holy Mountain, Ermeneia eis tas Epta Catholicas Epistolas (Commentary on the Seven Catholic Epistles), 3rd ed., Thessaloniki: Ekdoseis "Orthodoxos Kypsele", 1986, pp. 495–496 (in Greek).

following: "And what is Babylon? Nothing other than this perishable world, in which nothing is free from the sway of the adversary and good is mingled with evil" (*Patrologia Graeca*, Vol. 106, 688B, 713D, 729C).

According to the Hesychastic ethos, the students of John's *Apocalypse* should not focus on chapter 13, but they should understand that chapters 4 and 5 constitute the theological centre of John's *Apocalypse*. In particular, the "*New Song*" (*Revelation*, 5:9–10) is the Christological centre of John's *Apocalypse*:

> You are worthy to take the book, and to open the seals thereof, because you are slain, and with your blood you purchased men for God from every tribe and language and people and nation. You have made them to be a kingdom and priests to serve our God, and they will reign on the earth.

Orthodox Christians, as a "holy nation" (*1 Peter*, 2:9), a "peculiar people, zealous of good works" (*Titus*, 2:14), are "partakers of Christ" (*Hebrews*, 3:14), Who fulfills history, since he is "the Alpha and the Omega, the beginning and the end, the first and the last" (*Revelation*, 1:4,8; 2:8; 4:8;11:17; 21:6;22:13).

Being "fellow–members of Christ's body" (*Ephesians*, 3:6), the faithful do not suffer by existential anxiety or fear, because they believe that "greater is He that is in us [the uncreated Grace of God], than he that is in the world [Satan]" (*John*, 4:4) and "stronger" (*Matthew*, 12:29; *Mark*, 3:27; *Luke*, 11:22). In fact, Satan is the archetype of spiritual death and existential failure, whereas, being "partakers of Christ", the faithful become 'uncreated' according to Grace (i.e. according to God's uncreated energies), and, therefore, they participate here and now in the 'eschaton'.

As a consequence of the above–mentioned approach to the *Apocalypse*, Hesychasm leads also to a spiritual condemnation of terrorism in general and of 'apocalyptic war', which is an extreme form of terrorism, in particular. The total antithesis between Hesychasm and terrorism is based on the former's refusal to subordinate the spirit to historical expediencies or necessities. In contradistinction to the Hesychasts' relation to the transcendent and the ecclesiastical community, a terrorist is a totally practical and pragmatic actor who internalizes his historical condition in a negative sense and believes that the ultimate meaning of his existence is the achievement of a historical goal, and, therefore, he justifies the evil and actively takes the side of the evil. In the context of Western Christianity, the ethos of the Society of Jesus (Jesuits), of the Holy Inquisition and of the Orange Order is a characteristic example of the degeneration of Christianity as a result of the adoption of the aforementioned terrorist mentality (i.e. an extremely practical and pragmatic spirit) by religious authorities.

For a Hesychast, heroism means that one refuses to subordinate the spirit to historical expediencies or necessities, without negating the value of history. In other words, according to the Hesychasts' way of understanding heroism, a heroic person undertakes his historical responsibilities, while remaining *spiritually* independent from historical results, since he believes that the end of history is not a historical goal. Thus, such a person is historically active, but his existential hopes are not exhausted in history. On the contrary, according to the psychology of a terrorist, heroism is identified with warlike achievements or with competition in general. Hence, apart from war and competition, there is no other activity that can spiritually nourish a person that endorses the terrorist's approach to heroism.

The significance of any historical entity *per se* is determined either by nature or by established historical conventions, and, therefore, it can be approached only in utilitarian terms, and not in terms of a personal relationship. On the other hand, for a person who refuses to subordinate his spirit to historical necessities, the significance of any historical entity is a matter of personal choice. Hesychasm averts and condemns totalitarianism, because Hesychasm refuses to transform the spirit into a historical institution, i.e. it keeps the spirit constantly transcendental and, therefore, irreducible to practice. This is the essence of the tradition of the Hesychastic communion.

Within the framework of the Hesychastic communion, one's relationship with the absolute good (Divinity) is always personal and, hence, free, and not determined by any logical or other necessities. On the other hand, terrorism is a form of totalitarianism, and, therefore, a violation of human rights, because it wishes to transform the spirit into practice. The ultimate aim of totalitarianism is to eliminate theory (i.e. spiritual vision) from human life —in accordance with Karl Marx's eleventh thesis on Feuerbach[186] or in accordance with the Nazis' apocalyptic historicism— and to establish the absolute domination of practice, or historical action.

The essence of terrorism is the subjugation of the spirit to historical expediencies or necessities. Hence, terrorism is not conducted only by non–state actors but also by states. The fundamental characteristic of a terrorist is not his political, legal, or ideological status, but his absolute commitment to the pursuit of his historical vindication and his refusal to recognize and endorse any trans–historical principles and values. In other words, at a fundamental level, terrorism is a cultural attitude.

Given the cultural character of terrorism, the secular political antiterrorist methods of the Western liberal states are unable to fight terrorism, because they are unable to refute the cultural core of terrorism. Far from being unable to refute the cultural core of terrorism, the Western liberal states endorse a practical and pragmatic approach to history, and, therefore, there is a significant yet elusive cultural affinity between Western liberal states and terrorism. Even though, in the context of neoliberal institutionalism, Western states condemn terrorism and totalitarianism, their attitude towards terrorism and totalitarianism is neither consistent nor sincere. They condemn terrorist and totalitarian phenomena only when such phenomena are opposite to the interests and the value–system of the dominant Western elites. But the modern West has not condemned the cultural essence of terrorism and totalitarianism, i.e. is the spirit of pragmatism and practicality, which proclaims the achievement of historical goals as an end in itself. On the contrary, Hesychasm's antithesis to terrorism and totalitarianism is consistent and sincere, because it is founded on the spirit's autonomy from history.

The significance of the spirit's autonomy from history and of philosophical life has been acknowledged and vigorously defended by the great American statesman Benjamin Franklin, who wrote in a letter to David Hartley (4 December 1789): "God grant, that not only the Love of Liberty, but a thorough Knowledge of the Rights of Man,

---

186   According to the well–known Marx's eleventh thesis on Feuerbach, "Philosophers have hitherto only interpreted the world in various ways; the point is to change it". In general, Marx's Theses on Feuerbach —which are eleven short philosophical notes written by Marx as a basic outline for the first chapter of his book The German Ideology (1845)— identify political action as the only truth of philosophy.

may pervade all the Nations of the Earth, so that a Philosopher may set his Foot anywhere on its Surface, and say, 'This is my Country'".

The essential characteristic of the Western interpretations of the classical Greek philosophy is that they confine truth within the human intellect. Additionally, the reaction of Western scholars against the intellectual tradition of neoclassicism continued to maintain that truth is a creation of man. Thus, by differentiating the logical foundation of truth (rationalism) from the historical foundation of truth (historicism), the West caused a split between reason and historical becoming.

On the contrary, the classical Greek philosophy and the Hesychasts endorsed a metaphysical attitude according to which every being and thing in the world is united with its *logos*, or purpose, and, therefore, inherent in every being and thing in the world is a meaning that transcends the corresponding being or thing itself. Thus, ancient and medieval Greek philosophers and theologians seek truth not through a relationship with beings and things themselves but through a relationship with the *logos*, or purpose, of beings and things. The classical Greek philosophy and the Hesychastic spirituality do not disdain historical action, but they emphasize that history is hierarchically inferior to spirit.

For instance, according to Plato, a sculpture exists because it is the embodiment of a genus, and, therefore, the creation of a sculpture denotes an itinerary from amorphy to form. In other words, from Plato's perspective, a sculpture is a creative act because it is a conception and an imitation of the corresponding genus. The imitation of a genus, in turn, is a creative act not because it represents something but because it gives a material form to a genus, and, therefore, it highlights the ultimate purpose, i.e. the truth, of a being. When imitation simply represents something (representational art), it reduces to several complicated techniques, such as those cultivated by the Renaissance, but it lacks the spiritual purpose that imitation has in the context of Plato's, Aristotle's and Byzantium's aesthetics.

Thus, in the context of Plato's and Aristotle's philosophy and in the context of Hesychasm, authentic creativity is intimately related to tradition. This is not a contradictory attitude, because, through tradition and due to tradition, Plato, Aristotle and the Hesychasts avert the sanctification of action *per se* and the establishment of mechanistic systems. For Plato, Aristotle and the Hesychasts, 'tradition' means the transfer of a transhistorical *logos* from the past to the future, and, hence, the present is meaningful because and to the extent that it operates as the bridge through which the transcendental truth of beings and things is transferred from the past to the future.

6

ETHICS, JUSTICE AND HESYCHASM

ACCORDING to 2 *Samuel*, 3:7, moral values are the foundation of one's authority. In philosophical language, 'morality' is a conscious state in which the consciousness of existence formulates judgments. In other words, moral consciousness is the consciousness of existence itself when the latter operates as a judge. The thesis that moral consciousness is innate is corroborated by the fact that, even though moral consciousness is *affected* by social structures, it is not *created* by social structures. Moral consciousness internalizes and reflects social values, and it may be forced to comply with social values, but it can always judge and criticize social values, articulate its own notion of a 'good society' and even revolt. Hence, moral consciousness is not a mere creation of society. Moral consciousness transcends any established social structure.

Moral consciousness is composed of three operational components: the sentimental component (including the sentiments of respect, pride, indignation and guilt), the intellectual component and the volitional component. The sentimental component, the intellectual component and the volitional component of moral consciousness are inseparable from each other, but the sentimental component is the most powerful one, because it plays the predominant role in the formation of moral consciousness.

The intellectual component of moral consciousness (e.g. a concept), may be characterized by a high level of ambiguity, and, therefore, moral consciousness may not be able to make decisions on the basis of a given intellectual element, but, if moral consciousness has a clear sentimental orientation, then it may be able to make a clear and accurate evaluation of the situation in which it has to act. Moreover, the volitional component of moral consciousness may be weak, and, therefore, it may be unable to lead moral consciousness to a clear decision, but, if moral consciousness has a clear sentimental orientation, then it may remain strong and vigilant and make clear decisions.

THE PROBLEM OF ETHICS

In the context of modern philosophy, the most influential moral theories are those of Jeremy Bentham, John Stuart Mill, Adam Smith and Immanuel Kant. In the sequel, we shall analyze and evaluate these moral philosophies, and we shall compare and contrast them with Hesychasm.

Jeremy Bentham (1748–1832) attempted to found liberalism on utilitarian principles. His political thought is in essence a quantitative theory of pleasure, and his moral philosophy consists in a "felicific calculus", which has been explained and summarized by J.V. Orth[187] as follows: the value of a pleasure in isolation is determined by intensity, duration, certainty, propinquity, fecundity and purity. Additionally, since Bentham was concerned with the common good, he argued that the value of a pleasure is also determined by the extent of the pleasure or the number of persons affected by it.

According to Bentham's "felicific calculus", the quality of pleasures is ultimately determined by their quantity or at least by their intensity. Therefore, the most important defect of Bentham's moral philosophy is that it is unable to address qualitative issues as such.

Another important defect of Bentham's moral philosophy is his argument that the value of a pleasure depends on the number of the persons that are affected by it. The previous principle is problematic because of the following reasons: (i) Bentham emphasizes the fact that the same pleasure can be experienced by different human subjects, but this argument contradicts the subjectivity of conscious states. (ii) Bentham has not taken into account the fact that a person may accept that one has moral duties, but one may define them in

---

187 J.V. Orth, "Jeremy Bentham: The Common Law's Severest Critic", American Bar Association Journal, Vol. 68, 1982, p. 714.

accordance with one's own individual interests; hence, Bentham's moral philosophy may reduce to a justification of egoism. (iii) Apart from the possibility that Bentham's moral philosophy may reduce to a justification of egoism, Bentham's moral philosophy may also lead to the suppression of the individual, because Bentham argues for the protection of the general interest of society without having formulated any universal moral criterion capable of uniting different individuals into a harmonious whole. In other words, Bentham's moral philosophy lacks a universal Logos.

John Stuart Mill[188] (1806–1873), a student of Francis Place and Jeremy Bentham, attempted to liberate utilitarianism from the antinomies and defects of Bentham's moral philosophy. According to Mill's moral philosophy, utility as a moral criterion is of a qualitative nature, and not of a quantitative one. J.S. Mill argues that, if one overlooks the qualitative dimension of pleasure, then he arrives at a moral theory "worthy only of swine". Additionally, J.S. Mill maintains that "it is better to be a human being dissatisfied than a pig satisfied".

In the context of Mill's moral philosophy, which was influenced by socialism, the general interest of society must be respected and get priority because of its intrinsic value and not merely because it may coincide with people's individual interests. Thus, Mill's utilitarian morality is founded on the following principle: do as you would be done by and love your neighbor. The previous principle implies that only a pleasure that is intrinsically noble is worthy to be experienced by man. In other words, for J.S. Mill, the keystone of utilitarian morality is the value of being human itself.

Indeed, J.S. Mill managed to improve Bentham's utilitarian moral philosophy. But J.S. Mill's moral philosophy has its own defects due to antinomies that are intrinsic to utilitarianism itself. Mill argues that there is an empirical criterion for the qualitative evaluation of pleasures and that this criterion is unerringly manifested in the consciousness of the most scientifically cultivated and knowledgeable people. The previous argument is not convincing, because even the consciousness of the most scientifically cultivated and knowledgeable people is not infallible.

---

188 See: Karl Britton, John Stuart Mill, Harmondsworth: Penguin, 1953; Roger Crisp, Mill on Utilitarianism, London: Routledge, 1997; Pedro Schwartz, The New Political Economy of J.S. Mill, London: Weidenfeld & Nicolson, 1972.

Furthermore, according to J.S. Mill, if no other factors (such as restrictions, coercion, etc.) interfere, consciousness is attracted, and it should be attracted, to the noblest pleasures. Thus, he makes a logically illegitimate inference from 'is' to 'ought', from 'is desired' to 'is worthy of desire'. G.E. Moore[189] has called the previous syllogism the "naturalistic fallacy".

Finally, J.S. Mill has not managed to give a satisfactory answer to the following question: since he maintains that pleasure is the ultimate criterion of morality, how can one argue that a concrete pleasure is superior to every other pleasure? In other words, without a criterion of morality that transcends pleasure, how can one create a universal hierarchy of pleasures?

Adam Smith (1723–1790), the founder of classical political economy, published *The Theory of Moral Sentiments* in 1759, and he is the main representative of the morality of sympathy. By the term 'sympathy', Adam Smith means the intuitive perception of the normative character of human behavior. Smith relates sympathy to approval as follows: "To approve of another man's opinions is to adopt those opinions, and to adopt them is to approve of them...But it is equally the case with regard to our approbation or disapprobation of the sentiments or passions of others"[190]. Similarly, he argues: "To approve of the passions of another...as suitable to their objects, is the same thing as to observe that we entirely sympathize with them; and not to approve of them as such, is the same thing as to observe that we do not entirely sympathize with them"[191].

Smith argues that sympathy, of which we must become worthy, must be pure, unconditional (i.e. immune to criticism) and universal (i.e. experienced by everybody, or at least by the majority of the people). However, the following question emerges: what should one do in case he does not know if others approve or disapprove of his actions? Smith has answered the previous question as follows: whenever people do not know if others approve or disapprove of their actions, they should act as impartial spectators of their own actions, so that one's own judgment can be used as a substitute for other persons' approval or disapproval of one's actions.

---

189   G.E. Moore, Principia Ethica, New York: Prometheus Books, 1988 (originally published in 1903).

190   Smith, The Theory of Moral Sentiments, ed. D.D. Raphael and A.L. Macfie, Oxford: Oxford University Press, 1976.

191   Ibid, p. 16.

Adam Smith's moral philosophy has the following defects: (i) Sympathy is not as universal as Smith contends, because it is not a necessary conscious state, and conscious states are characterized by subjectivity. (ii) Since moral consciousness has sentimental and volitional components, sympathy can be influenced by them, and, therefore, it cannot lead to the formulation of unconditional moral judgments. (iii) By arguing that an actor's own consciousness can be used as a substitute for the consciousness of a sympathizing spectator–judge whenever the first operates as an impartial spectator, Smith eliminates sympathy (resp. antipathy) in those fields in which sympathy (resp. antipathy) is presupposed (i.e. in the fields of moral deliberation and judgment), and this is a logical contradiction. Adam Smith has not managed to clarify if sympathy is a moral sentiment (as he has theoretically asserted), or if, alternatively, it is an expression of moral rationality (as it is implied by the role that Adam Smith has assigned to an impartial spectator in his moral theory).

In the history of modern philosophy, the most influential theory of moral rationalism was formed by Immanuel Kant[192] (1724–1804). Kant's moral theory signals a shift of the debate about morality from actions to intentions. His most influential arguments are found in *The Groundwork of the Metaphysics of Morals*, but he developed, enriched, and in some cases modified those arguments in later works, such as *The Critique of Practical Reason, The Metaphysics of Morals, Anthropology from a Pragmatic Point of View,* and *Religion within the Boundaries of Mere Reason.*

Kant adopts J.–J. Rousseau's thesis that nothing is absolutely good in this world or out of it except a good intention, and he adds that a good intention is good not because its consequences are good but because it is intrinsically good. Thus, for Kant, an act is moral if its sole motive is pure respect for the moral law. Moreover, Kant emphasizes that the moral law is a categorical imperative, i.e. it commands unconditionally.

According to Kant, the ultimate criterion of morality is the following: always act so that you can will that everybody shall follow the determining principle of your action. No rational being can really will a contradiction.

---

192 See: Bruce Aune, Kant's Theory of Morals, Princeton, NJ: Princeton University Press, 1979; Paul Guyer (ed.), Kant's Groundwork of the Metaphysics of Morals —Critical Essays, Lantham, MD: Rowman and Littlefield, 1998.

Kant emphasizes that the rational will imposes upon itself universal laws: A lying promise is a contradiction. Thus, no rational being can will that everybody should make lying promises, for, if everybody did, nobody would believe anybody and finally lying promises would prove to be self–defeating. Similarly, no rational being can will to disregard the welfare of others, because, if everybody did the same, the given being itself might someday become the victim of inhuman behavior.

The major defects of Kant's moral philosophy are the following: (i) Kant's argument that nothing is intrinsically and absolutely good in this world or out of it except a good intention is wrong. A characteristic counter–example to Kant's previous assertion is 'knowledge'; knowledge is an epistemological value and not an intention, but it is intrinsically and absolutely good, since knowledge is always morally superior to ignorance. (ii) Kant's thesis that the moral law is a categorical imperative leads to oversimplification. A characteristic counter–example to Kant's previous assertion is the following: if you know that someone asks you information about other persons in order to harm them, then it may be neither psychologically easy nor rational to be sincere. The logical power and consistency of Kant's moral theory presuppose the elimination of sensitivity and generally the elimination of the sentimental factor in moral life. Thus, Kant's moral philosophy inhibits the development of a fully integrated moral consciousness.

Kant's moral theory is founded on a coercive *ratio*, i.e. on an impersonal logic that commands unconditionally 'from above', and, therefore, it gives rise to a suffocating and oppressive social order, in which the human being is a slave of the social system's logic. On the contrary, as I explained in previous chapters of this book, Plato, Aristotle and the Hesychasts maintain that the *logos* of being transcends being *per se* but it is personally united with beings and it embraces beings from inside. Thus, from the perspective of Plato, Aristotle and the Hesychasts, *logos* is the foundation of social harmony, or communion.

In the context of Hesychasm, the truth of being is identified with the personal existence of God. God is not ontologically restricted by His essence, but He is "hyperousios", which in Greek means that He cannot be determined by any essential or natural characterization. Thus, the divine mode of being, as I argued earlier in this book, is defined as freedom and love. Additionally, God's mode of being stems not from essence, which would transform the Divinity into an ontological necessity and His Logos into a categorical command, but from the person and the freedom. Hence, it is love that hypostases God's being into a personal and trinitarian communion.

Having been created "in the image" of God in Trinity, the human being, or rather humanity, is one in essence according to its nature, but it exists in and through many hypostases in terms of its persons. Thus, man is a person, i.e. an–existential–otherness/distinctiveness–in–communion, and not merely an individual, i.e. a subdivision of the human nature as a whole. From the previous perspective, man transcends his biological hypostasis, i.e. his DNA, because he is a partaker of a transcendental logos, i.e. he is simultaneously a biological and spiritual hypostasis, exactly as the Incarnation of Logos teaches us.

In the light of the aforementioned theses, the human being need not be weighed down by the commands of its biological hypostasis (law of the flesh) nor is it obliged to cut loose from the sensible world by the categorical imperative or the call of logic. Instead, the moral code of a Hesychast is determined by and founded on the fact he relates to beings and things in the world by primarily relating to the beings' and things' *logoi* and not to the beings and things themselves. Thus, a Hesychast treats the beings and things in the world as bearers of transcendental *logoi* and not as objects that should be exploited according to a utilitarian world conception or that should be logically organized according to a rationalist world conception. In fact, this is the essence of spiritual vision, or *theoria* (theory), the ability to see each and every being and thing in the world not merely in terms of its physical substance but also in terms of its transcendental *logos*, which resides inside it. The ethics of Hesychasm is founded on the principle of holiness, which, in turn, is founded on the thesis that every being and thing in the world is united with its transcendental *logos*.

Without the spiritual vision of the ultimate significance, or the *logos*, of beings and things, i.e. without a deep awareness of the holiness of beings and things, we are confined to defective moral theories, such as those of Jeremy Bentham, John Stuart Mill, Adam Smith and Immanuel Kant. Hesychasm allows us to transcend the previous defective moral theories by elucidating the difference between 'being good' and 'being godly'. The difference between 'being good' and 'being godly' was originally emphasized by the Apostle Paul in *Ephesians*, 2:3. Only through being personally united with the universal Logos, that is, in Hesychastic terminology, only through being partakers of the uncreated energies of God, can we become good in God's sight.

Several secularized religious communities, which have chosen to compromise the Gospel of Christ with political and economic systems and necessities, transform Christian ethics into a recipe for social adjustment according to the commands of the social establishment. It is for this reason that several political and economic oligarchies around the world are concerned with religious affairs and with the so-called faith–based diplomacy. From the perspective of secularized religious communities, religion is a method by means of which a cultural elite can moralize people according to the values and norms of the social establishment and can oversee and guide the manner in which people manage and express their feelings of discontent and grief. On the contrary, in *John*, 16:20, we read that society's values can make the persons that are united with the transcendental Logos feel like misfits, and, in *Matthew*, 19:30, we realize that Jesus turns the world values around. Thus, as I have previously explained, the ethics of Hesychasm is based on and stems from the Hesychastic teleology.

THE PROBLEM OF JUSTICE

In the second half of the 20th century, Rawls[193], Nozick[194] and Elster[195] made some of the most prominent contributions to the theory of justice.

John Rawls starts from an imaginary "original position" in which people are placed. He assumes that, in this hypothetical situation, people do not have any knowledge about their talents, abilities and social status. Additionally, he assumes that these people are not aware of any particular purposes in life, but they only know that it will be useful to have various "primary goods", which, according to Rawls are "the principles that rational and free

---

193 John Rawls, A Theory of Justice, Revised edition, Cambridge, Mass.: Belknap Press, 1999 (originally published in 1971).

194 Robert Nozick, Anarchy, State and Utopia, New York: Basic Books, 1974.

195 Jon Elster, Local Justice, New York: Russell Sage Foundation, 1992; J. Elster and K.O. Moene (eds), Alternatives to Capitalism, Cambridge: Cambridge University Press, 1989.

persons concerned to further their own interests would accept in an initial position of equality as defining the fundamentals of the terms of their association"[196]. Rawls lists these "primary goods" as rights and liberties, opportunities and powers, income and wealth and the bases of self–respect. According to Rawls, everyone wants as many of these "primary goods" as possible, but, because, in the "original position", "no one knows his place in society, his class position or social status, nor does anyone know his fortune in the distribution of natural assets and abilities, his intelligence, strength and the like"[197], people are constrained to articulate general distributive principles.

Rawls's first maxim of justice is the following: "each person is to have an equal right to the most extensive basic liberty compatible with a similar liberty for others"[198]. The basic liberties of citizens are political liberty (i.e. to vote and run for office), freedom of speech and assembly, liberty of conscience, freedom of thought, freedom of the person along with the right to hold private property, and freedom from arbitrary arrest. In the context of Rawls's philosophy, this maxim of justice is a categorical imperative and may never be violated, even for the sake of the second maxim. However, various basic rights may be traded off against each other for the sake of establishing the optimal system of rights.

Rawls's second maxim of justice is the following: "social and economic inequalities are to be arranged so that they are both (i) reasonably expected to be to everyone's advantage, and (ii) attached to positions and offices open to all"[199]. For instance, according Rawls's second maxim of justice, it is fair that a doctor makes more money than a porter, because, if this were not the case, people would not study and train to become doctors and there would be no medical care. According to Rawls's syllogism, the fact that a doctor makes more money than a porter benefits not only him but the entire society, including the porter, since, in this way, he can have medical care.

---

196   Rawls, A Theory of Justice, p. 11.
197   Ibid, p. 12.
198   Ibid, p. 60.
199   Ibid, p. 60.

In his Tanner and Dewey lectures[200], Rawls has given further explanations about his theory of "justice as fairness". In the previous lectures, Rawls answered the criticism that his theory is indefensibly ahistorical, since it attempts to derive principles of justice entirely from general assumptions about human purposes. Rawls's response was that his theory reflects the traditions of a modern democratic state. Moreover, in the previous lectures, Rawls answered the criticism that his notion of primary goods embodies an unwarranted individualism. Rawls's response was that, in his theory, primary goods are to be understood in terms of a Kantian conception of the human subject as a moral agent that can follow public principles of justice and simultaneously devise and pursue its own ideals of good life.

Even though Rawls modified his original *Theory of Justice* in his Tanner and Dewey lectures and he admitted that his theory represents the ethos of the Western subject, his theory still has two important defects:

i. Rawls tries to find a balance between two goals: the goal of personal liberty (which is reflected in his first maxim of justice and expresses man's attraction to life) and the goal of social equality (which is reflected in his second maxim of justice and expresses man's concerns about the viability and sustainability of life). For this purpose, Rawls has adopted Kant's moral rationalism. Thus, Rawls's theory of justice has the defects of Kant's moral rationalism, which I explained earlier in this chapter.

ii. The second main defect of Rawls's theory of justice is that, even though Rawls tries to avoid the defects of utilitarianism through his "Kantian constructivism", his hypothesis about the "original position" is actually based on a form of utilitarianism. Therefore, Rawls's theory of justice is vulnerable to critical comments similar to the ones that I put forward against utilitarianism earlier in this chapter.

---

200 John Rawls, "Kantian Constructivism in Moral Theory", Journal of Philosophy, Vol. 77, 1980, pp. 515–572 (The Dewey Lectures); John Rawls, "The Basic Liberties and their Priority", in: S.M. McMurrin (ed.), The Tanner Lectures on Human Values, Salt Lake City: University of Utah Press, 1982, Vol. III.

From a social–anthropological perspective, Rawls's theory of justice is founded on a negative definition of liberty (i.e. 'liberty' as 'freedom from' and not as 'freedom for') and on a civilization of rights. Thus, Rawls's theory of justice is opposite to the ethos of the Hesychastic collective, which is founded on the mystery of communion and not on rights, in accordance with *Matthew*, 5:39–44, and *Philippians*, 2:5–11.

Robert Nozick has criticized Rawls's theory of justice from the viewpoint of libertarianism, which is a 20th century radical form of liberalism. A similar type of liberal thought has been articulated by Bruce Ackerman[201].

Nozick objects to the maxim approach altogether. According to Nozick, "to think that the task of a theory of distributive justice is to fill in the blank in 'to each according to his —', is to be predisposed to search for a pattern", but "no end–state principle or distributional pattern principle can be continuously realized without continuous interference in people's lives"[202].

Nozick proposes a 3–part "Entitlement Theory", which is founded on the following inductive definition of justice[203]: (i) *Principle of justice in acquisition:* If a person has acquired a holding in a just manner, then the given person is entitled to that holding. (ii) *Principle of justice in transfer:* If a person has acquired a holding in accordance with the principle of justice in transfer, from someone else entitled to the holding, then the given person is entitled to the holding. (iii) *Principle of rectification of injustice:* No one is entitled to a holding except by repeated applications of principles (i) and (ii). Thus, entitlement implies that "a distribution is just if everyone is entitled to the holdings they possess under the distribution"[204]. But not everyone follows these rules: "some people steal from others, or defraud them, or enslave them, seizing their product and preventing them from living as they choose, or forcibly exclude others from competing in exchanges"[205]. Hence, Nozick argues, the principle of rectification of injustice is necessary.

---

201   Bruce Ackerman, Social Justice and the Liberal State, New Haven, Conn.: Yale University Press, 1980.

202   Robert Nozick, "Distributive Justice", in J. Westphal (ed.), Justice, Indianapolis: Hackett Publishing Company, 1996, p. 17.

203   Nozick, Anarchy, State and Utopia, p. 151.

204   Ibid, p. 151.

205   Ibid, p. 152.

Entitlement theory is based on John Locke's ideas about 'natural rights'. In fact, in the fifth chapter of his *Second Treatise on Government*, Locke formulates and defends the principle of justice in acquisition and the principle of justice in transfer. Nozick's theory of justice is based on his self–ownership argument, which has been summarized by Will Kymlicka[206] as follows: (i) People own themselves. (ii) The world is initially owned by nobody. (iii) One can acquire absolute rights over a disproportionate share of the world, if he does not worsen the condition of others. (iv) It is relatively easy to acquire absolute rights over a disproportionate share of the world. Therefore: (v) Given that private property has been appropriated, a free market in capital and labour is morally required.

Nozick's key syllogism is that people own themselves, and, therefore, they also own their talents and productive abilities as well as whatever they can produce with those talents and productive abilities. Furthermore, Nozick stresses that, in a free market, one can sell the products of exercising his talents and productive abilities and that any taxation of the income from such selling "institute[s] (partial) ownership by others of people and their actions and labor"[207].

The three main defects of Nozick's theory of justice are the following:

i.   Nozick defines the autonomy of the individual in terms of 'self–ownership'. But he does not explain why self–ownership is only compatible with such strong property rights. Self–ownership is equivalent to such strong property rights only if one assumes that his ownership of himself is equivalent to his ownership of the commodities that he produces and/or purchases. But, if one makes the previous assumption, then he degrades himself into a commodity. If one degrades himself into a commodity, then he cannot logically prove that he is superior to other commodities or that he legitimately owns other commodities (since he is also a commodity).

ii. In its attempt to assign meanings and significances to

---

206   Will Kymlicka, Contemporary Political Philosophy, Oxford: Clarendon Press, 1990, p. 112.
207   Nozick, Anarchy, State and Utopia, p. 172.

things, consciousness has the continuous tendency to follow two psychological paths, i.e. extroversion and introversion, and the ego needs assistance from and cooperation with other egos. Nozick seems to ignore these things and to assume that the human being is characterized only by its self–ownership, as if it were an ontologically self–sufficient being. Nozick's principle of self–ownership does not take into account the essence of personhood, which is intimately related to the process of socialization.

iii. Nozick delineates human autonomy in purely economic terms without explaining why every other interpretation of autonomy is irrelevant. He ignores that the true autonomy of the human being presupposes that human life has many meanings (and thus it is not exhausted in the production and consumption of commodities) and that human beings can set various goals about which they can argue that they are worth pursuing. Furthermore, Harvard philosopher Michael Sandel, author of *What Money Can't Buy — The Moral Limits of Markets*[208], has analyzed the evils of 20th century U.S. capitalism and how it rocks the moral fiber of the U.S. In particular, in his previous essay, Sandel pointed out that, "when people buy and sell things under conditions of severe inequality or dire economic necessity", market exchanges are neither as fair nor as voluntary as Nozick and other market enthusiasts maintain.

Furthermore, since, as I argued in chapter 5, the beings and things in the world are united with their transcendental *logoi*, contra Nozick, we do not own what we have. This point is emphasized in the Bible in *Leviticus*, 25:23, and in *Numbers*, 31:25–30. Additionally, in *James*, 2:2–4, we read that it is wrong to judge a person by his economic possessions.

Jon Elster is a prominent representative of 'analytical Marxism' (an individualist reworking of Marx based on game theory) and

---

208 Michael Sandel, What Money Can't Buy —The Moral Limits of Markets, Oxford: Brasenose College (The Tanner Lectures on Human Values), 1998.

'methodological individualism'. Elster uses analytical theories, and especially rational choice theory, in order to develop scientifically rigorous theories of economics and morality. According to Elster, "rational choice theory is far more than a technical tool for explaining behavior"; "it is also, and very importantly, a way of coming to grips with ourselves —not only what we should do, but even what we should be"[209].

Elster's theory of social choice and his approach to distributive justice are based on his assumption that preferences are endogenous to rational choice models. Elster argues that individual preferences are formed through the process of political decision–making itself[210], and, therefore, individual preferences are not 'a priori' or exogenous. Even though Elster correctly draws attention to the ways in which preferences are modified through the process of political decision–making itself, he does not take into account the fact that, at some point, during the process of political decision-making, individual preferences must be aggregated into a single social preference ranking, which philosophically legitimates functionalism–structuralism.

Furthermore, if one is committed to the rationality postulate alone, as it is understood in classical microeconomics, he will, sooner or later, find himself in the path of operational insignificance. Elster himself (who started his research work with an almost obsessive commitment to rational choice theory), in his later writings, admitted that rational choice theory is not as powerful as he had initially contended. In his book *Explaining Social Behavior*, Elster argues as follows: "I now believe that rational–choice theory has less explanatory power than I used to think. Do real people act on the calculations that make up many pages of mathematical appendixes in leading journals? I do not think so... *There is no general non–intentional mechanism that can simulate or mimic rationality*"[211]. In other words, rational choice theory is not a substitute for teleology or for the transcendent.

---

209 Jon Elster, "Some Unresolved Problems in the Theory of Rational Behavior", Acta Sociologica, Vol. 36, 1993, p. 179.

210 Jon Elster, "The Market and the Forum: Three Varieties of Political Theory", in: J. Elster and A. Hyland (eds), Foundations of Social Choice Theory, Cambridge: Cambridge University Press, 1986, pp. 103–132.

211 Jon Elster, Explaining Social Behavior —More Nuts and Bolts for the Social Sciences, Cambridge: Cambridge University Press, 2007, pp. 5, 25ff.

"Do Not Judge": Judgment and Being

In *Matthew*, 7:1, we read Jesus Christ's teaching about judging: "Do not judge, or you too will be judged". In order to understand the ethical, and in fact the meta–ethical, content of the previous statement, we must keep in mind that the purpose of Christ's Gospel is not to moralize people but to teach them what is the divine mode of being and how to attain it. In essence, Christianity is not a system of morality, but it is a revelation of the path to man's deification. From the perspective of Hesychasm, in particular, morality is not mere adherence to a code, but it is rather the free actions of people acting in accordance with the Divine Logos, who is the ultimate source of the significance of beings and things in the world.

Furthermore, in the context of Christianity, God is neither a supreme judge nor man's superego, but He is the ultimate existential mirror in which man can look at himself and evaluate himself. Therefore, the New Testament teaches that Christ is not the grand master of a moral system, but he is the incarnation of the Divine Logos, that is the revealed channel of God's love in history. Moreover, as I have already argued, from the Hesychastic perspective, love is not a sentiment, but it is a mode of being and more specifically God's mode of being. Thus, in *John*, 13:34, Jesus Christ says: "A new command I give you: Love one another". Moreover: in *John*, 1:3–5, we realize that God's love is bigger than any problem; in *John*, 3:16, we realize that God sets the pattern for love; in *Luke*, 12:7, we realize that God's love is the basis for self–worth; and in *1 Corinthians*, 13:1ff, we realize that love is more important than spiritual gifts.

Hesychasm emphasizes that the purpose of the Church in general and of the clergy in particular is not to discipline people according to a set of moral rules, but their true purpose is to change people's minds in order to harmonize them with God's mode of being, which is love and freedom. Thus, Hesychasm proposes Hesychastic psychotherapy, which I explained in chapter 4, as a substitute for mainstream and coercive moral systems. Inherent in Hesychastic ontology is a Hesychastic meta–ethical attitude. In Hesychasm, the ultimate criterion of judgment is the extent to which man's mode of being reflects God's mode of being.

7

HESYCHASM AND THE SPIRITUALIZATION
OF GEOPOLITICS

MICHAEL Barnett, in his highly influential research paper "Social Constructivism"[212], recognized that international politics is shaped by such ideational factors as the goals, threats, fears, identities, cultures and other elements of the reality of consciousness that influence states and non–state actors within the international system. Hence, according to Barnett, every empirically significant study of international relations must be concerned with how ideas define international structure, how this structure defines the interests and identities of states and how states and non–state actors reproduce this structure[213]. The reality of international politics is socially constructed by cognitive structures that give meaning to the material world[214]. Additionally, as Zbigniew Brzezinski, former Advisor of the U.S. National Security Council under President Carter, has admitted, ideas mobilize political action and hence shape the world.[215]

---

212 Michael Barnett, "Social Constructivism", in: John Baylis, Steve Smith and Patricia Owens (eds), The Globalization of World Politics —An Introduction to International Relations, Oxford: Oxford University Press, 2011, pp. 148–165. Moreover, see: Emanuel Adler, "Seizing the Middle Ground: Constructivism in World Politics", European Journal of International Relations, Vol. 3, 1997, pp. 319–363.

213 Barnett, "Social Constructivism".

214 Adler, "Seizing the Middle Ground".

215 Zbigniew Brzezinski, Out of Control —Global Turmoil on the Eve of the 21st Century, New York: Collier Books, 1993, p. x.

In *Genesis*, 1:27–28, we read that God created humans "in his own image" and that he blessed them and said to them: "Be fruitful and increase in number; fill the earth and subdue it". In philosophical language, the previous Biblical text can be rephrased as follows: The Logos, or the Truth, of the cosmos is universal and exists independently of human consciousness, but the human being can personally and freely partake of the universal Logos and Truth, since the human being has been created "in the image of" God. In other words, the relationship between the universal Logos and the human being is neither mechanistic nor coercive, but it is personal and, therefore, free.

Furthermore, as Maximus the Confessor and several other Greek Church Fathers have pointed out commenting on *Genesis*, 1:27–28, under the condition that man remains connected to, or in communion with, the universal Logos, humanity is the wise royal species of the created cosmos. Thus, to the extent that man remains in communion with the universal Logos, man, as the ruler of the Earth, creates a harmonious world order on the Earth, a world order that reflects the communion that exists among the three Persons of the Holy Trinity (God the Father, or *Nous*; God the Son, or *Logos*; God the Holy Spirit, or *Spirit*). Moreover, to the extent that man remains in communion with the universal Logos, the creations of the human spirit, that is technology[216] and institutions, serve humanity and solve all its historical problems in accordance with the God–

---

216 For instance, Robert Solow has found that, in the United States, during the period 1909–1949, about one–eighth of the increment in labour productivity could be attributed to increased capital per man hour, and the remaining seven–eighths to a factor that is called "Solow residual" and consists of technological progress and other cultural factors that improve efficiency (R.M. Solow, "Technical Change and the Aggregate Production Function", Review of Economics and Statistics, Vol. 39, 1957, pp. 312–320). Paul M. Romer, an American economist and entrepreneur associated with the New York University Stern School of Business and with Stanford University, has put forward the following argument: "Economic growth occurs whenever people take resources and rearrange them in ways that are more valuable. A useful metaphor for production in an economy comes from the kitchen... History teaches us, however, that economic growth springs from better recipes, not just from more cooking" (P.M. Romer, "Compound Rates of Growth", in: http://www.econlib.org). Through science, technology, management and generally through institutions, the creativity of human consciousness can provide substitutes for several natural resources. For instance, antigravity, nuclear fusion and nanotechnology can solve all energy problems. Thus, all those gloom mongers who, under the guise of science, terrorize humanity by talking about the 'dangers' of overpopulation and the lack of food and energy resources simply degrade man from the living image of God into an economic animal exploited by the political and economic oligarchy.

given command "Be fruitful and increase in number; fill the earth and subdue it".

In *1 Corinthians*, 1:3, and in *Philippians*, 4:7, the Apostle Paul emphasizes that an international order, or the general notion of peace, is substantially different from God's peace, since the latter stems from and is founded on the truth that emerges from communion. Thus, John the Evangelist, in *John*, 14:27, characterizes true peace as a gift from the Holy Spirit.

On the contrary, when and to the extent that humanity substitutes either the reason of the human subject itself (rationalism/nominalism /historicism) or the reason of the created nature (biocentrism) for the universal Logos, the individual imaginary of men and human selfishness cause chaos and historical turbulence, since they injure the ability of man's soul to be in communion with the universal Logos. As a consequence of the previous injury in man's soul, men cannot create a communion among themselves, but at best they can create merely selfish associations and alliances. This world of division and selfishness is the reality of geopolitics in its worldly, "profane", secularized form.

Alexander Dugin, the father of the modern Russian geopolitical school, has pointedly observed that modern geopolitics is the product of the laicising and desacralising of a traditional science that is known as "sacred geography". In the context of sacred geography, Cardinal Points have special qualitative significances. In particular, sacred geography, in the context of "space symbolism", traditionally considers the East as the "land of Spirit"; for instance, this idea is mirrored in *Genesis*, 2:8: "the Lord had planted a garden in the East, in Eden". A similar understanding is peculiar also to other Abrahamic traditions (Islam and Judaism) and to many non–Abrahamic traditions, e.g. Iranian, Hindu and Chinese ones. In the context of sacred geography, the West has the opposite symbolic meaning, and it signifies a transition from completeness and spiritual freedom to need and natural necessities.

Furthermore, according to different systems of cosmic symbolism, the ancient traditions organized their "sacred spaces", founded their cultural centers, and interpreted the natural and political geography of the planet[217]. However, modern geopolitics is exclusively focused

---

217   See for instance: Diana L. Eck, India —A Sacred Geography, New York: Three Rivers Press, 2012; Kenneth Pletcher (ed.), The Geography of China —Sacred and Historic Places, Rosen Educational

on material affairs, leaving out of its analytical framework the spiritual aspects of geography.

UNDERSTANDING MODERN GEOPOLITICS

The term geopolitics (Geopolitik) was coined by the Swedish political scientist Rudolf Kjellén at the University of Gothenburg at about the same time as Friedrich Ratzel was structuring the academic discipline of political geography in Berlin[218]. Kjellén was strongly influenced by Ratzel, and he defined geopolitics as "the science which conceives of the state as a geographical organism or as a phenomenon in space"[219]. According to Kjellén, the state organism was engaged in a perpetual struggle for life and space, and only the fittest and most adaptable could be expected to survive and prosper. Both Ratzel and Kjellén were influenced by the Darwinism of the time and zoological research, and this fact signals an ontological degradation of the human being.

In the later 19th century, Alfred Thayer Mahan[220], the well–known United States Navy flag officer, geostrategist and historian, put forward the idea of the global dichotomy of land and sea power and laid stress on the importance of the latter for the security of the world's great maritime states. This theme was soon taken up in Great Britain by Sir Halford John Mackinder, who was an influential English geographer and Director of the London School of Economics. Mackinder[221] went further than Mahan by proposing an interpretation of world history based on geographical thinking. According to Mackinder, the underlying theme running through world history was the conflict between land power and sea power.

Mackinder maintains that the Earth's land surface is divisible into: (i) the "World–Island" (comprising of the interlinked continents of Europe, Asia, and Africa), (ii) the "offshore islands" (including the British Isles and the islands of Japan), and (iii) the "outlying islands"

Publishing, 2010; Jean Richer, Sacred Geography of the Ancient Greeks, trans. Christine Rhone, New York: State University of New York Press, 1994.

218 Bertil Häggman, Rudolf Kjellén —Founder of Geopolitics, Helsingborg: Center for Research on Geopolitics, 1988.

219 Rudolf Kjellén, Der Staat als Lebensform, Leipzig: Hirzel, 1917.

220 A.T. Mahan, The Influence of Sea Power on History, 1660–1783, London: Samson Low, 1889.

221 H.J. Mackinder, "The Geographical Pivot of History", Geographical Journal, Vol. 23, 1904, pp. 421–444.

(including the continents of North America, South America and Australia). The "Heartland"[222] lay at the centre of the world island, stretching from the Volga to the Yangtze and from the Himalayas to the Arctic; Mackinder has also called this vast land–locked region "the Pivot of World History".

Mackinder's Heartland was the area then ruled by the Russian Empire and after that by the Soviet Union, minus the Kamchatka Peninsula region. With its enormous economic potential and its inaccessibility to sea power, this region —argued Mackinder— would eventually evolve into the leading world power. It was up to the maritime states, led by the British Empire, to prevent this scenario from happening. During the Cold War, Mackinder's theory was used to provide a geopolitical underpinning for the global ideological confrontation in general and for Sovietology in particular[223].

During World War II, an American school of geopolitics emerged. Yale political scientist Nicholas Spykman articulated an analysis of the position of the United States "in terms of geography and power politics", in order to allow for the formulation of "a grand strategy for both war and peace based on the implications of its geographic location in the world"[224]. Spykman's geopolitical theory played an important role in reorienting American foreign policy from isolationism to "interventionist globalism". Drawing upon Mackinder, Spykman stressed the critical significance of what Mackinder termed "Inner or Marginal Crescent", i.e. the periphery, which he named the Rimland[225].

During the Cold War, Sovietology was a key area of research within the context of strategic studies in the United States. After the end of the Cold War, in the U.S. strategic studies Programs, the concept of Sovietology was succeeded by the concept of Eurasian studies, which is concerned with the methodical study of the post–Soviet space (including the Russian Federation and the other former Soviet republics). Hence, the research program of Eurasian studies is

---

222 H.J. Mackinder, Democratic Ideas and Reality —A Study in the Politics of Reconstruction, London: Constable, 1919.

223 R.E. Walters, The Nuclear Trap, Harmondsworth: Penguin Books, 1974.

224 N.J. Spykman, America's Strategy in World Politics —The United States and the Balance of Power, New York: Harcourt, Brace, 1942, p. 8.

225 D.W. Meinig, "Heartland and Rimland in Eurasian History", The Western Political Quarterly, Vol. 9, 1956, pp. 553–569.

a continuation of Sovietology with other means —namely, adjusted to the post–Soviet reality.

After the end of the ideological warfare between the U.S. and the Soviet camps, there emerged an ideologically unipolar world due to the worldwide spread and domination of the Western and primarily American model of liberal democracy, market capitalism and consumerist and hedonistic lifestyle, as it has been exemplified by Francis Fukuyama in his controversial book *The End of History and the Last Man*[226]. In that book, Fukuyama declared "the end of history", in the sense that, according to his analysis, after the end of the Cold War, there was no alternative to the ideology of the American camp and the world was (ideologically) unified, since there was a global conformity to the ideology of the American camp.

In essence, according to Fukuyama and according to the West's liberal democracy in general, the logos of the Western collective subject, as it is exemplified by the interests and norms of the Western political and economic oligarchy and as it is delineated by liberal scholars, is the perfect substitute for the ancient Greek philosophers' and for the Christians' universal Logos. In other words, through liberal democracy and globalization, the West attempts to restore the ethos and the mentality of the Pharaohs, who were substituting their own logos for the Divine Logos (*Exodus*, 5:1–2).

Capitalism, which is a necessary component of the West's liberal–globalist bloc, is an institution of society whose central value is the unlimited expansion of rational mastery in accordance with the physiocratic fallacy, which I explained in chapter 3. That is why capitalism may very well adjust to the absence of private property (e.g. in the case of the Soviet Union's state capitalism) and to a centralized, autocratic state (e.g. crony capitalism, fascism, etc.). What matters is the masters and possessors of natural resources and of human labour. In the context of this rational organization of human life, the population is privatized, in the sense that the population does not participate in political life. The outcome is that the affairs of the community are administered by a coercive monologue that corresponds to the capitalist imaginary. Voting every four, five or seven years for persons that you do not really know, on problems that you do not really understand and that the system has taken care to prevent you from understanding is an

---

226   Francis Fukuyama, The End of History and the Last Man, New York: Free Press, 1992.

illusion of participation and a degenerate form of liberal democracy. The domination of an oligarchy, which can be understood as the 'priesthood' of the capitalist imaginary, and the passivity and privatization of the people are the two pillars of the regime of liberal oligarchy. Liberal oligarchy is the dominant form of liberalism in the context of Western modernity and capitalism.

Fukuyama's argument about "the end of history" was soon qualified and partially refuted by Samuel Huntington[227]. In the 1990s, Huntington showed that, even though the ideological war between the U.S. capitalism and the U.S.S.R. socialism was over, there were new kinds of confronting entities —namely, civilizations. Huntington has written extensively about "the clash of civilizations" and the return of geopolitics. It is important to stress that, in the post–Cold War era, geopolitics returned in spite of the end of the ideological war between the U.S.A. and the U.S.S.R. Thus, Huntington explained to the Atlanticist elite that the establishment of a global system of Western monologue would not be as easy as the Atlanticist elite had originally assumed.

The renewal of geopolitics in the post–Cold War era has been strongly influenced by Zbigniew Brzezinski, who is one of the most influential American political scientists, geostrategists and statesmen. Brzezinski has played a key role in the creation of the post–Cold War Atlanticist geopolitical doctrine[228].

Mackinder has formulated the following hypothesis: "who rules the Heartland commands the World–Island; who rules the World–Island commands the world". Furthermore, Mackinder has argued that there are two ways in which one can control the Heartland: the one is controlling "from without" and the other is controlling "from within". Brzezinski, following Mackinder's geopolitical thought, has argued that the Atlanticists, or sea powers, should command the World–Island by encircling the Heartland (from Europe, from the Middle East, from the Persian Gulf, from the Indian subcontinent and from the Sea of China). This strategic plan for controlling the Heartland from without gives the Atlanticists the possibility to rule the world.

---

227 S.P. Huntington, The Clash of Civilizations —Remaking of World Order, New York: Simon and Schuster, 1996.

228 Zbigniew Brzezinski, The Grand Chessboard —American Primacy and Its Geostrategic Imperatives, New York: Basic Books, 1998.

On the other hand, in the post–Cold War era, Russia tries to control the Heartland from within. In other words, Russia tries to control the post–Soviet space in order to project its influence across the borders. In this context, in the beginning of the 21st century, Russia's geostrategic interests are strongly associated with the North Stream and the South Stream energy pipelines, whereas the U.S. pipeline diplomacy in the Caspian strives to bypass Russia, elbow out China and isolate Iran.

In the post–Cold War era, the Atlanticist geopolitical thought gave birth to two models of organizing political space worldwide: (i) unipolarity, which has been endorsed and promoted by the neoconservatives[229] and generally by leading members of the Republican Party in the United States, and (ii) multilateralism, which has been endorsed and promoted by the so–called neoliberal school of international politics and by leading members of the U.S. Democratic Party. According to the unipolar model, the U.S. should be the core of the world system, as a kind of liberal–democratic empire, and all other states should be organized around the U.S. on, more or less, the same strategic and ideological basis. On the other hand, according to the U.S. neoliberal school of international politics, or the U.S. globalists, the U.S. should partly give up its hegemonic pretensions and share its rule of the world with other powers, primarily with the powers that are close to the U.S. in terms of history and values[230].

Both the unipolar vision of the world (associated with the U.S. Republicans) and the multilateral, or globalist, model of the world (associated with the U.S. Democrats) share the ambition of imposing a unique model of organization, and, in fact, one *logos*, on the world,

---

229 Neoconservatism is an intellectual movement born in the 1960s inside the monthly review Commentary, which is is the journal of the American Jewish Committee. The most influential neoconservative scholars, such as Norman Podhoretz and his son John, Irving Kristol and his son William, Donald Kagan and his son Robert, Paul Wolfowitz and Abram Schulsky, refer explicitly to the political philosophy of Leo Strauss to such an extent that they describe themselves as "Straussians". The military and foreign policies of the Republican U.S. Presidents Ronald Reagan, George H.W. Bush and George W. Bush were strongly influenced by neoconservative advisors.

230 On 26 September 2012, at the European Forum for New Ideas" (EFNI), in Warsaw, Zbigniew Brzezinski gave a lecture entitled "The Role of the West in the Complex Post–Hegemonic World". In the context of that lecture, Brzezinski argued that "global domination by any single power is no longer a realistic international prospect", and that the Atlanticist powers "have no choice but to promote wider geopolitical cooperation".

and they differ only in methodological terms: the unipolar model is based on an explicitly hegemonic policy, according to which the national interest of the U.S. should become the measure of the national interest for all the other states, whereas the multilateral model is based on an implicit, or "soft"[231], hegemonic policy, according to which all the people are obliged to accept the value system and the dominant mentalities of the U.S.

The American globalists' or neoliberals' universalizing narrative of the unfolding of a rational system of world history, founded on American liberal democracy and capitalism, is simply a negative form of the American neoconservatives' and generally Republicans' imperialism. The American neoliberals, such as Joseph Nye Jr and Francis Fukuyama, though critical of the neoconservatives' imperialism, concluded that the exercise of the American "smart power" on non–Western countries through such operations as the "Arab Spring" and the insurgency against the Assad regime in Syria was ultimately for the best because it brought those countries into the evolutionary narrative of Western history, thus creating the conditions for the compliance of those countries with Washington's values and understanding of development. This is an arrogant and arrogating narrative.

The Moral Standing of the Atlanticist Geopolitical Thought

As I have already explained, in the context of Hesychasm and of classical Greek philosophy, 'evil' means lack of communion with the ultimate significance of being. Plato, Aristotle and the Hesychasts understand the ultimate significance of being as a Logos that is universal and transcendental —and, therefore, it cannot be manipulated or controlled by any particular human being or organization— and simultaneously it can be personally related to (and participated by) each human being. In the context of the previous understanding of Logos, there are simultaneously universalism and individualism. In contrast to the previous spiritual traditions, the Atlanticist geopolitical thought promotes the universal domination of the logos of the Atlanticist historical subject, and, therefore,

---

231   Nye Jr., Soft Power. Joseph Nye Jr. is a very influential American political scientist, statesman and former Dean of the John F. Kennedy School of Government at Harvard University. Moreover, he is the co-founder, along with Robert Keohane, of the "neoliberal theory" of international relations.

the Atlanticist geopolitical thought is inherently and inalienably connected with war, competition, authoritarianism, oligarchy and exploitation.

On 4 January 2013, Glen Greenwald wrote in *The Guardian* that the actions of the US officials ensure that the "War on Terror" will continue indefinitely, since US actions are the cause of that war[232]. Moreover, in the same article, Glen Greenwald mentioned that the U.S. is aware of the fact that terrorism is motivated not by hatred for the U.S. liberal–democratic system but by U.S. policy and aggression in the Islamic world. Exactly for this reason, Glen Greenwald maintains, the U.S. political elite continues this policy: U.S. leaders, officials of the National Security system and beneficiaries of the private military and surveillance industries accumulate political and economic power through the "war on terror".

Carroll Quigley, Professor of History at Georgetown University, where he was former U.S. President Bill Clinton's mentor, has analyzed the role and the strategy of the global financial elite in his seminal book *Tragedy and Hope — A History of the World in Our Time*. Quigley argues that the banking system's power over government is based on government financing and personal influence as well as on other pressures. Furthermore, Quigley points out that the history of the 19th and the 20th centuries shows that the advice given to governments by bankers, like the advice they gave to industrialists, was consistently serving the bankers' own interests, but it was often disastrous for governments, businessmen, and the people generally. Such advice, Quigley continues, could be enforced by manipulation of exchanges, gold flows, discount rates and even levels of business activity. The far–reaching aim of the powers of financial capitalism has been to create a world system of financial control capable of dominating the political system of each country and the economy of the world as a whole and being itself controlled in a feudalist fashion by the central banks of the world acting in concert on the basis of secret agreements[233].

In the 2010s, the Eurozone officially adopted the system of financial fascism by applying a series of bail–out Programs and by

---

232 Glen Greenwald, "The 'War on Terror' —By Design— Can Never End", The Guardian, 4 January 2013.

233 Carroll Quigley, Tragedy and Hope —A History of the World in Our Time, New York: Macmillan, 1966, pp. 62, 324.

initiating a bail–in strategy in Cyprus in April 2013. The notion of financial fascism has been explained by the Italian historian Gaetano Salvemini, who has written that fascism makes taxpayers responsible to private enterprise, because "the State pays for the blunders of private enterprise...Profit is private and individual. Loss is public and social"[234].

In her thought–provoking book *La Crise Sans Fin* (2012), the distinguished French philosopher Myriam Revault d'Allonnes of the École des hautes études en sciences sociales argues that the global crisis that broke out in 2008 is not simply a phase of a historical evolutionary process about which one can tell where it comes from and where it goes to[235]. Nor is it simply one of the known crises of the economic cycle, which will be succeeded by similar crises. Almost five years after the onset of this crisis, the world talks about "the crisis" ("la crise") —as Professor Myriam Revault d'Allonnes has pointed out— which is not like other crises, but it is a global crisis of finance, education, culture, interpersonal relations, family (including the institution of marriage) and the natural environment.

After analyzing the notion of crisis according to ancient, medieval and modern philosophers, Myriam Revault d'Allonnes concludes that 'crisis', more than a concept, is a metaphor that refers not only to an objective reality but also to a life experience. Hence, crisis narrates and demonstrates the difficulty of the early 21st century humans to envisage the orientation of their itinerary towards the future.

Furthermore, according to Myriam Revault d'Allonnes, at the dawn of the 21st century, it became clear that crisis as a concept and as an experience has been mutated: in its original meaning, crisis signifies the 'decisive moment' in the course of an uncertain process, which, nonetheless, can be diagnosed and, therefore, it can be managed towards the 'conclusion of the drama'; instead, as a result

---

234 Gaetano Salvemini, Under the Axe of Fascism, (1936) reprint ed. Lyle Stuart, 1971, p. 416. The relationship between the Eurozone and financial fascism was methodically analyzed by the distinguished French politician and economist Jean–Jacques Rosa in his book Euro Exit —How (and Why) to Get Rid of the Monetary Union, New York: Algora Publishing, 2012. Moreover, the international political and economic think–tank Schiller Institute has published several articles and research papers that explain the imposition of financial fascism in the Euroatlantic world in the 20th century.

235 Myriam Revault d'Allonnes, La Crise Sans Fin —Essai sur l' expérience moderne du temps, Paris: Seuil, 2012.

of the crisis that broke out in the first decade of the 21st century, humanity experiences the moment, or the challenge, of structural uncertainty about the causes, the consequences and the general dynamics of the issue. Thus, humanity cannot see the 'conclusion of the drama' in the historical horizon.

ALTERNATIVE GEOPOLITICAL RESEARCH PROGRAMS

The most important criticism against the ideological underpinnings of the Atlanticist school of geopolitics in the United States has been articulated by the paleoconservatives. Paleoconservatives in the 21st century often highlight their points of disagreement with neoconservatism, especially regarding issues such as military interventionism, multiculturalism, foreign aid (in the context of U.S. "smart power"), illegal immigration and large amounts of legal immigration (especially of culturally alien people), to which they are opposed[236].

Paleoconservatives are strongly critical of the neoconservatives and their sympathizers. Additionally, paleoconservatives often argue that they are not conservatives in the sense that they necessarily wish to preserve existing institutions or seek merely to control the growth of the government's powers. They do not wish to be closely identified with the U.S. Republican Party, because they seek the renewal of "small r" republican society in the context of the Western political tradition. In particular, Joseph Scotchie has argued for the classical republicanism, in the context of which the powers of the government are limited and the government is accountable to the citizens, and he has contrasted classical republicanism with the neoconservatives' imperialism.

Paleoconservativism emphasizes tradition and rootedness. Historian W. Wesley McDonald[237] argues that a humane social order is necessarily founded on a community of spirit reflected in religious dogmas, traditions, humane letters, social habit and custom and prescriptive institutions. James Kalb[238] argues that tradition succeeds where ideology fails, because tradition includes elements of the

---

236   Joseph Scotchie (ed.), The Paleoconservatives —New Voices of the Old Right, Transaction Publishers, 1999.

237   W. Wesley McDonald, Russell Kirk and the Age of Ideology, Columbia: University of Missouri Press, 2004.

238   James Kalb, The Tyranny of Liberalism, Intercollegiate Studies Institute, 2008.

human soul (such as habits and attitudes about things) that are hard to articulate rationally. According to Joseph Sobran, tradition does not imply "resisting change", but it demands from us to consciously decide what can and should be salvaged from "devouring time"[239].

Paleoconservatism has articulated an accurate criticism of the neoconservatives' imperialist policy and of the neoliberal theory of international relations, which is the intellectual foundation of the U.S. globalists. But paleoconservatism itself has an important intellectual weakness —namely, most paleoconservatives work within the scholastic paradigm of the medieval West (especially philosophical realism and Thomism), and, therefore, they cannot offer effective cures for the spiritual causes of neoconservativism and neoliberal globalization.

The most promising anti–doctrine against the Atlanticists' internationalism is Eurasianism, because Eurasianism is opposed to U.S. liberalism and simultaneously it is not a nationalist ideology but an internationalist one. In other words, Eurasianism is a form of anti–liberal internationalism.

The acknowledged father of Eurasianism is Alexander Dugin[240], who is one of the most influential faculty members of the Moscow State University and a leading Russian politologist. Dugin's Eurasianism is, to a large extent, a Russian anti–doctrine against the U.S. geostrategic models of unipolarity and multilateralism. According to Dugin, both the unipolar model and the multilateral model of the U.S. geostrategic elite are intimately related to the attempt of the Atlanticists to control Eurasia from without and thus achieve global hegemony. Additionally, Dugin maintains that both the unipolar model and the multilateral model of the U.S. geostrategic elite aim to counter any potential alternative hegemonic power and to destroy any civilization that could challenge the Western value system as the latter is construed and promoted by the U.S. In both cases, Eurasia is the political, the strategic and the cultural space that the West tries to overcome and control.

The attitude of the Russian school of geopolitics and of many Russian statesmen, including President Vladimir Putin, is to accept the role of Eurasia and to recognize Russia as the Heartland of

---

239 Joseph Sobran, "Pensees: Notes for the Reactionary of Tomorrow", National Review, 31 December 1985.

240 Dugin, The Fourth Political Theory.

Eurasia, i.e. as the centre of land power. Dugin has stressed that this Eurasian geopolitical identity is something new, because it is not an imperialist idea for the continuation of the tsarist empire, it is not a continuation of the Soviet Union with its ideology, and it is not a nationalist ideology of the Russian Federation itself as a nation–state. This new Eurasian geopolitical identity, Dugin maintains, is a new civilization proposal, and thus it refers to a geopolitical entity that does not have exact borders, since the limits of a civilization do not coincide with the borders of specific nation–states. Even though Russia is the Heartland of Eurasia, Eurasianism is a separate, new identity, because it is a kind of civilization that aims to unite not only the population of the Russian Federation but also all the people that live in the post–Soviet space and even some populations in Eastern Europe, in the Balkans, in Turkey, in Afghanistan, etc.

Dugin stresses that Eurasia is a separate civilization pole and that, therefore, it should not be compared with individual nation–states, but it should be compared with entire civilization poles, such as Europe, the Hindu civilization, the Chinese civilization, etc. This thesis has led the Russian school of geopolitics to a new vision for world architecture, which is neither unipolar nor multilateral (globalist), but it is multipolar.

According to Dugin, a multipolar world is a system of different civilizations, or a system of different regional hegemonies. In particular, Dugin following Carl Schmitt's terminology, has explained that his vision for a multipolar world comprises the following "Grossraums" (Great Spaces), i.e. regional hegemonies, which could create a worldwide system of balance of power:

- the North Atlantic, or 'Western', civilization with its two components, i.e. the American one and the European one (however, certain Continental powers in Europe, mainly Germany and France, tend to pursue a more autonomous role for Europe vis–à–vis the U.S.);

- Eurasia;

- the Islamic civilization zone;

- the Hindu civilization zone centered on the Indian subcontinent;

- the Chinese civilization zone (comprising of China, Taiwan and other Asian regions in which the Chinese influence is strong);

- a separate Latin American strategic space founded on Latin civilization, Roman Catholicism and local cultural traditions;

- a Japanese regional hegemonic system;

- an African, Trans–Saharan unified political space.

Dugin's model of multipolarity is not a proposal to return to balance–of–power arrangements among nation–states. Dugin is well aware that, in the 21st century, national sovereignty is an important legal concept, but it has reduced geopolitical relevance. Thus, Dugin's multipolarity model is a system of integrated regions, and, therefore, it is different both from the state–centric models of balance of power and from the globalist model, which is based on the idea of global integration and global monologue. Dugin's multipolarity model is a "polilogue" of different groups of people with their own temporalities, spaces, visions of cosmos, cultural identities, instead of subscribing to a globalization policy that is based on a Western monologue, which ultimately reduces to a melting pot and to an authoritarian world system. Thus, Dugin combines topography with man's soul into a kind of geography of soul, updating and expanding the ancient notion of sacred geography.

Inherent in Dugin's geopolitical theory is a notion of personhood, and, therefore, his theory is concerned with the protection and the expression of international–political actors' existential otherness. In fact, Dugin has pointedly argued that his multipolar geopolitical model is the only way to save the West from itself and also to protect the Rest from the West.

According to Dugin, the liberal model of globalization, which was set in motion by the West during the end of the 20th century, becomes more and more insecure, disastrous and self–destroying, being based on the quite weak, questionable and unjustified presumption of the universality of the 'Western logos'. This Western form of globalization is a 'monologue' that, following the Western genealogy of ratio, imposes an uniformed and standardized set of values, practices and technologies on different, heterogeneous cultures, societies and religions. Proceeding in this direction, Dugin maintains, the previous form of globalization will erode the Western values at its core, inevitably provoking global resistance against the new kind of colonialism and consolidate radical anti–Western forces all over the world.

Furthermore, Dugin has pointedly observed that the West is losing its own identity precisely at the moment when this identity seems to have become universal and reached the most distant areas of the Earth. The West is afraid of peoples' personhood and especially of peoples' existential otherness, because its goal is to impose a system of generalized conformity to a particular monologue, which is dictated by the liberal oligarchy that rules the West. In its attempt to eliminate the other's existential otherness, the West promotes nihilism on a global scale, and ultimately the West itself becomes one of the victims of its own nihilistic policy.

In *Out of Control*, Brzezinski, writing from a Western perspective, suggests that, in the end of the 20th century, the world clearly entered a historical phase in which it is "like a plane on automatic pilot, with its speed continuously accelerating but with no defined destination"[241]. In the same book, Brzezinski argues that "the global crisis of the spirit has to be overcome if humanity is to assert command over its destiny"[242], and he warns the West that it cannot claim a leading role in the management of international affairs if it is part of this "global crisis of the spirit". The liberal globalization project creates and promotes an international system that is dominated by rhetoric and values that are primarily consumption oriented and that reflects utilitarianism and hedonism and imposes conformity to a mechanistic economic order. This is a world order of self–complacent nihilism[243], through which a global political and economic oligarchy attempts to establish itself as a global Pharaoh, i.e. as the ultimate source of the world's fundamental significations and social 'correctness'.

---

241 Brzezinski, Out of Control, p. xiv.

242 Ibid, p. 230.

243 The word nihilism comes from the Latin terms 'ne' (= 'not') + 'hilum' (= 'a hilum'), i.e. it signifies 'uprooted', or spiritually hovering and disconnected people.

THE RESTORATION OF PERSONHOOD IN GEOPOLITICS

The Atlanticist geopolitical thought is a rationalist attempt to restore the political ethos of the Pharaohs with modern means and to establish the global domination of a Western monologue. The major Western institutions of global governance, such as the International Monetary Fund, the Eurozone, the Federal Reserve System, and a network of NGOs promoting human rights, biocentrism and "green development" (as a form of soft power, or advanced propaganda) serve the previous goal. In the context of the Atlanticist geopolitical thought and liberal globalization, the human being is ontologically degraded into a conformist, undifferentiated element of a system that reflects the established monologue.

But any international order is caused radically (in the ontological sense) by something else, i.e. by the intentionality of the consciousness of the international actors. Any international order is not a datum to be reckoned with by the particular members of the world system, but it is a creation of consciousness. Therefore, a humane and viable world order is a world order of particularity, i.e. a multipolar system in the sense of Eurasianism. Alexander Dugin's theory of Eurasianism gives rise to the ontology of freedom in the field of international relations, but there are risks involved, too.

The first risk involved in Dugin's Eurasianism is that, by over-emphasizing the actors' existential otherness and by isolating the actors' existential otherness from their socialization in the world system, Eurasianism can cultivate aggressive individualism (in this case, by the term 'individual', I mean an international-political actor, e.g. a state, a civilization zone, etc.), instead of promoting the idea of personhood. As I have already pointed out, a 'person' is a socialized individual, or an-individual-in-a-relationship. Therefore, international-political actors (e.g. states and civilization zones) can become 'persons' only if they are partakers of a truth that transcends international-political actors themselves. As a result of its participation in the transcendent, an international-political actor acquires an individual value (exactly due to its relationship with the transcendent), and the different international-political actors that are aware of their participation in the transcendent constitute an international-political society, i.e. they recognize each other as members of a truth that can be participated by each one of them but transcends every one of them. In other words, international-political actors can become persons only if they have a common, universal, existential mirror in which they can look at themselves and evaluate themselves.

The second risk involved in Dugin's Eurasianism is that it may cultivate the mentality that people are *necessarily*, i.e. ontologically, restricted by geopolitical categories or that people are *necessarily* prisoners of geopolitical divisions. On the contrary, due to the freedom of spirit, man is not a being of the earth, or *gaia*, but he is a being of a "place beyond heaven" according to the terminology that is used by Plato in *Phaedrus*. Humanity is determined by geopolitical necessities only if and to the extent that it compromises its spiritual freedom and therefore it decides to be ontologically self-degraded. Thus, according to *John*, 4:21-24, Jesus Christ said to a Samaritan woman that there would no longer be limitations of geography in worshiping God, for "God is spirit, and those who worship him must worship in spirit and truth". In other words, man's relationship with his existential purpose transcends geopolitics and sacred geography.

The ontology of particularity is a *condition sine qua non* for the creation of a world order worthy of human beings. However, we must answer the following question: how can we socialize the actors of the international system, and, furthermore, how can we prevent particularity from degenerating into aggressive and destructive individuality?

International relations are unthinkable without the event of communication. Hence, the event of communication in the international sphere manifests each world order not simply as something instituted, that is, historically *given*, but as something *constituted*, that is constantly realized (structured and restructured) as an event of intentional communication. Each actor of the world system (including what Dugin calls civilization zones) is ontologically founded on communication, which means that –contra nationalism and fascism– there is no such thing as pure international-political subject, conceivable in itself, and simultaneously –contra the U.S. model of multilateralism/globalism– communication is founded on a concrete and free person.

In world politics, as in the context of societal relations in general, the person (e.g. nation-states, alliances, civilization zones, etc.) cannot exist without communication, and, therefore, the globalists are right to the extent that they recognize and declare the ontological significance of communication. Simultaneously, communication should never deny or suppress the person, and, therefore, the anti-globalists (including the Eurasian movement) are right when they recognize and declare the ontological significance of otherness. The previous arguments lead us to what the Greek Church Fathers in general and the Hesychasts in particular mean by the term hypostatic mode of being, or personhood. In other words, Hesychasm urges us to think about international relations in terms of communion.

The Hesychasts' understanding of communion can operate as a very important spiritual underpinning of the United Nations and promote the idea of an 'international-political person'. The United Nations belongs to no particular international-political actor, since it is intrinsically international, and, therefore, in principle, it can serve every international-political actor. From this perspective, the United Nations has an unrivaled moral status in the international-political system.

The tradition of Hesychasm can further empower the United Nations by highlighting the United Nations as a global society of international-political persons. In the context of such a model of global society, each and every international-political actor can freely experience its existential otherness, but simultaneously it is socialized through its participation in a universal truth, i.e. in a truth that transcends history and individual interests. In particular, the universal truth that can transform the United Nations into a global society of international-political persons is the freedom of the human being from historical necessity and the acknowledgement of the human being as the universal mediator who unifies the world with its existential purpose. This image of a universe that reveals its vocation through man has been stressed by Maximus the Confessor and is particularly significant for an ontologically grounded humanism, which should be the spiritual core of every institution of global governance.

The aforementioned approach to international relations, which emphasizes the transformation of the international-political actors into international-political *persons* ('individuals-in-relationships') and the transformation of the United Nations into a global society of international-political persons, posits that "legitimized relationships" are the norm in a prescriptive sense, according to

C.R. Mitchell's terminology[244]. According to Mitchell, legitimized relationships are not the same as 'legal' or 'legalized' relationships; the latter are frequently based on coercion or on the threat of sanctions by the stronger against the weaker. The key characteristic of legitimized relationships is that the actors involved in them accept them as being beneficial and 'right'. This conception echoes the ethos of the Hesychastic collective and the Orthodox Christian principles of conciliarity and discretion. Furthermore, following Mitchell's theory of world society, the second fundamental characteristic of legitimized relationships is that they tend to be self-sustaining due to their acceptability by those involved. In contrast, non-legitimized relationships are those which contain elements of coercion and threat.

Dugin's multipolarity principle is a necessary presupposition for the establishment of a world society, since it protects each actor's existential otherness and leads to the creation of regional hegemonies founded on common culture and freedom of consciousness. Furthermore, the Hesychastic notion of personhood is the necessary spiritual underpinning of society in general. Without the principle of personhood, society reduces to a fragile association of individual interests or to a coercive rationalist order, in which individuals are aggregated like objects. In other words, without the principle of personhood, the attempt to create a society is chimerical. Therefore, in the political sphere, Hesychasm can be understood as the meta-political custodian of society and in general of the event of communion and furthermore as the most solid metaphysical foundation of humanism. By looking at politics from a meta-political standpoint, i.e. from outside the political sphere itself, Hesychasm can grasp the reason and the purpose of the entire political stage, since a Hesychast transcends mere individuality and understands that his identity is located in his communion with the universal Logos and with his fellow humans, who are also partakers of the universal Logos. The Hesychasts' humanism is based neither on the 'cogito' (I know) principle nor on the 'sum' (am) principle, but it is based on the declaration "Ye are gods" (*John*, 10:34), i.e. on the awareness that our humanity is based on and stems from our divinity.

---

244   C.R. Mitchell, "World Society a Cobweb: States, Actors and Systematic Processes", in: M. Banks (ed.), Conflict in World Society, Brighton: Harvester, 1984.

The Hesychastic principles of personhood and communion and the Hesychastic teaching about the deification of man imply that the human being is ontologically and morally prior and hence superior to any historical entity (state, nation, etc.), since "God created humankind in his image" (*Genesis*, 1:27). Even though human beings are shaped by the historical communities to which they belong, their value and their existential purpose transcend every historical community. This is the essence of the Hesychastic cosmopolitanism. Thus, even though each community may have its own ethics (i.e. its own concrete morality stemming from a rational social order where rational institutions and laws provide the content of conscientious conviction), the value of the human being as a potential god overrides every system of social ethics. From the previous perspective, Hesychasm provides a metaphysical underpinning for the Universal Declaration of Human Rights and for a world order centered on the divinity of man.

Furthermore, Hesychasm implies that there are superior and inferior civilizations, according to the degree to which each civilization recognizes the divinity of man and helps man to become aware of and actualize his potential divinity. Hence, inherent in Hesychasm is a call for a continuous progress of humanity towards higher levels of consciousness and Grace.

BIBLIOGRAPHY

For the study of classical Greek and Latin philosophers, I used Oxford's scholarly editions and Penguin Classics. For the study of Greek Church Fathers, I used J.P. Migne's *Patrologia Graeca*. For the study of Latin Church Fathers, I used J.P. Migne's *Patrologia Latina*. For the study of the New Testament, I used the Nestle–Aland editions. For the study of the Old Testament, I used the *Septuagint* and the *Biblia Hebraica Stuttgartensia*.

Abbé Guettée, *The Papacy*, New York: Carleton, 1866

Ackerman, B., *Social Justice and the Liberal State*, New Haven, Conn.: Yale University Press, 1980

Adler, E., "Seizing the Middle Ground: Constructivism in World Politics", *European Journal of International Relations*, Vol. 3, 1997

Archbishop Chrysostomos, *A Guide to Orthodox Psychotherapy*, Lanham: University Press of America, 2007

Aune, B., *Kant's Theory of Morals*, Princeton, NJ: Princeton University Press, 1979

Baird, F.E. and Kaufman, W., *From Plato to Derrida*, New Jersey: Pearson Prentice Hall, 2008

Barnett, M., "Social Constructivism", in: John Baylis, Steve Smith and Patricia Owens (eds), *The Globalization of World Politics — An Introduction to International Relations*, Oxford: Oxford University Press, 2011

Barth, K., *Church Dogmatics — A Selection*, trans. and ed. G.W. Bromiley, Edinburgh: T.&T. Clark, 1961

Basil the Great, *On the Human Condition*, trans. and intro. by Verna Harrison, Crestwood, N.Y.: St. Vladimir's Seminary Press, 2005

Bauer, W., *Orthodoxy and Heresy in Earliest Christianity*, trans. and ed. R. Kraft and G. Kroedel, Philadelphia: Fortress Press, 1971

Bedzow, I., *Halakhic Man, Authentic Jew — Modern Expressions of Orthodox Thought from Rabbi Joseph B. Soloveitchik and Rabbi Eliezer Berkovits*, New York: Lambda Publishers, 2009

Berger, P.L. and Luckmann, T., *The Social Construction of Reality — A Treatise in the Sociology of Knowledge*, Garden City, N.Y.: Doubleday & Co., 1966

Bergson, H., *Time and Free Will — An Essay on the Immediate Data of Consciousness*, tr., F.L. Pogson, Montana: Kessinger Publishing Company, 1910

Bishop of Nafpaktos Hierotheos, *Orthodox Psychotherapy*, trans. Esther Williams, Levadia, Greece: Birth of the Theotokos Monastery, 1994

Black, B., "The Abolition of work", in B. Black, *The Abolition of Work and Other Essays*, Port Townsend, WA: Loompanics Unlimited, 1985

Bourke, V.J., "Rationalism", in D.D. Runes (ed.), *Dictionary of Philosophy*, Totowa, NJ: Littlefield, Adams and Company, 1962

Bowle, J., *A History of Europe*, London: Heinemann, 1979

Britton, K., *John Stuart Mill*, Harmondsworth: Penguin, 1953; Roger Crisp, *Mill on Utilitarianism*, London: Routledge, 1997

Brzezinski, Z., *Out of Control — Global Turmoil on the Eve of the 21st Century*, New York: Collier Books, 1993

Brzezinski, Z., *The Grand Chessboard — American Primacy and Its Geostrategic Imperatives*, New York: Basic Books, 1998

Byron, R., *The Byzantine Achievement*, Mount Jackson, VA: Axios Press, 2010 (first published in 1929)

Cairnes, J.E., *The Character and Logical Method of Political Economy*, London: Macmillan, 1888

Castoriadis, C., *The Imaginary Institution of Society*, London: Polity Press, 1987 (originally published in 1975 by Éditions du Seuil)

Chadwick, H., *Boethius*, Oxford: Oxford University Press, 1981

Chrestou, P.K., "Neohellenic Theology at the Crossroads", *The Greek Orthodox Theological Review*, Vol. XXVIII, 1983

Cipolla, C.M., *Before the Industrial Revolution — European Society and Economy 1000–1700*, 3rd edition, trans. C. Woodall, New York: W.W. Norton & Company, 1993

Copleston, F., *A History of Philosophy*, Vol. 2: Augustine to Scotus, Kent: Burns & Oates, 1999 d'Allonnes, M.R., *La Crise Sans Fin — Essai sur l' expérience moderne du temps*, Paris: Seuil, 2012

Dawson Jr., J.W., "Gödel and the Limits of Logic", *Scientific American*, Vol. 280, No. 6, 1999

Dawson Jr., J.W., *Logical Dilemmas — The Life and Work of Kurt Gödel*, Wellesley Mass.: A.K. Peters, 1997

Dickinson, J. (ed. and trans.), *The Statesman's Book of John of Salisbury*, New York: Knopf, 1927

Dugin, A., *The Fourth Political Ideology*, U.K.: Arktos Media Ltd., 2012

Eck, D.L., *India — A Sacred Geography*, New York: Three Rivers Press, 2012

Einhard, *The Life of Charlemagne*, trans. S.E. Turner, New York: Harper & Brothers, 1880

Ekonomou, A.J., *Byzantine Rome and the Greek Popes — Eastern Influences on Rome and the Papacy from Gregory the Great to Zacharias, A.D. 590–752*, Lanham, MD: Lexington Books, 2007

Elster, J., "Some Unresolved Problems in the Theory of Rational Behavior", *Acta Sociologica*, Vol. 36, 1993

Elster, J., "The Market and the Forum: Three Varieties of Political Theory", in: J. Elster and A. Hyland (eds), *Foundations of Social Choice Theory*, Cambridge: Cambridge University Press, 1986

Elster, J., *Local Justice*, New York: Russeell Sage Foundation, 1992

Elster, J., *Explaining Social Behavior — More Nuts and Bolts for the Social Sciences*, Cambridge: Cambridge University Press, 2007

Elster, J. and Moene, K.O. (eds), *Alternatives to Capitalism*, Cambridge: Cambridge University Press, 1989

Florovsky, G., *Christianity and Culture*, Vol. 2, in *The Collected Works of Georges Florovsky*, 2nd printing, Belmont, MA: Nordland Publishing Company, 1974

Foucault, M., *Language, Counter–Memory, Practice*, ed. D.F. Bouchard, Ithaca, N.Y.: Cornell University Press; Oxford: Blackwell, 1977

Freud, S., *On Metapsychology*, The Pelican Freud Library, Harmondsworth: Pelican, 1975–1986, Vol. 11

Fryde, E., *The Early Palaeologian Renaissance (1261 — c. 1360)*, Leiden: Brill, 2000

Fukuyama, F., *The End of History and the Last Man*, New York: Free Press, 1992

Gadamer, H.–G., *Truth and Method*, London: Sheed and Ward, 1975, p. 263

Gautier, P. (ed.), *Michaelis Pselli Theologica*, Vol. I, 11, Leipzig: Teubner, 1989

Geanakoplos, D.J., *Constantinople and the West*, Madison: University of Wisconsin Press, 1989

Gewirth, A. (ed. and trans.), *Marsilius of Padua, the Defender of the Peace*, New York: Harper and Row Publishers, 1956

Grant, M., *The Civilizations of Europe*, London: Weidenfeld and Nicolson, 1965

Gregoriou tou Palama — Hapanta ta Erga (Gregory Palamas — Complete Works), ed. P. Chrestou, Thessaloniki: Paterikai Ekdoseis "Gregorios ho Palamas", 1981–1986

Greenwald, G., "The 'War on Terror' —by Design— Can Never End", *The Guardian*, 4 January 2013

Guthrie, W.K.C., *Orpheus and Greek Religion —A Study of the Orphic Movement*, revised edition, Princeton, N.J.: Princeton University Press, 1993

Guyer, P. (ed.), *Kant's Groundwork of the Metaphysics of Morals — Critical Essays*, Lantham, MD: Rowman and Littlefield, 1998

Häggman, B., *Rudolf Kjellén —Founder of Geopolitics*, Helsingborg: Center for Research on Geopolitics, 1988

Habermas, J. and Ben–Habib, S., "Modernity versus Postmodernity", *New German Critique*, No. 22 (Special Issue on Modernism), 1981

Harris, G.S., *Turkey —Coping with Crisis*, Boulder, Colo.: Westview Press, 1985.

Hawking, S. and Mlodinow, L., *A Brief History of Time*, New York: Bantam, 2005

Hegel, G.W.F., *Phenomenology of Spirit* (originally published in 1807), trans. A.V. Miller, Delhi: Motilal Banarsidass, 1998

Heidegger, M., *Being and Time*, New York: Harper & Row, 1962

Hilgenfeld, A., *Die Ketzergeschichte des Urchristentums*, Leipzig, 1884

Holland, T., *Millennium*, London: Abacus Books, 2009

Hosein, Sheikh Imran N., *Jerusalem in the Qur'an*, New York: Masjid Dar–al–Qur'an, 2003

Hothersall, D., *History of Psychology*, 4th edition, New York: McGraw–Hill, 2004

Hultgren, A.J., *The Parables of Jesus —A Commentary*, Michigan: Wm. B. Eerdmans Publishing, 2002

Huntington, S.P., *The Clash of Civilizations — Remaking of World Order*, New York: Simon and Schuster, 1996

Johnston, D. (ed.), *Faith–Based Diplomacy — Trumping Realpolitik*, Oxford: Oxford University Press, 2003

Kadloubovsky, E. and Palmer, G.E.H. (trans. and eds), *Writings from the Philokalia on Prayer of the Heart*, London: Faber, 1951

Kalb, J., *The Tyranny of Liberalism*, Intercollegiate Studies Institute, 2008

Karmiris, J., *A Synopsis of the Dogmatic Theology of the Orthodox Catholic Church*, trans. Rev. G. Dimopoulos, Scranton: Christian Orthodox Edition, 1973

Kierkegaard, S., *The Kierkegaard Reader*, ed. J. Chamberlain and J. Rée, Oxford: Blackwell, 2001

Kjellén, R., *Der Staat als Lebensform*, Leipzig: Hirzel, 1917

Kockelmans, J.J. (ed.), *Contemporary European Ethics*, New York: Anchor Books, 1972

Koenig, H.G., McCullough, M.E. and Larson,D.B., *Handbook of Religion and Health*, New York: Oxford University Press, 2001

Kolakowski, L., *Main Currents of Marxism*, 3 vols, Oxford: Oxford University Press, 1978

Kymlicka, W., *Contemporary Political Philosophy*, Oxford: Clarendon Press, 1990

Lacan, J., *The Four Fundamental Concepts of Psycho–Analysis*, trans. Alan Sheridan, New York: W.W. Norton, 1978

Larchet, J.–C., *Introduction à Saint Maxime le Confesseur, Ambigua*, Paris: Suresnes, 1994

Larchet, J.–C., *La Divinization de l' Homme Selon Saint Maxime le Confesseur*, Paris: Éditions du Cerf, 1996

Larchet, J.–C., *Thérapeutique des Maladies Mentales — L' Expérience de l' Orient Chrétien des Premiers Siècles*, Paris: Les Éditions du Cerf, 1992

Lavelle, L., *Traité des Valeurs — Théorie Générale de la Valeur*, Paris: PUF, 1951

Le Senne, R., *Le Mensenge et le Caractère*, Paris: F. Alcan, 1930

Lévi–Strauss, c., *The Raw and the Cooked*, trans. John and Doreen Weightman, Chicago: The University of Chicago Press, 1969

Lipsius, R.A., *Der Gnosticismus*, Leipzig, 1860

Louth, A., "The Ecclesiology of Saint Maximos the Confessor", *International Journal of the Study of the Christian Church*, Vol. 4, 2004

Mackinder, H.J., "The Geographical Pivot of History", *Geographical Journal*, Vol. 23, 1904

Mackinder, H.J., *Democratic Ideas and Reality — A Study in the Politics of Reconstruction*, London: Constable, 1919

Mahan, A.T., *The Influence of Sea Power on History, 1660–1783*, London: Samson Low, 1889

Makrygiannis, I., *Apomnemoneumata* (Memoirs), Athens: A. Karavia Publications

Marcel, G., *Man Against Mass Society*, trans. G.S. Fraser, St Augustine's Press, 2007

Marcel, G., *Being and Having*, trans. K. Farrer, Westminster: Dacre Press, 1949

Marcel, G., *The Mystery of Being*, Vol. 1: *Reflection and Mystery*, trans. G.S. Fraser, and Vol. 2: *Faith and Reality*, trans. R. Hague, London: The Harvill Press, 1951

Marquis de Sade, *Justine, Philosophy in the Bedroom and Other Writings*, London: Arrow Books, 1965

Marshall, P.J. and Williams, G., *The Great Map of Mankind*, London: J.M. Dent and Sons, 1982

Marx, K., *A Contribution to the Critique of Political Economy*, trans. N.I. Stone, New York: International Library Publishing, 1904 (originally published in 1859)

Marx, K., *Critique of Hegel's Philosophy of Right*, trans. A. Jolin and J. O'Malley, Cambridge: Cambridge University Press, 1982

McDonald, W.W., *Russell Kirk and the Age of Ideology*, Columbia: University of Missouri Press, 2004

McGuckin, J.A. (ed. and trans.), *The Book of Mystical Chapters — Meditations on the Soul's Ascent, from the Desert Fathers and Other Early Christian Contemplatives*, Boston, Mass.: Shambhalla Publications, 2002

Meinig, D.W., "Heartland and Rimland in Eurasian History", *The Western Political Quarterly*, Vol. 9, 1956

Milbank, J., *Theology and Social Theory — Beyond Secular Reason*, Oxford: Blackwell, 2006

Mitchell, C.R., "World Society a Cobweb: States, Actors and Systematic Processes", in: M. Banks (ed.), *Conflict in World Society*, Brighton: Harvester, 1984

Moore, G.E., *Principia Ethica*, New York: Prometheus Books, 1988

Myrdal, G., *The Political Element in the Development of Economic Theory*, London: Routledge & Kegan Paul, 1953

Nederman, C.J., "Bracton on Kingship Revisited", *History of Political Thought*, Vol. 5, 1984

Nicodemus of the Holy Mountain, *Ermeneia eis tas Epta Catholicas Epistolas* (Commentary on the Seven Catholic Epistles), 3rd ed., Thessaloniki: Ekdoseis "Orthodoxos Kypsele", 1986

Norris, C., *Derrida*, London: Fontana, 1987

Novoseltsev, A.P., *The Eastern Slavs and Russia in the 9th–10th Centuries*, Moscow: Gosudarstvennoe Izdatel'stvo, 1965

Nozick, R., "Distributive Justice", in J. Westphal (ed.), *Justice*, Indianapolis: Hackett Publishing Company, 1996

Nozick, R., *Anarchy, State and Utopia*, New York: Basic Books, 1974

Nye Jr. J., *Bound to Lead —The Changing Nature of American Power*, New York: Basic Books, 1991

Nye Jr., J., *Soft Power —The Means to Success in World Politics*, New York: Public Affairs, 2004

O' Collins, G. and Farrugia, E.G., *A Concise Dictionary of Theology*, New Jersey: Paulist Press, 2000

Obolensky, D., *The Byzantine Commonwealth —Eastern Europe 500– 1453*, Crestwood, N.Y.: St. Vladimir's Seminary Press, 1971

Orth, J.V., "Jeremy Bentham: The Common Law's Severest Critic", *American Bar Association Journal*, Vol. 68, 1982

Pangle, T.L., "Introduction", in T.L. Pangle (ed.), *The Rebirth of Classical Political Rationalism —An Introduction to the Thought of Leo Strauss*, Chicago: University of Chicago Press, 1989

Papademetriou, G.C., *Introduction to Saint Gregory Palamas*, New York: Philosophical Library, 1973

Paton, H.J., *The Moral Law —Kant's Groundwork of the Metaphysics of Morals*, London: Hutchinson University Library, 1948

Philip K. Hitti, *History of the Arabs*, London: Macmillan, 1970

Philokalia ton Hieron Neptikon (Philokalia of the Holy Neptic Fathers), Athens: Ekdotikos Oikos "Aster", 1974–1976

Pirenne, H., *Medieval Cities —Their Origins and the Revival of Trade*, trans. F.D. Halsey, Princeton: Princeton University Press, 1952

Pletcher, K. (ed.), *The Geography of China —Sacred and Historic Places*, Rosen Educational Publishing, 2010

Portal, R., *The Slavs*, London: Weidenfeld and Nicolson, 1965

Previte–Orton, C.W., *The Shorter Cambridge Medieval History*, Cambridge: Cambridge University Press, 1952

Price, H., *Time's Arrow and Archimedes' Point — New Directions for a Physics of Time*, Oxford: Oxford University Press, 1996

Psellos, M., *De Omnifaria Doctrina*, ed. L. G. Westerink

Quigley, C., *Tragedy and Hope — A History of the World in Our Time*, New York: Macmillan, 1966

Rawls, J., "Kantian Constructivism in Moral Theory", *Journal of Philosophy*, Vol. 77, 1980 (The Dewey Lectures)

Rawls, J., "The Basic Liberties and their Priority", in: S.M. McMurrin (ed.), *The Tanner Lectures on Human Values*, Salt Lake City: University of Utah Press, 1982, Vol. III

Rawls, J., *A Theory of Justice*, Revised edition, Cambridge, Mass.: Belknap Press, 1999

Rawls, J., *Justice as Fairness — A Restatement*, ed. E. Kelly, Cambridge, MA: Harvard University Press, 2001

Richer, J., *Sacred Geography of the Ancient Greeks*, trans. Christine Rhone, New York: State University of New York Press, 1994

Romanides, J.S., "Notes on Palamite Controversy and Related Topics", Part II, *The Greek Orthodox Theological Review*, Vol. IX, Winter 1963–64

Romanides, J.S., "Notes on Palamite Controversy and Related Topics", Part I, *The Greek Orthodox Theological Review*, Vol. VI, Winter 1960–61

Romanides, J.S., *The Ancestral Sin*, trans. G.S. Gabriel, Ridgewood, New Jersey: Zephyr Publications, 2002

Romanides, J.S., *To Propatorikon Hamartema* (Ancestral Sin), Athens, 1957

Romer, P.M., "Compound Rates of Growth", in: http://www.econlib.org/library/Enc/EconomicGrowth.html

Rosa, J.–J., *Euro Exit — How (and Why) to Get Rid of the Monetary Union*, New York: Algora Publishing, 2012

Runciman, S., *The Great Church in Captivity — A Study of the Patriarchate of Constantinople from the Eve of the Turkish Conquest to the Greek War of Independence*, Cambridge: Cambridge University Press, 1986

Salvemini, G., *Under the Axe of Fascism*, (1936) reprint ed. Lyle Stuart, 1971

Samuelson, P.A. and Nordhaus, W.D., *Economics*, 14th edition, New York: McGraw–Hill, 1992

Sandel, M., *What Money Can't Buy — The Moral Limits of Markets*, Oxford: Brasenose College (The Tanner Lectures on Human Values), 1998

Sartre, J.-P., *Being and Nothingness*, trans. H.E. Barnes, New York: Washington Square Press, 1992

Scanlon, T.M., "Rights, Goals, and Fairness", in J. Waldron (ed.), *Theories of Rights*, Oxford: Oxford University Press, 1984

Schaff, P. and Wace, H. (eds), *A Select Library of Nicene and Post-Nicene Fathers of the Christian Church*, Grand Rapids, MI: Wm. B. Eerdmans, 1991, Vol. 7

Schwartz, P., *The New Political Economy of J.S. Mill*, London: Weidenfeld & Nicolson, 1972

Scotchie, J. (ed.), *The Paleoconservatives — New Voices of the Old Right*, Transaction Publishers, 1999

Searle, J., *The Rediscovery of the Mind*, Cambridge, Mass.: MIT Press, 1992

Sellars, R.W., "The Spiritualism of Lavelle and Le Senne", *Philosophy and Phenomenological Research*, Vol. 11, 1951

Shevchenko, I., *Byzantium and the Slavs*, Harvard Ukrainian Research Institute, 1991

Skinner, Q., *The Foundations of Modern Political Thought*, 2 Vols, Cambridge: Cambridge University Press, 1970

Smith, A., *The Theory of Moral Sentiments*, ed. D.D. Raphael and A.L. Macfie, Oxford: Oxford University Press, 1976

Sobran, J., "Pensees: Notes for the Reactionary of Tomorrow", *National Review*, 31 December 1985

Solovyov, V., *Divine Sophia — The Wisdom Writings of Vladimir Solovyov*, ed. by Judith D. Kornblatt, New York: Cornell University Press, 2009

St. John Damascene, *An Exact Exposition of the Orthodox Faith*, trans. E.W. Watson and L. Pullan, in Vol. 9 of *Nicene and Post-Nicene Fathers*, Second Series

St. Maximus the Confessor, "Peri Theologias kai tes Ensarkou Oikonomias tou Hyiou tou Theou, Pros Thalassion" (Regarding theology and the incarnate oeconomy of the Son of God, to Thalassios), in *Philokalia ton Hieron Neptikon* (Philokalia of the Sacred Neptic Fathers —hereafter, *Philokalia*), Athens: Ekdotikos Oikos "Aster", 1975, Vol. 2

Spykman, N.J., *America's Strategy in World Politics — The United States and the Balance of Power*, New York: Harcourt, Brace, 1942

Strangas, Archimandrite Th.A., *Ecclesias Ellados Istoria* (History of the Church of Greece), Vol. 2, Athens, 1970

Symeon the New Theologian, *Hymns of Divine Love*, trans. G.A. Maloney, Denville, N.J.: Dimension Books, 1975

Symeon the New Theologian, *Method of Holy Prayer and Attentiveness*, Greek text and French trans. I. Hausherr, "La méthode d'oraison hésychaste", *Orientalia Christiana*, Vol. IX, 2, No.36, Rome, 1927, p. 164.

Thunberg, L., *Microcosmos and Mediator — The Theological Anthropology of Maximus the Confessor*, 2nd edition, Chicago: Open Court Publishing Company, 1995

Titchener, E.B., "Wilhelm Wundt", *American Journal of Psychology*, Vol. 32, 1921

Tsirpanlis, C.N., *Introduction to Eastern Patristic thought and Orthodox Theology*, Collegeville, MN: The Liturgical Press, 1991

Ullmann, W., *Principles of Government and Politics in the Middle Ages*, London: Methuen, 1961

Vasiliev, A.A., *A History of the Byzantine Empire*, Milwaukee: University of Wisconsin Press, 1958

Vattimo, G., *The End of Modernity — Nihilism and Hermeneutics in Postmodern Culture*, trans. J.R. Snyder, Baltimore: Johns Hopkins University Press, 1988

von Balthasar, H., *Presence and Thought — An Essay on the Religious Philosophy of Gregory of Nyssa*, trans. Mark Sebanc, San Francisco: Ignatius Press, 1995

Walters, R.E., *The Nuclear Trap*, Harmondsworth: Penguin Books, 1974

Ware, T. (Bishop Kallistos of Diokleia), *The Orthodox Church*, Harmondsworth: Penguin Books, 1963

Ware, T., *The Orthodox Church*, second edition, London and N.Y.: Penguin Books, 1993

Weber, M., *The Protestant Ethic and the Spirit of Capitalism*, New York: Dover, 2003

Wilson, N.G., "From Byzantium to Italy: Greek Studies in the Italian Renaissance", *The Sixteenth Century Journal*, Vol. 25, Autumn, 1994

Wilson, N.G., *Scholars of Byzantium*, London: Duckworth, 1983

Wundt, W., *Logik*, Vol. 3, Stuttgart: Enke, 1921

Yannaras, C., "The Distinction Between Essence and Energies and Its Importance for Theology", *St. Vladimir's Theological Quarterly*, Vol. 19, no. 4, 1975

Yannaras, C., *Orthodoxia kai Disi sti Neoteri Hellada* (Orthodoxy and the West in Modern Greece), Athens: Domos, 1993

INDEX